LAWN PEOPLE

Lawn People

How Grasses, Weeds, and Chemicals
Make Us Who We Are

By

PAUL ROBBINS

TEMPLE UNIVERSITY PRESS
Philadelphia

PAUL ROBBINS is Professor in the Department of Geography
and Regional Development at the University of Arizona. He is the author
of *Political Ecology: A Critical Introduction*.

Cover photograph: National Archives (306-PS-59-13580).

Temple University Press
1601 North Broad Street
Philadelphia PA 19122
www.temple.edu/tempress

♾

The paper used in this publication meets the requirements
of the American National Standard for Information Sciences—
Permanence of Paper for Printed Library Materials,
ANSI Z39.48–1992

Library of Congress Cataloging-in-Publication Data

Robbins, Paul, 1967–
Lawn people : how grasses, weeds, and chemicals make us who we are /
Paul Frederick Robbins.
      p.   cm.
Includes bibliographical references and index.
ISBN-13: 978-1-59213-578-3   ISBN-10: 1-59213-578-1 (hardcover: alk. paper)
ISBN-13: 978-1-59213-579-0   ISBN-10: 1-59213-579-X (pbk.: alk. paper)
   1. Lawns—United States.   2. Lawns—Weed control—United States.
      3. Lawn ecology—United States.   I. Title.

SB433.15.R63 2007
635.9'647—dc22   2006038426

020909-5

For Sarah Moore

CONTENTS

ACKNOWLEDGMENTS

I MUST ADMIT THAT the book is not ultimately my own idea. The original concept came from an undergraduate paper turned in for a Water Resource Management class I taught at the University of Iowa in 1996. Dara Houdek's work for that course—a class otherwise primarily focused on big bureaucracies and economies (such as the Army Corps of Engineers and the Los Angeles Chamber of Commerce)—focused on the water quality implications of her own lawn, and opened my eyes to a class of problems that would occupy me for the next decade. When I last heard, Dara was a master instructor at the Appalachian Mountain Club, far from her family's lawn. I owe her the debt of this idea.

Marielle Brinkman and her colleagues at the Battelle Memorial Institute do some of the analytical chemistry described in this book; work that demonstrates that lawn chemicals do not stay put. Not only has her work on public health and safety been an inspiration, but her carrying it out in a laboratory institution otherwise known for developing weapons of mass destruction is a wonder. She is a well-hidden but paramount example of those Donna Haraway has called "allies" in the laboratory.

The National Science Foundation (NSF) Program in Geography and Regional Science funded much of the research described in this volume (Project #0095993). I am deeply indebted to the NSF and several anonymous reviewers for being willing to throw the dice on this project.

At the Ohio State University (OSU), the Urban Landscape Ecology Project (ULEP) and all of its affiliated faculty and staff have been a source of constant help and inspiration, especially John Cardina who believes weeds are nature too. Susan Clayton at College of Wooster has been a terrific partner in this research, as has ULEP's guiding spirit, Parwinder Grewal.

The OSU's Department of Geography earned its reputation for rich inquiry coupled with methodological rigor. This tradition has rubbed off on me to a degree (though not as much as one might have hoped), but not without the constant encouragement of Larry Brown, who supported this project when it was still just a seed of an idea, along with several of my other misguided endeavors. I will miss my other colleagues at OSU. Among them especially are graduate students, whose research labor is at work throughout this book, including not only Julie Sharp (who surveyed the industry and conducted the interviews in Kingberry Court) and Trevor Birkenholtz (who painstakingly digitized lawn coverage), but also Annemarie Polderman and David Kadonsky (who labored over statistical models).

To conversations I had with Joel Wainwright I owe the basic notion–so central to this book–that turfgrass produces "subjects". Only he could have convinced me that Louis Althusser might have the most useful things to say about lawns. Julie Guthman similarly provided grim insight into the bulimic nature of green consumption. Fortunately, J. P. Jones and others here at the University of Arizona's Department of Geography and Regional Development encouraged me to rant about this thesis and pretended to believe it. Sallie Marston (and Vinnie the amazing rescue Greyhound) provided generous hospitality for writing. Bob Toborg, Frank Forgione, and Dave Feroe remain the gold standards for clarity and common sense. Peter Wissoker is the kind of editor every writer needs, and ferried earlier versions of this text through several dreadful drafts, also facilitating Denis Wood's frank, constructive, and thorough critiques. Alex Holzman saw the project through to the end. Sarah Moore, as always, makes a writing life worth living.

Finally, this work and its conclusions rest on the backs of those who were willing to share the details of their lawn lives with unknown researchers. This includes all those who opened their private domestic yards both over the phone and in person, but also those members of the industry who took the time to respond to questions and explain the complexity of the economy in which they invest their labor.

Of course, none of these people can be held responsible for the contents of the book. I hope they all will forgive any negative associations created in the preceding paragraphs, by unnecessarily linking them to my own deeply personal and obsessive fixation with grasses and chemicals.

INTRODUCTION

S TARING OUT FROM THE PORCH of my house in Columbus Ohio on a late spring morning a few years ago, not long after I purchased the property, I noticed something disturbing about the yard and, simultaneously, about myself. My eyes had become fixed on a bald patch of ground in the shade where the grass had retreated and where the yard had come to favor a dull green moss, mixed with clover. Everywhere else, the yard had become covered with a purple-flowered ivy. I found the mint smell of the dusty vine pleasant; at least I had earlier in the week as I walked through it on a shortcut to the sidewalk. Now, however, I looked on it with concern, since I had been warned the day before that this was "Creeping Charlie" (*Glechoma hederacea*), an aggressive plant that would soon devour my lawn. It wasn't long after this that the usual junk in my mailbox—and there was lots of it that spring—began to seem more interesting to me. It was clear from colorful flyers that there were a staggering range of options available to me for dealing with the idiosyncratic qualities of my front yard, most of them involving a labyrinth of "steps programs" to rid myself of my problems. These "helpful" instructions had been sent to me by a number of companies and services, and they explained when, where, and how to take care of the grass. What disturbed me was that these flyers and procedures had begun to linger in my mind as I lay in bed at night. My lawn was keeping me awake.

As a self-described environmentalist with absolutely no interest in gardening or home maintenance, I felt a twinge of guilt accompanied by ecological anxiety. This became most acute when I considered the option of actually applying some of the chemicals that were being marketed to me (perhaps at night when no one was looking!). Why was it that weeds had never bothered me until the day I was responsible for "caring" for a lawn? How did the needs of the grass come to be my own? Something unpleasant was happening. In brooding about the grass, my role in its care, and my relationship to the vast economy designed to manage it, I was becoming a slightly different kind of person, a sort of . . . "lawn person."

How Did This Happen?

Nearby in suburban Reynoldsburg only a year earlier, neighbors of Ketha Robbins (who is no relation to the author) trespassed on her property in the middle of the night, mowed her lawn and ripped up the saplings that were growing there. Robbins' decision to restore the forest in her backyard by ceasing to mow and pull weeds had clearly inflamed something in those who lived around her. Though the city found that Ms. Robbins had not violated the spirit of municipal 6-inch maximum lawn height law, a jury of her peers—lawn people through and through—had spoken in a single act. While at the time of writing the civil case remains pending in municipal court, the matter has been effectively settled by a frighteningly coordinated social action.[1]

Who Are These People, and How Did They Get This Way?

This profile of a simultaneously zealous and anxious community is not unique to Columbus, Ohio. A survey of U.S. households conducted in 2001,[2] asking people how they manage their lawns and how they feel about the risks and hazards associated with turf care, suggests a nation of similarly ambivalent citizens. The survey revealed that those who apply chemicals to their lawns (controlling for income and education) are statistically *more likely* than nonchemical users to believe that "home lawn-care practices generally have a negative impact on local water quality" and that "lawn-care services have a negative impact on local water quality." People who use chemicals tend to think they are worse for the environment than those who do not.

This is at first surprising, but on closer examination seems somewhat familiar. Contemporary cities are populated by people with many similar ambivalent and anxious desires. Driving a sports utility vehicle (SUV) brings with it a complicated calculus of global environmental change, public safety, and one's own risk. Drinking coffee presents a blinding array of options, from organic to fair trade, all linked to the dawning awareness of connectivity between simple daily behaviors and broader ecological and economic systems. Every checkout counter decision between "paper" or "plastic" appears to present a negotiation between mounting landfills and clear-cut forests. And no one is more intimately aware of such connections, it would seem, than the average people who face these ecologies and economies, and whose actions are so closely tied to those broader worlds. But the fact that being a lawn person is similar to a whole class of other urban ecological behaviors does not, in and of itself, untangle the mystery of why the contradiction occurs.

Why Participate So Fully in Something That Makes One Anxious, Especially Something That Takes Time, Capital, and Effort?

The Lawn is Urban Ecology

Certainly the aggregate effects of the ambivalent labor of lawn people are self-evident. Covering a total area roughly the size of the state of Iowa,[3] the lawn is one of the largest and fastest growing landscapes in the United States. The lawn also receives more care, time, and attention from individuals and households than any other natural space. In many North American communities, the lawn represents a continuous intensively managed parkland connecting mile-upon-mile of grass: unmistakable, unbroken, ubiquitous (Figure I.1). Inputs into the lawn—in time, labor, money, and chemicals—have never been higher than they are today, and the rate of increase in the last decade is startling. Outdoor household fertilizer usage more than doubled just between 1994 and 1999, from 21 million households to 49 million. Between 1988 and 1989, use of outdoor insect control chemicals (most of which were applied to lawns), grew by 44%.[4] Behind such changes is a growing national and international lawn care and lawn chemical industry. One in five U.S. households used a lawn care company in 1999. With 24 million households spending an average of $55 each, U.S. home-owners spent a total of 1.2 billion dollars just on outdoor insecticides in 1999. Total U.S. consumer sales on lawn care (separate from gardening and other outdoor investments) topped 9 billion dollars that same year.[5]

Lawns also represent an urban ecological problem on a vast scale. In the United States, the chemicals of lawn maintenance–including dichlorophenoxy-acetic acid (2,4-D), glyphosate, diazinon, and dicamba–are significant contributors to nonpoint source water quality problems that continue to elude solution almost 30 years after the passage of the Clean Water Act.[6] Lawn pesticides are applied on a scale to rival agricultural toxins; 23% of the total 2,4-D applied in the United States is used on lawns; 22% of glyphosate, 31% of chlorpyrifos, and 38% of dicamba used nationally is applied to home lawns.[7]

But the actual care, feeding, and reproduction of this vast expanse of greenery is the business of countless, independent, individual people. As with many urban ecological dilemmas–including problems such as household garbage disposal and commuter-driven carbon dioxide emissions–this makes the problem a staggeringly complex puzzle. It is hard to get one's head around these problems precisely because they are driven by the disaggregated choices of countless individuals, each of whom is living within a labyrinth of complex daily

0   150   300 Feet   N

FIGURE I.1   The unbroken urban grassland: lawns form a contiguous monocultural park.

decisions. Millions of choices govern daily activities such as trash disposal and automobile use, and combine to form the urban environment.

Of course, the very *ordinariness* of these daily decisions makes them easy to overlook, even as they combine to create large effects. The most frequent encounters between human beings and other life forms, after all, occur in the most mundane places: the kitchen, the bathroom, and the backyard. Because such interactions are mundane, however, does not make them trivial, especially given that these household spaces and interactions are constant and ubiquitous. The use of household antibacterial soap may influence the evolutionary selection of bacteria and the creation of super-germs.[8] People influence water quality through flows of raw sewage propelled with each flush of the toilet. The average car in the United States expels its own weight in carbon into the atmosphere every year through daily driving. Average individuals perform all of these actions every day.

So the consensus across the country to manage and care for turfgrass through the use of chemical inputs and crew-cut mowing must be viewed as more than a coincidence, and the effects of this consensus—on ourselves, our health, and our economy—all demand exploration and explanation. Why do we do it and what effect does all this activity have on us as people and as communities?

Urban ecological research actually tells us very little in this regard. Most research on urban environments, even where it pertains to nature and nonhuman elements such as water, trees, and waste, has tended to emphasize the role of vast bureaucracies, engineering firms, and planning offices. The harnessing of Los Angeles' water, a topic of countless books (and the movie *Chinatown*), was the product of a cabal of planners and developers. So too, it was large-scale planning and the demands of city health officials that reversed the flow of the Chicago River in 1900. But the environmental realities of the twenty-first century, including landfill overflows, greenhouse gas emissions, and chemical use and exposure, are as much the work of individuals as states or firms.

In this sense, the lawn is a very good place to start unraveling how urban ecologies work more generally, and how the ecology of cities makes us certain kinds of citizens. To explore and understand the lawn in its ecological, economic, and social context then, is to ask new questions in the nascent field of urban ecology. How do individuals fit in larger urban ecologies and how do they get to be the kind of people they are?

This brings us back to the dilemma of Ketha Robbins who, until further notice, will have a lawn in her backyard no matter what she may prefer, her homestead extending in a small way the growing sea of lawns in urban America. How did her neighbors come to form their priorities and aesthetics? And what form of urgent neighborliness would drive neighbors to behave so . . . well . . . unneighborly?

To answer "they behave that way because the lawn is important to them" is entirely unsatisfactory. Why do we want what we want? What places demands on us: neighbors, large companies, family, and even the turfgrass itself? How do we come to understand and trade-off our aesthetics, environmental values, and community desires? What are the implications for our health and our communities? In this sense, the questions that need to be asked extend beyond the boundaries of the lawn, to something larger in our ecological polity.

This is a book about the North American lawn then, its ecological characteristics and its political economy. But it is, more intimately, about nature's influence on us, and its role in producing certain kinds of communities and

individuals. The volume aims to describe the array of linkages that the contemporary turfgrass yard makes to complex ecosystems, vast chemical production economies, community values and priorities, and personal aesthetics and
obligations. More generally, the book posits a larger argument, that the lawn is
a system that produces a certain kind of person–a turfgrass subject. The volume
will therefore be more than a summary and consolidation of previously written
academic work. Instead it intends to provide a novel explanation of how daily
life is not only manipulated by an enormous and growing economy of landscape
management, but also how it is controlled and disciplined by a nonhuman
actor–the lawn itself.

This is by no means the first book on the lawn, nor will it be the last, I trust.
Bormann, Balmori, Geballe, and Vernegaard's *Redesigning the American Lawn:
A Search for Environmental Harmony* (from 1993) grew from an innovative
interdisciplinary seminar at Yale intended to capture the elements of design,
landscaping, and ecology necessary for imagining an alternative to front lawn
monoculture. This excellent brief treatise shows how better design might point
the way toward less demanding and more sustainable outcomes.[9] Michael Pollan's short 1991 essay explored the same topic more succinctly by simply asking
Why Mow? His approach to the question, recording his ongoing personal experiment of replacing his lawn slowly but surely with garden, also emphasizes the
arbitrary nature of the lawn aesthetic.[10]

Virginia Scott Jenkins' now-classic 1994 volume, *The Lawn: An American
Obsession*, carefully and exhaustively traces the arrival of the turfgrass lawn to
America and its expansion into a ubiquitous ground cover, with serious attention to the environmental problems that such a transformation entailed. This
work is especially notable for the way it emphasizes the remarkably recent history of a landscape that seems so quintessentially normal and timeless to many
of us.[11]

One of the most serious academic treatments the lawn has received is
Georges Tessyot's 1999 collection *The American Lawn*, which provides an
exhaustive genealogy of the lawn as a landscaping phenomenon. In particular,
this book unites the lawn with other aesthetic movements both in the history of
art and architecture.[12] Pointed more squarely at social analysis, Fred Schroeder's
1993 *Front Yard America* interrogates the history of the American lawn in terrific detail, empirically dispensing with "natural" explanations for its existence
(see Chapter 1) and pointing to the relatively recent emergence of the "democratic" front yard. More than this, Schroeder's book stands in defense of the yard
as a product of urban democratic history, even while he criticizes some of its
"unintended" economic and ecological side effects, including water and chem-
ical-hungry turfgrasses.[13]

The most recent (2006) and accessible work, Ted Steinberg's *American
Green*, provides exhaustive evidence of the lengths Americans will go to achieve
the perfect lawn. Laid out in the form of an environmental history, the work

shows the step-by-step rise of the lawn aesthetic and the technologies required to fulfill it, including some disturbing and startling facts about lawn mower injuries, among other graphic and visceral stories. This book provides one of the most readable approaches to the problem, one that might be put in front of an extraterrestrial visitor to help both describe and explain American culture.[14] All these books and essays emphasize, justifiably, that Americans love their lawns, viewing them as signs of opulence, leisure, and achievement.

The search for alternatives to the lawn has spawned a noble industry of its own, on the other hand, and most outstanding in this regard are *The Landscaping Revolution* and *Requiem for a Lawnmower*, by Sally and Andy Wasowsky. Combining common-sense solutions with acknowledgment of dynamic ecology (especially the implications of increasing water scarcity), these books provide realistic alternatives for people who want to replace lawns with something else.[15]

While I would direct any serious student of the lawn (or of vernacular culture more generally) to these excellent works, this book begins where they leave off. While I draw heavily on the insights of these previous explorations, the volume diverges in its emphasis on explaining the work the lawn does on us as individuals, communities, and cities. The book also adopts an approach that focuses especially on broader political economy, since while the lawn is of course a fundamental product of American imagination–a symbol–it is also a vast and coercive economy. More specifically, monocultural lawn cultivation imposes a set of economic relationships between grasses, weeds, chemicals, companies, and people.

It is not enough, this book suggests, to argue that the peculiar history of America (along with Australia and other places where turfgrass lawns prevail) led to a series of unrelated pressures to produce this relationship. The depth, ubiquity, and resilience of the resulting pattern requires us to consider, rather, the relationship between these various forces and actors. Do turfgrasses, chemical companies, communities, and individuals simply co-inhabit the world as an unfortunate accident, or is there a political, economic, and sociocommunal bond between them? If so, how does it function and how might it be shattered? How do lawn *workers* (we who maintain these landscapes) become *subjects* of the turfgrass economy? How do turfgrass relationships coerce firms and communities to create altogether new kinds of people? To answer these questions, this volume depends on quite a bit of primary data (interviews, measurements, surveys) to get a clearer picture of why people and grasses do what they do. The original research draws on three years of funding from the National Science Foundation (Award #0095993), and was conducted between 2001 and 2004. The research involved a range of methods including a national survey; some air photograph analysis; a survey of lawn chemical applicators; an investigation of business reports; and interviews with homeowners, business owners, and university extension agents. The details of how this work was conducted and the more exhaustive data that resulted are available for review in Appendix B. These have been left out of the main body of the text to make room in the volume for the arguments to follow.

The Rest of the Volume

Chapter 1 briefly presents a portrait of lawn people and their curious characteristics and beliefs, specifically showing how lawn chemical users are more likely to be concerned about using chemicals than nonusers. It then lays out the conceptual architecture of the approach taken in the book, interrogating the assumptions with which the lawn is typically viewed, in order to offer a hypothesis to explain this curious contradiction. Specifically, this chapter points to the instability of several apolitical ideas about people, communities, and economies, including the notion that environmental outcomes like the lawn are simply the product of *culture, choice,* and economic *demand,* and that nonhuman actors such as turfgrass have little or no influence on the outcomes that involve them. The chapter offers an alternative, explicitly political approach, which points to the mutual tyranny that individuals, communities, firms, and lawns exert over one another. It further argues that it may be useful to think about the lawn as a kind of sociotechnical system, which produces a political and economic turfgrass subject–that sort of urban/suburban person whose identity is interpellated (literally from the French, "called" into self-recognition) by the high-input lawn, and whose life is disciplined by the material demands of the landscapes they inherit, create, and maintain.

    Chapter 2 critically evaluates the idea that the lawn is an expression of American culture, rather than of economy and politics. Surveying the history of both the idea and practice of lawn maintenance in the New World, the chapter points to the way lawn grasses have come to thrive as part of a larger pattern of ecological conquest since 1492. It also emphasizes the way the lawn has, since its inception, been proffered as an instrument both for maintaining growth in contemporary urban development and for creating a responsible domestic American citizen: a responsible, domestic kind of person. Rather than simply being an artifact of culture then, the lawn is better understood as a vehicle for creating certain kinds of cultural subjects.

    Chapter 3 examines what turfgrass lawns *require* (especially in terms of chemical inputs and labor) to maintain the green, monocultural aesthetic most valued by lawn people. Surveying the ecology of turfgrasses and the demands of lawns, the chapter concludes that not only are inputs required but that, should anything like the ideal be maintained, the multiple needs of this kind of lawn over seasons and years become the necessary concerns of lawn owners and so govern their behaviors from day to day, and season to season. The rhythms of turfgrass become those of suburban communities and subjects.

    Whether or not these inputs represent a meaningful hazard to lawn people themselves or the larger ambient ecosystem, and whether that hazard has become more or less acute over the last century, is the focus of **Chapter 4**, which surveys the history of the lawn chemical industry and the risks associated with the current dominant suite of lawn chemicals. Based on both toxicology and on analytical chemistry, evidence is amassed to show the specific ways that these lawn chemicals escape after treatment to influence the broader environment and to enter homes and accumulate and persist as a chronic hazard. The chapter demonstrates that the hazards that concern lawn people are quite real, though fraught with uncertainty, making their position necessarily one of anxiety and unease.

Is this risk an incidental or fundamental part of the economy that produces lawn chemicals? **Chapter 5** addresses this question through an examination of the lawn chemical economy—including chemical formulators (companies that produce consumer products), chemical application companies (who come to your home to spray), and the chemical production companies that ultimately supply them. The results show that there are increasing demands and constraints placed on the industry not only by the market and regulation, but also by the limits created by nature: seasonality and variability. These constraints have resulted in stalled growth, consolidation, and debt. As a result, there have been aggressive recent efforts to secure new markets both by increasing the inputs of current users and by turning nonchemical users into chemical users. This cascade of influences, from producers to providers to homeowners, suggests that pressures within the economy have necessarily led to the externalization of risk onto consumers and workers. They have also led to innovations in direct marketing to bombard homeowners with symbols that reflect a specific urban subject, using images connecting lawn maintenance to community and family.

But how is this manifested in lawn people's decision making and experience? **Chapter 6** examines the motivations and doubts of lawn chemical users through review of national survey results and in-depth interviews with cul-de-sac dwellers. The results show how anxious homeowners reconcile their behaviors with their beliefs, usually through consideration of collective good, community values, and moral obligations. These results reveal that lawn people do not simply "choose" to maintain their lawns, but instead act under the burden of reconciling a range of contradictions in both economy and community.

In the face of such pressures, do alternatives exist and are they realistic? Recently, a range of alternatives to the chemical-input lawn care have emerged, taking the form both of institutional/legal controls, as well as informational and advocacy organizations and new products. **Chapter 7** briefly discusses these changes and reforms, pointing to areas of achieved success (e.g., Canadian chemical bans) as well as potential success (e.g., organic lawn approaches). The chapter emphasizes, however, the degree to which these alternatives face steep social and legal opposition. It also raises questions about how effective alternatives can be if they follow the apolitical logics of free consumer choice and moral citizenship inherent within the existing lawn economy.

Chapter 8 offers a summary of the findings, stressing the way people become turfgrass subjects, through a coercive economy, fraught with uncertainty and anxiety, mediated by a moral dedication to community and family. In so doing, it briefly raises several related questions about the role of anxiety in political and economic change as well as the role of objects in the world around us in making us who we are. Is anxiety politically emancipatory, and do progressive activists need to understand it better? And if objects and landscapes are constantly acting on us, our economies, identities, and polities, has the time come to reconsider the problem of environmental "influences," long eschewed for fear of environmental "determinism"?

The book concludes then, that whereas the aesthetic of the lawn may be old, indeed ancient, the turfgrass subject is new: the urban person who is concerned about nature but uses chemicals, who supports the Kyoto Protocol but drives an SUV, who recycles fervently while constantly wasting more and more. Rather than condescendingly dismissing such inconsistencies as "cognitive dissonance" as is common to apolitical critique, the book advances an alternative, which emphasizes the range of constraints on our alternatives and that stresses the way the biotechnical machines we make increasingly make us who we are.

What the book does *not* argue, however, is that grasses are in and of themselves "bad." The often-vaunted value of turfgrass is true. Grasses on rooftops can help to cool the urban heat island. In agricultural watersheds they can buffer and decompose toxins. Grown as an alternative energy source, grasses can sequester carbon. In urban watersheds, they can slow storm water runoff and reduce noise pollution. In this sense grasses are "good," if such a distinction can be applied to a huge family of species.[16] Turfgrasses predate us in this world and will no doubt outlast us; they are no more pernicious than we are.

Having said this, the specific form the modern lawn takes—large, monocultural, and chemically demanding—is by no means a good thing, nor is it the only landscape physically available to us around our homes. More than this, the poorly hidden costs and risks associated with the contemporary lawn are numerous and expanding. Lawns are by no means the only, or indeed the easiest, urban ecological option. And collectively, as we increasingly know them, they represent a self-imposed burden and hazard.

Similarly, this book does *not* argue that American middle class homeowners (a community from whence the author emerges) are a bunch of dupes or shills for capital, unable to think for themselves. Such condescending and classist forms of cultural criticism are both unconvincing and empirically wrong. So too, they suffer from what Fred Schroeder accurately calls "the Philistine Effect" where "vernacular culture usually appears in the historical record as objects of censure, ridicule, contempt or pity."[17] On the contrary, it is my intention to write as a lawn person myself; a middle class homeowner and neighbor, until recently one with a lawn and a mower–a deeply embedded participant in that which I observe, with no more scorn for my neighbor than I hold for myself.

Even so, as I hope to show here, there are clear tensions between our many contradictory desires; we want to be good citizens, good consumers, and good environmental stewards, a triumvirate that may simply be unachievable. Born of class-based identities and community ideologies, the specific forms that these honest desires take are all further enmeshed in a larger political economy. Simply because we wish to avoid classist analysis, does not mean we should avoid class analysis.

CHAPTER 1

Explaining Lawn People

W E SPOKE WITH SUZANNE at her home in 2001. A resident of a small Midwestern subdevelopment, she told us about her problems with lawn care, especially chemicals, and how she and her family have reconciled themselves to their use, despite disturbing effects.

> One of our dogs was very allergic to the [lawn chemical] treatment. In the spring when they would start to fertilize, his paws would just get raw and bleed. We would have to take him to the vet two or three times a week and they would do these whirlpool treatments and finally we realized it was the lawn chemicals. So, for a couple of days after we had the grass done we would put these little booties on the dog. Otherwise it would really hurt him, and he would just bite and chew at his paws and they would bleed all over the place. We felt so badly for him.

Clearly, Suzanne and her family were not insensitive to the plight of the animal, and the alternate solution they devised—dog booties—makes a certain kind of sense, but only if changing lawn care practices and priorities is overlooked entirely, along with the possible implications that these treatments might have on people in the household or children in the neighborhood. Why not stop using pesticides? Is it something peculiar about Suzanne?

A Profile of Lawn People

For decades, researchers in environmental sociology, geography, and marketing have attempted to explain these kinds of behaviors, along with the embrace of alternatives. Empirically comparing ecologically motivated consumers ("greens") with environmentally disinclined ones ("browns"), this research has tried to explain a range of behaviors such as purchasing green products, recycling, or engaging in environmentally related political action. Generally, the approach tests sociodemographic (rich/poor), geographic (North/South), partisan (Republican/Democrat), and personality (selfless/selfish) characteristics to see what kinds of people behave in what sorts of ways.[1]

Studies suggest, for example, that women, older people, more highly educated people, and people from higher social classes engage in more environmentally protective behavior than men and less-educated people or those of poorer social class.[2] People residing in areas of higher property values have been shown to be more likely to recycle and donate to altruistic causes.[3] Urbanites appear to claim greater environmental concern than rural residents, though this gap closes when actual behaviors are examined.[4] Based on this kind of previous research, one might predict that demographic, geographic, personality, and community characteristics all combine to make people behave the way they do. If we are to believe these kinds of sociodemographics of green behavior, a profile of a high-intensity, lawn chemical user *should* look something like this: males, older people, less educated people, or people with lower incomes should be more likely to use lawn chemicals than females, younger people, or people with higher education and incomes. Rural residents and people in Southern and Western census regions should be more likely to use lawn chemicals than urban residents and people in Midwestern and Northeastern census regions. People who believe that residential lawn care behaviors have no impact on water quality should be more likely to use them than people who are environmentally informed and believe that residential lawn care behaviors do affect water quality problems.

The results of our own national survey (see Chapter 6 and Appendix B for more details) present a totally inverse picture and contradict the expectations outlined above. The positive and negative directions of statistically significant relationships are summarized in Table 1.1.

The survey results show that whether someone uses lawn chemicals (professional lawn care, do-it-yourself chemicals, or both) is related to all of the influences described above (region, neighborhood, and environmental concerns), but in almost the reverse of the expectations laid out previously. Lawn chemical users tend to have higher income and higher housing values, be better educated, and be older than nonusers. They live in nonrural (urban or suburban) settings, more often in the Midwest and South than the Northeast or West. They are also more likely to have neighbors that use chemical inputs.

What is perhaps most remarkable is that people who use chemicals on their lawn tend to be more likely to believe that lawn care has a negative effect on local water quality than people who do not. This somewhat counterintuitive finding (consider that those who do *not* claim lawn chemicals are a problem are less likely to actually use them!) certainly suggests that values and ideas (what

TABLE 1.1 Predictors of U.S. Lawn Chemical Use: Direction of significant relationship, positive (+) or negative (−)

Parameter	Chemical Use
Income	+
Rural	−
Neighbors use lawn chemicals	+
Housing Value	+
Education	+
Claim that lawn chemicals generally have a negative impact on local water quality	+
Claim that lawn-care services have a negative impact on local water quality	+
Claim that neighbors' lawn care practices have a negative impact on local water quality	+
South or Midwest	+
Age	+

people believe) do not translate into behaviors (what people do). As a general profile, people who use chemicals do so despite claiming they have negative impact, especially if their neighbors use chemicals. These people either claim that there is a negative impact but do not *care*, or they act despite their misgivings. As we shall demonstrate later, the latter attitude is far more common than the former one; lawn people worry a lot about what they do, although their behavior is not always altered by that belief.

Clearly, Suzanne is in no way aberrant. Something is at work on her that puts the lawn before the dog, which allows her to reconcile potential evidence of more general risk, and which forces her to live simultaneously with her lawn and her anxiety. Well-educated, affluent, and fully cognizant of a technological hazard, she chooses to maintain her current practices rather than seek out alternatives.

Lawn chemical use is only one facet of lawn care, of course, and myriad other behaviors are relevant to understanding people's relationships with their lawns. Yet this initial result already upsets some simple assumptions about people's thoughts and actions, and raises some straightforward questions. What makes lawn people act this way? What influences their behaviors? How do people reconcile the complex outcomes of their decisions?

Interrogating Assumptions in Apolitical Ecology

The ability to explain beliefs and practices like these is diminished by several typical assumptions that we tend make about human beings and their environmental behaviors. Specifically, there is a tendency to think about lawns, and other landscapes and practices, in a largely *apolitical* way. Apolitical thinking is taken to mean here, simply, the view that decisions and behaviors are free from coercion, suggestion, power, and exploitation. Apolitical ecology, the dominant approach to thinking about the things people do and the places people make, includes several more specific tendencies, including (1) a focus on free individual *choices*, (2) a propensity to assign *culture* a driving role in understanding group behavior, (3) a predisposition to think of economic activities and the behavior of firms as meeting consumer *demand*, and (4) an inclination to think about human actions, whether those of individuals or companies, as *sovereign* relative to the influence of nonhuman actors, objects, and animals. Each are worth considering in turn.

First, apolitical ecology holds that most outcomes, ecological or otherwise, are the product of choices. People choose to recycle or they do not, to commute to work or not, to use responsibly produced products or not. Similarly in this way of thinking, companies choose to make their products safer, choose methods of advertising, and choose the prices and characteristics of their products. Indeed, choice is such a fundamental assumption about human behavior that it is hard to imagine any other way of thinking about what we do. This view also influences how we think about ecological reform. To make a cleaner, safer, less toxic world, individuals must be supplied with more and better information about hazards, hidden impacts, and invisible costs. With better knowledge will come better behavior.

Where we admit that people's behaviors may be less than fully "rational," there is a further tendency to think about aberrant, regional, or specific kinds of behaviors as expressions of "culture." Culture, in this case, is taken to mean the way certain groups of people do things—habits of action and understanding shared by communities, families, tribes, states, and nations. These, in turn, are understood to produce certain kinds of landscapes—social and natural environments that express something not just about individual decisions, but a collective identity.

From an apolitical way of thinking, moreover, economic actors (specifically, people and firms who supply goods and services to individuals), do so in an effort to meet, or perhaps exploit, the already existing demands of individuals and culture groups. These firms, it is also generally assumed, have a certain range of free choice themselves, and can produce safe or dangerous products, preserve or destroy ecosystems, and decrease or maintain risk, just as they please. Finally, there is a tendency in apolitical ecological thinking to consider people–human beings–as the sole sovereign actors in creating and maintaining the world around them. In this way of thinking, if nonhuman nature ever had influence or power over people it was only in the remote past, before absolute dominion was eventually obtained by humanity, at least in the world of human affairs.

For understanding the lawn, this apolitical way of thinking has several implications. First, it suggests that people freely choose to have, maintain, and care for lawns. Second, it means that this desire (to the degree that it overrides some rational thinking on the part of individuals) is born of a collective culture, specifically something deeply "American." Third, it means that this nearly time-less individual and collective demand is met by an industry that has inevitably grown to meet that demand, spawning a multibillion dollar economic sector driven by consumer desire. Finally, it suggests that the lawn is not natural in any sense, but is a wholly manufactured and humanized landscape. It is influenced and quite literally produced by people and companies who are not, in any mean-ingful way, influenced in return by the passive grasses from which the lawn is constituted.

But in the hesitant practices of lawn people lies a hint that things are not always so apolitical as they might immediately seem. Clearly people who par-ticipate in intensive lawn care, as described previously, have mixed desires, and indeed feel more ambivalence about lawn care than those who do not. This sug-gests outside influences on free choice, if not outright coercion. More gener-ally, there are theoretical reasons to imagine that apolitical ways of thinking about behavior, culture, economy, nature, and risk, are problematic. Concepts and evidence from "political ecology," an alternative way of thinking about the power-laden nature of human interactions with the environment, undermine notions of choice, freedom, culture, and the autonomy and impotence of the nonhuman world.[5]

Do People Get to Choose What They Do, or Even What They Want?

It is perhaps inevitable that we imagine ourselves creatures of choice, especially in contemporary America. Stores are filled with a dazzling array of consumer options. The general affluence of North American people give them enhanced freedoms of choice, as do the promises of democratic government. Environ-mentally, people clearly make decisions every day: to drive, walk, or take the bus; to recycle or simply throw away the trash; and to apply or not apply chemicals to their lawn.

Sociobehavioral research starting from this assumption of free choice has tried in the past to examine why having or expressing concerns about the envi-ronment generally fails to actually coincide with what people really do, whether that is recycling, donation, or conservation.[6] People who "talk green" may fail to "act green" because they lack full information or may be skeptical of infor-mation,[7] because they believe that environmental problems are too complex to be solved by individual action,[8] or because they believe that environmental protection is the responsibility of the government.[9]

Research like this been has criticized for poor sampling, obsolete data, conflation of attitudes with behavior, and conflicting results.[10] It has also been subject to the complaint that environmental consciousness has become so mainstream in modern society that environmental concern cannot be assigned to certain demographic groups.[11] Green consumer studies are also hindered by a lack of specificity. People with a general concern for global environmental problems such as climate change or wildlife extinction may be fully unaware of local environmental issues like groundwater pollution, especially when they are not directly affected by such problems.[12] At the same time, concern for the environment takes many forms, including the belief that the balance of nature should not be disturbed, or that economic growth has limits, or that certain relationships between humans and nature are ordained by God, or that humans must change to meet nature's demands.[13] Compressing these beliefs into a single measure of environmental concern masks the relationship between environmental attitude and behavior.

Whatever problems such research may have on its own terms, political ecology questions the approach altogether and begins from an different point of view. Specifically, research in this field has directed itself to the fact that individual actions are not the result of "free" decisions by any means. Commuters are forced by rents and housing costs to live further and further from their places of work, resulting in more drive time, more fuel use, and more carbon emission. Increased packaging of almost every imaginable consumer item means a mounting pile of garbage for households to sort, recycle, destroy, or dump, all on their own time. Urban residents of the United States are far more likely to think themselves masters of their own destiny than people living elsewhere in the globe, but it is increasingly clear that the range of choices open to even the most apparently wealthy and powerful people in the world is severely restricted. Although political ecologists Piers Blaikie and Harold Brookfield originally intended their comments to describe rural peasant producers, their twenty-year-old assertion remains cogent: any explanation of local phenomenon (e.g., application of lawn chemicals) is nested within a wider context of pressures and coercions. Their claim that "there is no 'correct' scale for an investigation of land managers and their decisions"[14] is as true for the lawn manager in Ohio as it is for the grower of millet in India. Any meaningful explanation of human behaviors, they suggest, must follow a chain, which:

> starts with the land managers and their direct relations with the land (crop rotations, fuelwood use, stocking densities, capital investment and so on). The next link concerns their relations with each other, other land users, and groups in the wider society who affect them in any way, which in turn determines land management. The state and the world economy constitute the last links in the chain.[15]

In other words, lawn people may make their own landscapes, but not always the landscapes of their own choosing (in a geographic paraphrase of Karl Marx).[16] The constraints in such arrangements begin to appear as soon as one starts looking for them; in the household, in the community, in the marketplace, in the rules and laws of the state, in the restrictions and opportunities available at any number of levels.

As a result, just as Blaikie and Brookfield long ago insisted for the interpretation of agricultural land use practices, castigation of lawn people as "ignorant," "stupid," and "conservative" misses the point, in so far as they operate within boundaries and constraints, and because "where there is a known set of practices and behavioral responses, it is . . . much easier for the [manager] to adhere to an established pattern than to make changes." What we need to understand and empirically evaluate in the case of the lawn then (as we explore in this volume), are the contextual pressures of real estate, community, and municipality, which may or may not together *enforce* high-input lawn care choices.[17]

More forcefully, it might also be suggested that even these enforced "choices" reflect no real freedom for these practitioners. As some critical materialist philosophers suggest instead, the intentions, plans, and concepts of the future these individuals hold–which are all prerequisite to making choices–might be seen as *consequences* of social processes rather than as causes. That is, what people want might in and of itself be a product of who they are and the role they play in the society and economy.[18]

This is not to say that people do not take action, nor make history happen. Nor is it to say that people want things because they are told to want them. Instead, a political ecology of lawn people asks us to look at our actions and desires differently than we typically do, by assessing our role in occupying certain political places and serving certain economic functions. It is somewhat disturbing to think of ourselves in this way, of course, but as we shall see below, it opens the possibility of admitting the power certain things (like lawns) often have over us.

Are Landscapes Expressions of Culture?

If our choices are not unconstrained and the scope of what we desire may be somewhat circumscribed, it might be tempting to think that our "culture"–the way of thinking and doing in which we were raised and live–might be the central influence on us. We make and create things, it would be sensible to assume, the way people within our culture do.

Following this line of thinking, common sense thinking as well as generations of good academic scholarship has tended to view landscapes like lawns as "cultural." Landscapes–those assemblages of buildings, plants, machines, infrastructure, light, color, and sound that provide the backdrop for our myriad daily actions–can be viewed as being shaped by human action, but usually in the constantly reinforced patterns of our larger community. In this way of thinking, certain kinds of people, from particular cultural backgrounds, tend to produce and live in certain kinds of landscapes. Amish people produce Amish landscapes. Chinese produce Chinese landscapes. Americans produce American landscapes.

Such an apolitical perspective on culture lends itself to a specific view of the lawn. The lawn landscape, although not unique to America, does appear to predominate here in a way that it does not even in its regions of origin in the Old World. Americans have tendencies, such as being gregarious and neighborly and romantic about yeoman farming, which are unique to their history on this continent and which might make their desire for lawns seem almost inevitable. In this way of thinking, American Lawns are an outward, unconscious, expression of American collective psyche.

But even the Scotts company, a dominant firm in lawn care chemicals and services, insists in its own messages to shareholders and consumers that "beautiful lawns don't just happen."[19] To make this landscape normal, as we shall see, requires repeated representation both of the aesthetic ideal and the enormous battery of consumer goods and services that make it possible. This closely echoes the thinking of geographer Don Mitchell, who observes that distinct, meaningful, cultural objects like the modern lawn "are actively *made*," that culture is not just a "realm" but also an industry, and that cultural representation usually furthers political and economic effects and purposes.[20]

And following on the related work of sociologist Sharon Zukin, average consumers and homeowners are not the only people who produce and reproduce these cultures. In the case of the lawn, advertisers, investors, chemical lab technicians, developers, and a host of other players provide the "critical infrastructure" that makes this landscape not only possible, but also impossible to unimagine.[21] A large cast of characters and objects together act to give cultural meaning to turfgrass, all as part of a larger system of economic production.

For theorists like Antonio Gramsci, upon whom both Mitchell and Zukin draw, apparently willing participation in practices like applying lawn chemicals—practices that make us uneasy or indeed fill us with dread—test the boundaries between consent and coercion. As queried above, how much have we "chosen" to act as we do? Moreover, coming to call such coercion "cultural" begins to seem more problematic, indeed somewhat sinister. Gramsci refers to the enforcement of consent, in such cases, as evidence of *hegemony*: the pervasive power to turn enforcement into something that appears to happen "spontaneously," or is uncritically experienced as something inevitable, something like "culture."[22] In sum, culture and the industries of cultural production that undergird it can be understood as being inextricably linked not only to the economy that they serve to perpetuate, but also to hegemonic habits that cause us to take them for granted, to make them "cultural" in the first place. In a political ecological view of the lawn then, the very insistence on the cultural aspects of lawn maintenance is essential for rendering invisible its political and economic core, including the coercive requirements in maintaining the landscape and the industry such behaviors support.

Are Hazards an Accidental Byproduct of Capitalist Ecology?

But the landscapes we produce, cultural or otherwise, are not simply ideas, representations, or even exchanges of capital. Rather, they have concrete material characteristics and effects. In the case of lawn people, what is notable about the material nature of this aesthetic is that it is perceived as physically bad for water quality (and dogs, and children, as we shall see) by the people who maintain it. This raises questions about hazards and the accepting of risk.

A "hazard" refers to objects or processes, whether "human made" (nuclear waste) or natural (volcanic gases), that might harm people or the ecosystems on which they depend, and will be used in this text specifically to refer to real or potential undesirable problems that come from maintaining a lawn, especially chemical externalities.[23] "Risk," on the other hand, refers to the probability of a (typically negative) outcome occurring, or more generally encompasses the way people think about and calculate their behaviors with a knowledge, however uncertain, of potentially negative outcomes for themselves or the world around them.[24] In considering lawn people then, as described briefly above, we see a type of individual who acknowledges a potential hazard in lawn maintenance behavior, but whose risk calculation involves the decision to continue such behaviors, nonetheless.

But as we shall see, many of us do take risky actions with a vague trust (driven by somewhat apolitical thinking) that companies and service providers would not knowingly put them at risk. Even assuming so critical a configuration of culture and economy as explored above, where lawn culture may be perpetuated to serve narrow economic interests, it is indeed hard to imagine a system in which an economy would inflict actual hazards upon the consumers and environments upon whom it depends for survival.

Certainly the lawn chemical industry is adamant on both this point and its underlying logic. James Allen, Executive Director of "Responsible Industry for a Sound Environment," a standing committee of the pesticide industry's association, insists not only that lawn chemicals are safe, but are tested some 120 times before release, ". . . lawn chemicals add more than beauty. They have health and environmental benefits as well."[25] This is more than sloganeering; the essential logic of apolitical free market environmentalism holds that the producer of a product designed to protect a landscape or resource would certainly be uncompetitive if the result were the reverse. To the degree that hazards are possible outcomes of certain facets of industrial ecology, these can be relegated to factors beyond the control of the seller: consumers may use products in an incorrect or irresponsible fashion, for example by applying excessive chemicals

and failing to follow safety instructions. Or in a worst case, such negligent externalities, in the form of hazards to consumers or the environment, might be seen
as the unfortunate risk choices of a few bad apples, negligent firms acting outside the realm of capitalist logic and ethics.

Critical economic theory, however, is less sanguine on the illogic of industrial hazards to the environment. For observers like theorist James O'Connor,
it is clear that "capital"—including investors, companies, and those who operate and plan for them, no matter how well-meaning—is essentially incapable of
"preventing itself from impairing its own conditions."[26] This is because the economy tends to be constantly riddled by crisis. As the ongoing stress of competition tends to cause prices to fall, uncompetitive firms disappear and survivors
continue to innovate ways of shedding costs and responsibilities. Just like consumers, investors, owners, advertisers, and planners, guided by even the most
sharpened corporate ethics, must operate under conditions that are not entirely
(or even partly) under their control.

For producers especially the cheapest and most efficient techniques must be
embraced, and costs must constantly be shed. These costs include a huge range
of enormous expenses for which insufficient revenue exists, including expenses:

> to cleanup or repair the legacy of ecological destruction from the past;
> monies required to invent, develop, and produce synthetics and "natu-
> ral" substitutes as means and objects of production and consumption;
> the huge sums required to pay off oil sheiks and energy companies (e.g.,
> ground rent and monopoly profit); the garbage disposal costs; the extra
> costs of congested urban space . . .[27]

In this way of thinking, such costs, including especially the costs potentially coming from risky production, must either be realized in corporate
reinvestment, borne willingly by the broader public, or ignored altogether.
Given the profoundly competitive state of globalized trade, the first option is
impossible, the second increasingly rare, and the third not only logical but
increasingly inevitable.

At the same time, however, critical approaches to environmental impact
suggest that such costs are never borne evenly. Congestion, pollution, and the
urban hazards produced by economic growth have repeatedly been demonstrated to seek out the most politically and economically disempowered communities,[28] as well as environments for which there have historically been few
vocal representatives (e.g., wetlands–formerly known as "swamps"). As Erik
Swyngedouw observes then, there is no such thing as the unsustainable city in
general, but there are a series of urban and environmental processes that neg-
atively affect some social groups while benefiting others. A just urban socioenvironmental perspective, therefore, always needs to consider the question of
who gains and who pays . . .[29]

What might this mean for lawn care? It suggests that lawn chemicals and other inputs might represent a solution for increasingly competitive global markets looking for buyers of available goods and services. And excessive sales and usage of such inputs, rather than being bad for business, may be one of the few avenues to sustain economic growth in larger global energy and chemical sectors. Rather than an incidental outcome of bad corporate behavior, chemical hazards may be the inevitable consequence of decisions made by perfectly rational and well-meaning economic players. The distribution of such hazards, moreover, may be unevenly realized throughout the city, or externalized further out into environments beyond the urban boundary.

But the diffuse nature of contemporary hazards and the uncertainty surrounding them poses a final further problem for understanding lawn people. Specifically, modern urban people inhabit what Ulrich Beck describes as a "Risk Society." This means that there are a great many new and previously undreamed hazards in contemporary life (man-made herbicides and pesticides among them), but also that society more generally has geared towards calculating and managing those hazards both by creating a new technical knowledge elite and also by "individuating" risk decisions.[30] Individuation is here understood to mean the way "people are invited to constitute themselves as individuals: to plan, understand, design themselves as individuals and, should they fail, to blame themselves."[31] Their increasingly complex risk decisions become part of their biographies, moreover, part of defining who they are (e.g., "environmentalists," "conservatives," or "good neighbors").

Combining this insight with the critical economy of O'Connor, a clear pattern emerges. Under tightening economic conditions and in the face of crises, producers may not only be forced to shift increasing hazards downwards and outwards to consumers and workers, but also to present contemporary urban residents, like lawn people, with increasingly complex risk choices, the burden of which is increasingly the individual's to sort out, internalize, and live with.

In sum, if viewed apolitically, the problem of chemical hazards tends not to include considerations of (1) who gains and loses in risk decisions, (2) what logics and forces act on firms making such decisions, and (3) what responsibilities contemporary consumers are increasingly faced with, under the conditions of risk and uncertainty that result. A political approach to the risk ecology of the lawn, which addresses all these issues, seems relevant for understanding the problem.

Is Nonhuman Nature an Inactive Player in Urban Life?

A final problem in apolitical thinking about ecology takes the form of common assumptions about the environment itself. It is quite normal for most of us to think about "nature" as something that is both *outside the city* and as something, even where it is present, that is *passively molded* by human action.

In the first case, the concepts of "urban," "city," and "society" have typically been contrasted with their inverse "others"–"rural," "country," and "nature." Historically, these oppositional categories actually emerged in the process of urbanization itself, through literary and cultural expressions during the era of industrialization.[32] Such oppositional thinking persists in our own lives. Trying to get far from the city and "get away" to nature on our vacations, we constantly remind ourselves of these binaries and distinctions.

But this habit of thinking is just that, a habit. As Matthew Gandy reminds us in *Concrete and Clay*, his environmental history of New York City,

> It is paradoxically in the most urban of settings that one becomes powerfully aware of the enduring beauty and utility of nature. It is the reshaping of nature that has made civilized urban life possible. Nature has a social and cultural history that has enriched countless dimensions of the urban experience. The design, use, and meaning of urban space involves the transformation of nature into a new synthesis.[33]

Indeed, a growing body of urban history has come to emphasize the way cities are nothing but nature–metals, glass, and water–flowing through political and economic conduits. These previously free materials become "fixed" in the built environment but are very much a part of the social and political life of urban areas. Thinking this way, we can begin to see the lawn as a crystallized form of these raw natural materials and ecological forces, tempered, constrained, and spread across neighborhoods during the process of urban growth and housing development.[34]

Of course, nature is more than just passive, manipulated, resources. In reality, uncontrolled nature, or wilderness, exists all around us, pushing through the cracks in the sidewalk, nesting in the trees of vacant lots, and prowling the dusty hills outside of subdivisions. As William Cronon famously observed, our ongoing urge to scan the vistas of "authentic wilderness"–jagged mountains and dense forests–has blinded us to the nature all around us. In admiring the "wildernesses" close to home, including abandoned farms and neighborhood ponds, he explains: "What I celebrate about such places is not just their wildness, though that certainly is among their most important qualities; what I celebrate even more is that they remind us of the wildness in our own backyards, of the nature that is all around us if only we have eyes to see it."[35]

Many of these wild places and conditions are quite unintended outcomes of our own actions. Urban people are constantly making incidental natures, interacting with nonhuman species to create environmental outcomes of startling complexity. The lesser kestrel, a bird of prey currently on the brink of extinction, thrives in some cities of the Middle East, where it nests in clay roof tiles in areas of urban growth, just as the recovery of the peregrine falcon, a threatened species in the United states, is partly predicated on its New York City rooftop nests.The dramatic return of many northern shortgrass prairie species to the Rocky Mountain Front Range, including the bald eagle, is in part enabled by the closure of Rocky Mountain Arsenal, a military toxic dump only eleven miles from Denver Colorado now teeming with wildlife.

More radically, these nonhumans might be viewed as active agents, players in society, politics, and economy, who act outside of our volition to surprising effect, sharing our urban world but also transforming it. For this reason, Jennifer Wolch has come to describe the city as "Zoöpolis," a city of many species. Whereas urbanization puts animals at risk by driving them from the landscape and fragmenting their habitats, she points out that with urban growth an "animal town" emerges that shapes the city itself by attracting and repelling development and forcing interactions on people who can no longer insist on the clean partition between human and nonhuman habitat. Cougars prowl the subdivisions of the Santa Monica Mountains, with economic implications for the real estate industry that brought people and the big cats into increasing contact in the first place.[36]

In this sense, we might think of the lawn not simply as an ecological *product* of human action, aesthetics, and economics. Instead it is an environmental *actor* that forces behaviors, adaptations, and adjustments not only on individuals, but on whole municipal economies, and on the practices of firms that feed, grow, and tend them. Such an actor might be seen to behave and misbehave in its constant interaction with the homeowner and other species (earthworms, grubs, and dandelions most notably). To do so suggests understanding the lawn as autonomous, following its own rules and taking advantage of sociopolitical circumstances even as it is itself taken advantage of by other actors.

As theorist of science Bruno Latour describes microbes, for example, such an understanding raises questions about any simple explanation of political and economic history where one human actor or group is said to have their way over another. "There are not only social relations, relations between man and man. Society is not just made up of men, for everywhere microbes intervene and act . . ." Explaining their interactions in the world of humanity, Latour explains, these microbes "form alliances that complicate those relations in a terrible way."[37]

And as we shall see, the demands of turfgrasses are an immediate and profound influence on homeowners, which set people about tasks that keep them busy throughout the growing season. Given the labor performed by people for other domesticated crop species, as Denis Wood has asked regarding cereal grains–especially maize, which cannot reproduce on its own without its human servants–"who's to say which species has domesticated which?"[38]

The Mutual Tyrannies of Urban Political Ecology

To say this, however, is to say more than that there is a "tyranny" of the lawn over people, an often-asserted comment that only scratches the surface of the problem. At the same time that lawn grasses are obediently served by homeowners, the explosive growth of grass provides opportunities for other actors, especially those in the lawn care industry, who literally capitalize on grass's ubiquity in order to turn local community desires into profits. Simultaneously, however, the fickle habits of grasses may present obstacles and problems for firms who would try to profit from them; those firms are forced to constantly to adapt and alter their strategies. The emergent picture is that of a system of objects; firms, communities, and people are chained together in such a way that they tyrannize one another.

In such a network of associations, each of the separate pieces is not independent, but is instead made to be the way it is by virtue of its relationship to all the other parts. In this way, the term *network* might be used in the sense offered by Latour: It is both a process with its own momentum that gathers together, enrolls, and connects human and nonhuman actors (people, grasses, chemical companies) under its own momentum; and an "achievement" that stabilizes when all the varying actors are in place. In such a network, individuals or organisms do not have free "agency" (will and capacity of their own), but are instead given the capacity or incapacity to act only by virtue of their position in a complex of different elements. In such a model, "power," as Murdoch observes, "lies not in the properties of actors but in the relationship established between them." Nor is the identity of each actor independently formed and then joined to the whole. Instead, each becomes what it is through its specific relation to the other, through a process academic theorists describe as "translation." As Donna Haraway insists, "through their reaching into one another, through their 'prehensions' or graspings, beings constitute each other and themselves. Beings do not pre-exist their relatings."[39]

This notion of power (which reflects the approach of Michel Foucault)[40] means that one actor can no more volunteer to change the system than it can to change itself. It also means, however, that transformations can occur at a range of scales and locations, not simply at some central location, contrary to the hierarchical assumptions of some social science theory, where large-scale global actors are assumed to dominate and explain local effects and conditions. A single community—a set of local ecological conditions or political institutions—can transform itself and its role in the larger system, creating momentum for regional effects, enrolling and transforming other actors. This approach to social, political, and economic causes and effects is skeptical of the hierarchy of scale and the top-down tendencies typical of most explanations in the social sciences.

Lawn People: "Interpellation" of a Political and Economic Subject

Taken together, this proposition that the lawn is a political and economic network also should provide us with a better portrait of ourselves. But this is not because by seeing the lawn we are seeing an external expression of something internal to us. Rather it is because the lawn, among myriad other objects of daily life, constitutes who we are. In daily life, this means that personal identity, the way people imagine themselves as members of their families and communities, might be as much a product as a driver of lawn care.

To begin to understand how this might work, we need to think of the role of ideology in guiding both our behaviors and our sense of self. No one does anything (including lawn care) simply because someone else tells them to. There must be some tacit *idea*, based on one's notion of oneself, that such actions are right and good. There must be some process, moreover, where people are called upon to be right and good, where this makes them upstanding citizens and where such citizenship comes to be associated with these few specific performances of good neighborliness. This system of ideas, this ideology, must seem natural and indeed essential to us as people, otherwise mounting anxieties (about chemical application as one obvious example) might cause us to think twice.

The dominant system of ideas prevailing in a society, its *ideology*, according to Louis Althusser,[41] functions by appearing nonideological–indeed by denying and repelling its own ideological character. It cannot be ideology if we think of it that way; it must be intuitive (or from within), not an idea from without. Likewise, we must feel that only other people (Economics professors, AM talk radio hosts, communists) have ideologies, never ourselves.

Moreover, Althusser argues, such systems of ideas must be material, not just synapses in the brain, since they are embodied, institutionalized, repeated, and lived. You have to act them out. Social agents have ideas (e.g., lawn aesthetics) but these are also actions (e.g., chemical application) and part of a practice (e.g., lawn care). These practices, Althusser adds, in his somewhat off-putting mechanical terminology, are defined by the *material ideological apparatus*, a whole system of ideas through which the elements of the economy (labor, chemicals, surpluses, etc.) are represented back to individuals as a necessity and a sensible, immediate, daily way of life (home, community, and nature).[42]

As such, Althusser insists in his essay *Ideology and Ideological State Apparatuses*, all this ideology can only operate by constituting individuals as *subjects*. The term "subject" has critical dual meaning here. It asserts "free" subjectivity and an actor who acts freely–as in the subject of a sentence–while simultaneously implying a "subjected being, who submits to a higher authority." This dual identity is essential to the function of ideology to erase the ideological character of the economy. The individual as subject must act freely while submitting fully. Subjects must "work by themselves" without evident coercion. Only then can the system of production and flow of surplus from the economy (to lawns and chemical firms for example) remain stable.[43]

Althusser further argues that the mechanisms through which social participants are called upon, "trained," and "have their roles assigned" to them in a capitalist society require a process of recognition, where the subject comes to recognize herself as a subject and responds accordingly. The subject must be "hailed," literally (from the French) named, recognized, and most importantly self-recognized, or in Althusser's term: *interpellated*. In explaining this concept, Althusser draws on the example of a policeman calling to an individual on the street; in the moment the individual turns in recognition of the call, guiltily, he become the subject.[44] This explanation seems compelling for social structures such as law enforcement, or perhaps the Church, since it helps us to understand how apparently noneconomic institutions produce economic effects by assigning stable roles to subjects, who then go about playing their roles in capitalist society. Yet it really says very little about the daily interactions that actually dominate people's lives and human behaviors in nature, economy, and community. In the case of vast ecologies, what does the interpellating? Not the Church, nor the police. Who calls to the lawn chemical user so that they consistently respond as lawn workers? Whose voice does the lawn owner hear as they open the door and look out on the grass, checking the moisture to determine whether it is time to mow?

We hope to demonstrate here that it may be the lawn itself. Desire and diazinon are demanded by lawns, if not by the grasses that constitute them. When the lawn needs cutting, when wild mints or fungi rival its constituent species, when it becomes dry, its signals are apparent to homeowners, whose response is an act of subjection, not only to the lawn, but also to the ideology of community and the international economy of turf maintenance.

So, in gazing into their landscapes, responding to the demands of the grass, and answering these calls, individuals become new kinds of political and economic subjects. As the turf draws its demands from the culture and the community, it helps to mold the capitalist economy into specific forms, and helps to produce peculiar kinds of people–Turfgrass Subjects. It is only these sorts of subjects who can together constitute lawn communities and produce lawn chemical economies. And they do so, working by themselves, in an effort to purify, tend, and maintain an object whose essential ecology is high maintenance, fussy, and energy-demanding. The lawn, an object, helps to constitute the subject.

But for any or all of this to be plausible, to begin to imagine things like hegemony, networks, and interpellation in something so common and apparently desirable as the turfgrass lawn, some traces of these forces must be evident in the history, economy, and daily practice of lawn care. For lawn people to have gotten the way they are by dint of complex over-determined political and economic forces, rather than by free choice, culture, and consumer demand, several things must be empirically true about the modern lawn.

First, the modern lawn cannot be an expression of culture outside of a political and economic history in which property, citizenship, and proper consumer behavior are conjoined. Second, lawns (although not necessarily grasses) must at some level require the inputs invested in them by people, and these demands must enforce human practices and behaviors. Third, chemicals for lawns must also represent real problems, ones born of a risk society where hazards and the burden of risk calculation are shed downwards and outwards. Fourth, input-producing firms must be compelled for broader economic reasons, to eschew lower-input alternatives and to shift risk ecology to consumers. Finally, if this view of the lawn has any leverage, the lawn cannot be something that people simply say "no" to, despite their best intentions, and switch off as a kind of consumer preference. Lawn people must act to some degree against their better judgment in their risk calculation. The range of viable alternatives must be truncated by formal and informal structural barriers.

In this book, each of these assertions will be taken in turn, evaluating how lawns, chemicals, firms, and people must together require one another, stubbornly enforcing their mutual positions, characteristics, strategies, and identities. We will, in the process, reveal the way contemporary urban political ecology is a system of mutual relations, held together in what might be called (following Maria Kaika), a space of flows.[45] These networks of power in the lawn economy, it will be further demonstrated, are not simply knitted together by a flow of value or capital. Rather, they are also joined together by a flow of chemicals, which are, quite simply, bad for children, wildlife, and other living things. They are real, material, and have effects we can understand and normatively judge.

To begin with, however, we must critically evaluate one of the most fundamental assumptions about lawns, that they are an expression of American culture. To this question, we turn first.

Is the Lawn an Expression of American Culture?*

G RASS PREDATES HUMAN CIVILIZATION and occupies places well beyond the confines of the human-inhabited and -dominated world. Perhaps as many as 68 million square kilometers of land are under grassland and pasture.[1] This remarkable figure demonstrates the hardiness of grasses, members of the Poaceae family. A further testimony to the flexibility and adaptivity of grasses is that although they are the youngest group of flowering plants, the grass family has the third largest number of species and is found in even the most extreme climatic conditions. In this sense, *grass* (distinct from the "lawn") cannot be considered an expression of culture in any simple way.

The evolutionary history of grasses, especially turfgrasses, is notably intertwined with that of humanity, however. Many of the earth's grasses have co-evolved with domesticated livestock and their wild ancestors over the last 100,000 years. The major cool-season turfgrasses such as Kentucky Bluegrass, familiar to most homeowners, emerged for the most part from the same geographic location as domesticated cattle, in the ancient Near East. Evolutionary selection for grazing tolerance likely produced the turfgrasses we recognize today. As a result, these turfgrass species grow densely, close to the surface of the soil, and depend heavily on horizontal, rhizomatic growth (rather than seeds) for reproduction.

Our relationship with grasses is therefore prehistorically deep and turfgrass cover has been with human civilization for a very long time, in some form or another. The term *turf* is derived from the Sanskrit word *darbha*, meaning tuft

* Reprinted from Robbins, P. and T. Birkenholtz. (2003). Turfgrass revolution: measuring the expansion of the American lawn. *Land Use Policy* 20:181–194, with permission from Elsevier

of grass. Of the fifteen major world crops today, ten of them are grasses (including wheat, maize, millet, and rice).

The depth of this historical relationship has led many observers to posit a natural and genetic affinity of humans to the lawn in its modern form. This argument can take several forms. Sometimes it is argued that our desire for the lawn is an evolutionary outcome of the experiences of our savanna-dwelling Australopithecine ancestors, whose desire for an open plain of grasses with a view to the horizon for both predators and prey, was handed down to us in the form of the back yard. Other arguments suggest that the lawn originally emerged as a practical matter of clearing woods and forest and keeping wild and fearful landscapes at a safe distance from the home, perhaps also serving as a firebreak.

As Fred Schroeder points out, these speculations, all of which tend to naturalize our current landscape choices as timeless and inevitable, have little empirical basis. The total absence of the home lawn throughout history, especially in Germany and England, where one would most expect to find its "deep roots," is notable. So, too, the dominance of walls (rather than open and contiguous front yards) is the rule rather than the exception not only historically, but geographically.[2] House construction in rural India and the rest of the world demonstrate that the front yard, where such a thing can be said to exist at all, is often a living and working space, usually enclosed or subdivided from adjacent properties by walls, and typically bereft of ground cover, especially grass. The term *lawn*, moreover, referring to a managed grass space, dates to no earlier than the sixteenth century.[3] The lawn is an historically recent development, specific to certain places and times, and most certainly not natural, hard-wired, or inevitable.

The Manor House Tradition: Labor, Land, and Grass

We know from European medieval art that cultivated lawn spaces were represented as part of the garden ideal of paradise. Medieval art work depictions of the Garden of Eden included something like open grass, as did the *prairie émaillée* ("dotted meadow") traditions of fifteenth century tapestry.[4] These ideals were not realized in the real-world landscape until the seventeenth century, however, when palatial plans first began to incorporate large areas of turfgrass as part of manor design. According to art historian Monique Mosser, the distinction between a rambling grass meadow and a "lawn" was established in France during the 1500s, where estate gardeners tended to both. As somewhat arbitrary Renaissance aesthetic, the lawn emerges in this period as a form of architectural expression.

In the following century, however, grass would only "take off" as a major land cover as part of a larger political and economic transition. When the turfgrass aesthetic was exported from the Continent to England in the 1700s, the meadow was left behind and the manicured lawn became more universal. This transition

FIGURE 2.1   Front yards: most people in the world do not have turfgrass front yards. Fronts of homes in Columbus Ohio (A) and Rajasthan India (B).

to lawns was definitively realized as cultivated, mowed, and tended fine grass on manor estates, demanding significant available land and labor inputs. The rise of this landscape, therefore, speaks less to the spread of a culture than the total transformation of land tenure and control of labor.

The emergence of the manor house lawn was specifically afforded by the creation of enclosures throughout the British Isles. The enclosures in the

Scottish Highlands during the 1700s, as a prominent example, led to a decline
in productive farming and an increase in the cultivation of open grasslands on
estates for the purposes of deer hunting. Cottagers and small garden tenants on
English estates were replaced with cultivated turf grass, managed by new armies
of professional gardeners. Paintings of landscapes from the period shows the
range of tasks–scything, rolling, and weeding–to which labor was increasingly
dedicated.[5] An acre of lawn, for example, required at least a day of labor from
three skilled workmen to mow, using the traditional scythe of the period.[6] This
labor, like the labor that would fuel the industrial revolution, could only be made
available through a massive agrarian transition of displacements. From its inception, then, the lawn was an elite political creature and an economic investment,
whose creation and cultivation allowed the spread of turfgrass, initially tied to
the privilege of the aristocracy and the expropriation of property. Lawns were
English "culture," but more clearly they were an expression of proto-industrial
land politics and a labor economy in transition.

The continued rise of this elite English lawnscape in the 1800s also in no way
assured or determined its migration and translation to North American popular
imagination. Indeed, the lawn was so profoundly changed in its transition–from
the English manor tradition, where lawns are grand and enclosed, to the American one, where lawns are small, contiguous, and tied to home life–that no real
corollary to the American suburban lawn exists in England to this day. The export
and translation of the lawn aesthetic to what would become the United States
and Canada, moreover, was predicated on a prior ecological transformation
throughout the Americas.

Ecological Imperialism and American Turf

The indigenous grasses of the Americas are numerous and diverse. This tremendous variety was largely supplanted by aggressive European fodder grasses during the colonial era, a transition that was only later followed in the nineteenth
and twentieth centuries by the establishment of lawn grasses, nearly all of which
are also from outside the Americas.

Indigenous American grasses range from the annuals that dominated the
Native-altered landscapes of New England to the perennials that evolved under
the grazing and trampling of the North American bison. In the first case, where
open parkland was visible in northeastern landscapes at the time of the Pil-
grims, it was the result of Native American use of fire. The periodic burning of
New England forests opened gaps for immediate succession of annual grasses.
These, in turn, provided good habitat for wild grazers (such as deer) and open
range for successful hunting.

Indigenous perennial grasses in the American West, on the other hand, were
heavily influenced by the unique conditions of bison grazing. Heavy grazing
and trampling by these massive herds not only maintained floral diversity on the

prairie,[7] it also influenced the development of grass species evolution, especially in the formation of prairie bunch grasses.[8]

None of these native grasses much resembled the varieties that arrived with the first European settlers in the sixteenth century. Old World species were adapted to cattle and sheep grazing, forming dense, low-lying, turf mats. New World species, on the other hand, evolved under complex regimes of periodic fire and drought, and under grazing by wild ungulates rather than domesticated ones, since no grazing animals were domesticated by New World cultures (with the exception of the llama in the Andes). Although hardy, these indigenous New World grassland communities could not survive the combined onslaught of grazing and agriculture that would come with colonialism. Settlers were disappointed with the quality of grazing they found on first arriving in North America. In New England, wild grass species such as Bluejoint (*Calamagrostis canadensis*) and Fowl Meadow-Grass (*Poa palustris*), among others, were ubiquitous but made poor forage for domesticated cattle.[9] As a result, settlers busily introduced a number of European plants, including clover, as well as some Asian and African grasses. At the same time, a number of Old World grasses and herbaceous weeds volunteered in pastures, including Couch Grass (*Elymus repens [also known as Agropyron repens]*), Knotgrass (*Paspalum distichum*), and the Dandelion (*Taraxacum officinale*); these found little competition from local species and so spread rapidly. The result was a total transformation of the types and distributions of grasses across the continent, especially east of the Mississippi River.

The seeds of these Old World species hitchhiked to the Americas in the stomachs of livestock, and spread under intense grazing pressure. Colonists in New England, according to environmental historian William Cronon, mistakenly assumed that the heavy grazing by their introduced cattle "improved" the quality of the local grasses, which they initially found to be of little use. For the most part, however, the grazing and manuring of these animals actually served to spread exotic Old World perennial pasture grasses, replacing the indigenous annuals altogether.[10]

Many of these grasses were deliberately introduced whereas others undoubtedly invaded under their own momentum. One key member of the latter group of unintended additions to New World ecology was *Poa pretensis*, a grass that was known of in ancient Greece, later renamed "English Grass" (when mixed with clover), and known to us today as Kentucky Blue. The species was probably a hitchhiker, arriving in America incidentally, its seeds making the overseas passage by riding in hay and manure. Initially, it would probably have been a weed in agricultural fields in the colonies of the East Coast. With a strong foothold, however, its expansion was rapid, spreading south and west from the Virginia colonies after 1584. Settlers arriving in the trans-Appalachian West in the early 1800s encountered the species in the area of Kentucky (named for the Caintuck wilderness), which lent the grass its new name. The grass had either outpaced the settlers and crossed the mountain range itself or, more likely, it had come south and east from early French settlements at Kaskaskia and Vincennes.[11] Either way, the exotic plant was already ubiquitous, forming wide pastures over large areas of the Ohio River Valley.

The landscapes west of the Mississippi were somewhat more resistant to change than their Eastern counterparts. These prairies were dominated by hardy species that had been grazed by bison for centuries. These creatures helped to select for tough, disturbance-adapted grasses such as Buffalograss (*Buchloe dactyloides*) and Blue Grama (*Bouteloua gracilis*), and their trampling and grazing benefited the health and diversity of the range, making it less vulnerable to invasion. Indeed Buffalograss is the only remaining indigenous North American grass to be used as a contemporary ornamental turfgrass. Even so, where this grazing regime was lost through the extirpation of the buffalo and the arrival of livestock, many of the benefits of this so-called "grazing effect" were lost, as was much of the native diversity.[12] Although checked therefore, the invasion of Euro-Asian and African grasses continued from coast to coast. To this day, the most common roadside species in North America are exotic, including Orchard Grass (*Dactylis glomerata*), Timothy (*Phleum pratense*), and other foreign *Gramineae* (grass species).[13]

Most importantly, the success of these invaders is not strictly a result of their innate "superiority" over native species. Rather, these species benefited from the westward progress of their allies, including grazing animals and new settlers who modified the landscape in tandem. Alfred Crosby has labeled this pattern of succession a form of "ecological imperialism," where Europeans settlers brought with them a vast set of species or *portmanteau biota*, so called for constituting their biological traveling luggage. These allied species included diseases, songbirds, housecats, weeds, cattle, and horses, which progressed like a phalanx of mutually supporting elements across the Americas, displacing native species and supporting the coercive efforts of human occupation. The rapidity of this transformation and its dramatic ecological success occurred during the "era of exploration," according to Crosby, because previous efforts at colonization (during the Crusades, for example) encountered environments in Asia and Africa where existing sets of diseases, flora, and fauna, were well enough integrated and networked to provide a solid defense.[14]

In this way, Crosby demonstrates that environments and societies create one another, or more abstractly, they are "mutually produced." The success of grasses depends on the success of the human settlement efforts that surround them, and vice versa. While these introduced Old World grasses benefited from European behaviors (grazing, and so forth), so too, settlers catered to the needs of the grasses, by planting and weeding, and animal grazing as they went.

The contemporary lawn does not deviate from this pattern. As shown in Table 2.1, the dominant turf grasses of the United States–used in lawns, playing fields, parks, and golf courses–are all introduced species. Moreover, many are species that arrived in the New World as forage plants for cattle. In

TABLE 2.1   Most Common North American Turfgrass Species and their Origins

Warm Season Grasses	Origin	Cool Season Grasses	Origin
Bahiagrass *Paspalum notatum*	Central or South America	Annual ryegrass *Lolium multiflorum*	Eurasia
Bermudagrass *Cynodon spp.*	Africa	Colonial bentgrass *Agrostis tenuis*	Eurasia
Kikuyugrass *Pennisetum clandestinum*	Africa	Creeping bentgrass *Agrostis palustris*	Europe
St. Augustinegrass *Stenotaphrum secundatum*	Mediterranean and Gulf of Mexico (?)	Kentucky bluegrass *Poa pratensis*	Eurasia
Zoysiagrass *Zoysia spp.*	East Asia	Perennial ryegrass *Lolium perenne*	Eurasia/Africa
		Red fescue *Festuca rubra*	North America, Africa, Eurasia
		Tall fescue *Festuca arundinacea*	Eurasia

this sense, the expansion of the lawn in the twentieth century is only part of an ongoing legacy of grassland transformation since 1492.

The establishment of lawn grass species is clearly not, therefore, a simple expression of an aesthetic culture of the lawn, at least not an expression of that culture innocent of the larger political, economic, and ecological transformations that precede it, are independent from it, and that are driven by a totally distinct set of violent forces. Equally significant, this early history provides one of the first analytical clues for understanding the social ecology of the turfgrass lawn: like the pasture systems that came before them, the lawn and its human allies work together, mutually select one another, and evolve as a team, or a network. Turfgrass "acts" on people even as people act to produce grass.

The American Lawn Tradition

Thus equipped with a range of exotic turf species, a New World landscape tradition was free to adapt to emerging political and economic conditions in America. The lawn's first appearance in America comes as a design feature in pre-Revolutionary public and institutional landscapes. In the English style, estates from New England to the Deep South had terraced lawns from as early as 1712. The style and appearance of these lawns varied widely, however. Some were laid out in geometric patterns, while others followed the more recent "naturalistic" movement of English estate gardening. In either case, the landscape styles, as well as grass species themselves, were imported.[15]

More commonly, lawns appeared as public mustering grounds and commons thorough New England. As in the later construction of Washington, D.C., with its many planned lawn spaces uniting monumental architectural features, lawns were made possible through community and state action and investment and were still in no way tied to a domestic aesthetic. Whereas small collectively managed New England commons differed from the displays of state power in the District of Columbia, lawns in both cases were public commons. Individual homeowners were far less likely to have lawns on their property, although George Washington's lawn at Mount Vernon and Jefferson's lawn at Monticello undoubtedly helped to establish the lawn ideal amongst a cultural elite.[16]

Interpellating a Genteel Subject: Andrew Jackson Downing

There had been an uneven history of large-scale, English style lawnscapes in America before the middle of the nineteenth century. The aesthetic had been tied to the reproduction and representation of state power and elite opulence. Average Americans had no grass lawns, if indeed they had open front or back lots at all.[17] This would at last begin to change in the latter half of the 1800s.

The first and greatest popularizer of the lawn in the nineteenth century was Andrew Jackson Downing, whose *Treatise on the Theory and Practice of Landscape Gardening, Adapted to North America* (first published in 1841) extended the ideal of lawns to the American home. This book, coupled with Downing's other works, was aimed at creating a country-residence style of dwelling, with plenty of space for "pleasuring" and "amusement." In particular, the "Graceful School" of landscape gardening (as opposed to the more rough-hewn Picturesque) aimed at open, grassy, pastoral landscapes. Downing's volume is dominated, as a result, by images of rolling, open designs with well-mown and maintained turf: "whose curves are expressive of grace, surfaces of softness, and growth of richness and luxuriance . . . The keeping of such a scene should be of the most polished kind, -grass mown into a softness like velvet . . ."[18]

While he insisted that "effects like these are within the reach of very moderate means,"[19] the ideal actually operated at a scale of land (as many as five hundred acres) and labor (hundreds of man hours per year) far beyond the average homeowner's means. Downing's enthusiastic support for the lawn waned somewhat in his later writings as a result, when the labor burden required for its construction and maintenance became more apparent. Indeed, the intensive requirements of human labor for cutting with a scythe, as described previously, had not changed much since the century before. In his later writing, Downing in fact advocated sheep rather than human labor for lawn maintenance,[20] a call that was echoed by other horticulturalists from the period.[21]

The principal drive for the advocacy of these otherwise largely unknown pastoral landscapes was directly and normatively guided at *creating* or at least

maintaining, rather than simply catering to, a certain kind of citizen. In particular, the goal of Downing's landscape development was not only to visibly establish the power of an emerging landed middle-class elite, but also to reinforce a
sense of community. In the context of rapidly diversifying and increasingly dense
urban growth, this effort was aimed at preserving a form of genteel citizenry,
bound by an harmonious aesthetic. For Downing, the urgency of this aesthetic
was the result of the demographic and transportation upheavals of the antebel-
lum period:

> to this innate feeling, out of which grows a strong attachment to natal
> soil, we must look for a counterpoise to the great tendency towards con-
> stant change, and the restless spirit of emigration, which form part of
> our national character; and which, though to a certain extent highly nec-
> essary to our national prosperity, are, on the other hand, opposed to
> social and domestic happiness.[22]

The benefits of this form of landscape development, Downing suggested,
would be extended beyond the gardens of country estates to the population
more generally, forming a collective benefit from elite private aesthetic
development:

> the sylvan and floral collections, the groves and gardens, which surround
> the country residence of the man of taste, are confined by no barriers
> narrower than the blue heaven above and around them. The taste and
> treasures, gradually, but certainly, creep beyond the nominal bound-
> aries of the estate, and reappear in the pot of flowers in the window, of
> the luxuriant, blossoming vines which clamber over the porch of the
> humblest cottage by the way side.[23]

For this reason, where the aesthetic was extended to smaller, more densely
settled suburban environments, early advocates and builders strongly argued
against fencing. In Llewellyn Park in New Orange New Jersey, a prototype suburb constructed in the 1850s, "no-fence" agreements gave these smaller lots the
appearance of a single estate with unblocked views and continuous swards of
grass.[24] Lawns would be connected to one another in an unbroken sea.

As explained by art historian Therese O'Malley, this approach to landscape
design marked an unusual combination of simultaneously exclusive and collective values: "Downing's cult of domesticity and community promulgated an indi-
vidualistic yet communitarian ethic. Although his theory has been discussed as
reflecting exclusivity and elitism, in fact it promoted a community ideal, and the
critical tenet that place could create community."[25]

In this design philosophy lay the roots of contemporary contiguous lawns,
and their public role in holding communities together (even to this day, as we

shall see). So in the specific vision for expanding the lawn beyond the manor house and to the newly settled areas of the city, Downing's concept was realized in the roots of the suburban lawn as a culture of community, in which individuals maintained a private yard for public consumption. This kind of "urban subject" was imagined as a bulwark against the chaos of demographic and class upheaval, and the lawn was intended to play a crucial role in cementing and maintaining this identity, this kind of American subject.

Interpellating a Populist Subject: Frederick Law Olmsted

A more populist expression of these same values followed a few years later in the work of Frederick Law Olmsted. Olmsted is well known and celebrated for his work in designing the landscapes of New York's Central Park and the Fens in Boston. He and his followers constructed parks in a number of other American cities including Buffalo, Milwaukee, and Chicago. The design of these spaces all followed Downing's central landscape themes by following a pastoral aesthetic that united English gardening styles, swards of grass, and flowing water. These parks and landscapes were intended with a paternalistic and communitarian goal as well: to better the moral conditions of urban dwellers, especially the working class, by allowing them access to groomed and civilized natural environments.[26]

To facilitate such a social and moral order, the aesthetic of these American parks was imagined with an eye towards rolling, open, grassy spaces. According to Olmsted, "It should be the beauty of the fields, the meadow, the prairies, of the green pastures, and still waters."[27] These parks should, moreover, continue in the rejection of the broken, rugged, romantic, "Picturesque" style of landscape, which cannot be guarded against the "occurrence of opportunities and temptations to shabbiness, disorder, indecorum, and indecency, that will be subversive of every good purpose the park should be designed to fulfill."[28]

In this sense, the order of the design, which depended to a large degree on public turfgrass areas as large, contiguous, monocultural, open spaces, was expected to extend and map itself into the order of the polity. Open space would lead to open activities, open community interaction, and open moral sociability. As Albert Fein observed for Olmsted's development of the Chicago suburb of Riverside, with its large grassy communal spaces following the Des Plains River, the town "would be distinguished by a physical form that encouraged communal activities . . . the strength of the open-space plan, still apparent, lay in the variety of uses made possible by its design."[29]

What is perhaps most notable about Olmsted's legacy is that these very *constructed* natural environments—Boston's "Emerald Necklace" was built on polluted mudflats—are largely not recognized as such today. Niagara Falls and Yosemite, both carefully reworked in Olmsted's designs, ironically represent for

most observers the perfection of pristine nonhuman nature. As Anne Whiston
Spirn notes:

> Olmsted was so skillful at concealing the artifice that both the projects
> he had so brilliantly constructed and the profession he had worked so
> hard to establish became largely invisible. Today the works of the pro-
> fession of landscape architecture are often not "seen," not understood
> as having been designed and deliberately constructed, even when the
> landscape has been radically reshaped.[30]

In this sense, Olmsted's legacy is not just making grassy landscapes, but
naturalizing them so that they appear inevitable, timeless, and appropriate. His
insistence, therefore, on extending Downing's Americanization of the romantic
English garden tradition, with its dependence on large lawn features, must have
gone no small way toward making these exotic features seem normally American. With the rise of public lawns, coupled with the emergence of golf courses
and baseball fields,[31] carefully clipped and intensively managed grass was everywhere, and gave the impression of having always been so.

Again however, as in Downing's vision, lawns were to be drivers of a moral
urban citizenry and a new type of American subject. Rather than expressing
American culture, therefore, lawns were designed to *produce* it.

The American Lawn Aesthetic Crystallizes

It was at this time, near the turn of the twentieth century, that more popular
and broadly accepted aesthetic expectations for the private lawn emerged. The
unification of the borrowed aesthetics of the English landed gentry, merged
with the budding sensibilities of a rising middle class, brought with it a unique
set of landscape goals, centered on grass. The specific characteristics of this
American lawn became increasingly codified.

As Samuel Parsons, the Superintendent of Parks for New York for a decade
and chief landscape architect for projects in Washington, D.C. and Philadelphia,
explains in his popular treatise on gardening from 1891, the home lawn firstly
must be open and largely monocultural, in the landscape gardening tradition of
previous centuries.

> I want it understood that the lawn is to be open; there may be allowed
> a few outlying trees and shrubs and flowers, but the lawn is to be prac-
> tically open, closely cut greensward, suitable for people to walk about
> on and children to play on without obstruction. If this end is not accom-
> plished, I consider the lawn a failure.[32]

This open grass space, however, might be individuated, to a small degree, as
private space, but definitely not fully enclosed: "I would not, as a rule, emulate

the strict exclusiveness of our English brethren who, in so many cases, shut themselves in with great stone walls . . ."[33]

Finally, in its management and upkeep, the lawn will reflect on the moral sensibilities of its owner: "In this country especially, we see a great many poor lawns and very few good ones, and a poor lawn should be considered as inexcusable a home feature as a ragged or soiled carpet."[34]

It is at the end of the nineteenth century, therefore, that a unified vision of the public, the private, and the moral emerged–all linked to a specific monocultural ecology. From the elite homes of Downing's landscaping to the increasingly common parks born of Olmsted's movement, more people became familiar with the lawn as a classed and moralized landscape (with its specific rules and standards) and with the assumed connection between a type of landscape and a type of person. Indeed, the proselytizing zeal of proponents such as Downing and Parsons in the waning years of the nineteenth century seems to suggest that this landscape aesthetic and its associated urban subjects both had to be created by forceful visionaries who assigned a coherent moral constellation between grasses, yards, and people before most Americans even had the opportunity to act them out.

Democratic Landscape: The Spread of the Modern Lawn

The space in which the average American could produce her own version of such an aesthetic, however, remained scarce in the early twentieth century. Urban areas were at the time modeled on high-density row housing and apartment blocks. The walking city of this period was largely devoid of yards, even for the very wealthy. [35]

Those suburbs that had begun to emerge, following early commuter rail lines outward from cities such as Philadelphia and Chicago, were significant for their elite status. The landscapes of early commuter rail suburbs–Lake Forest, Chicago, and Westchester County, New York, for example–were notable for their social pretensions, careful planning, and manicured topography. Here Parson's rules of lawns were well kept, along with Olmsted's rustic style bridges and winding pathways. A vast majority of urban populations, however, continued to dwell in dense city neighborhoods.[36]

The streetcar suburbs of the following decades offered more land, at lower prices, to a new class of homeowner. This growth was not, however, a simple, inevitable, or natural extension of growing affluence. Rather, as Kenneth Jackson notes in his comprehensive history of the suburbs, *Crabgrass Frontier*, it required the emergence of a class of suburban developers and real estate specialists who lobbied municipalities for services, directed the extension of transportation, and drew the new spacious property lines for construction. The central incentive of these entrepreneurs, needless to say, was to convert *as much land as possible* from agriculture to home lot.[37] All of this directed effort at land conversion meant a concomitant expansion in the ratio of lot to home. Although not spacious in the way imagined by Downing, and far too small for the park-like landscapes of Olmsted, the one-tenth of an acre allotted to these houses did leave room for yards, an unprecedented luxury for middle class homeowners.

Now the previous normative social goals of engineering an urban American subject through lawns was, for the first time, mixed with the commercial interests of the firms interested in fostering and maintaining urban growth. New homeowners with lawns were not simply moral subjects, therefore, but economic ones.

The next burst of suburban growth–in the period after World War II–was equally tied to emerging industries. Spurred by the automobile, and the rise of the Federal Housing Authority in 1934 and its bolstering by the GI Bill (of Rights) in 1944, new growth exploded throughout the country. Automobiles opened new cheap land for development and subsidies revolutionized financing such that more people could buy property. More homes were built, and the size of both houses and home lots increased concomitantly. Housing starts numbered 619,000 in 1941, up from a mere 93,000 in the 1933 depths of The Great Depression. Lot sizes expanded to more than one-fifth of an acre, with more open space.

The availability of inexpensive land meant suburbs of decreasing density. The new larger lots were quickly filled by horizontal housing ("Ranch") styles, including an increasing number of single-story units and bungalows. The average square footage of housing over the period did not increase substantially, but the house footprint did as Americans moved from multi-story buildings to Ranch homes.[38] The size of lots outraced the size of homes, however, and lawns throughout the country continued to grow appreciably. This trend would level off in later years, but the boom period of the postwar era meant that large lawns were available to many people for the first time.

At the dawn of the twenty-first century, these aesthetic expectations play themselves out on a scale previously unknown. The coverage of lawn is vast and continues to grow, but does so unevenly, in line with the uneven development of the urban economy. Based on calculations from air photography and tax assessment (described in Appendix B), some 23% of urban areas are covered in turf, and future growth in turfgrass area in the United States and Canada can be expected as cities expand. Indeed, the largest lawns and the largest ratio of lawns to total lot areas continue to lie on the outskirts of development where cheaply available, converted farmland commonly provides ample room for turfgrass. These areas also have the most recently-built housing, so that every year, despite an overall decrease in lot size nationally, there is a growing area of lawn spreading outwards from the urban core.

But the uneven availability of such suburban developments, along with their "exclusive" character (often determined by class or race) determines who

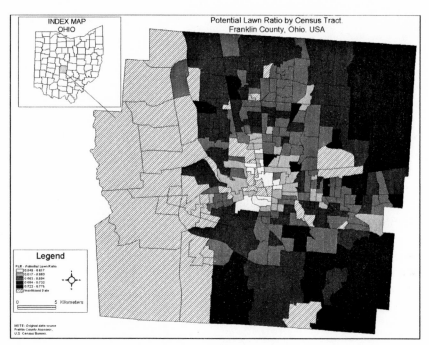

FIGURE 2.2   Potential lawn ratio, Franklin County, Ohio.
Reprinted from Robbins, P. and T. Birkenholtz. (2003). Turfgrass revolution: measuring the expansion of the American lawn. *Land Use Policy* 20:181–194, with permission from Elsevier.

inhabits areas with the largest lawns. By way of example consider the case of Franklin County Ohio, a typical suburban development zone surrounding the growing city of Columbus. Figure 2.2 shows the ratio of lot to house size. The heavily shaded areas represent properties which, regardless of their size, have the houses with the largest proportions of open space surrounding them and are typically dominated by turfgrass. Like most all North American cities, the large areas of lawn are most apparent in the affluent suburbs in the sprawling fringe of the city. Indeed the size of household lawns is statistically correlated with income.

More fundamentally, the unevenness of the lawn's distribution across the city means that different urban residents experience markedly different kinds of daily ecology. Wealthier, largely white residents of the urban fringe are more likely to spend more time tending to the lawn or paying for its management, and to invest more mental and emotional energy negotiating the complex desires and anxieties that are tied to lawn care. Although not exclusively a white middle-class phenomenon, the incidence of lawn people follows closely the geographic class and race contours of the contemporary city. If it is an expression of culture, therefore, it is by no means everyone's culture, and to the degree that the lawn is acting to create the citizens of Downing's and Olmsted's imagination, the structural patterns of urban development enforce an uneven pattern of subjection.

Lawn Culture for Lawn Subjects

In summary, the American lawn, although it forms a coherent aesthetic, has never been the expression of a regional American cultural sensibility. Instead, it has at various times played a number of symbolic roles in the ecological metabolism of a shifting political economy. In its European roots, it was an embodiment of emerging labor and land arrangements tied to expropriation of agrarian property. In its early American development, it was an expression of political ecological transitions of colonial development and imperial ecology. In the nineteenth century, it was a vehicle through which certain kinds of urban subjects might be formed, whether Downing's urban agrarian gentry or Olmsted's civilized city dweller. In its explosive growth in the twentieth century, it formed the quasi-common property for an emerging suburban citizenry.

And at each point, the lawn was as much a vehicle for the creation and maintenance of social systems as it was a product of those systems. In every period it served to mediate broader ideologies of citizenship and property, interpellating urban subjects as it went. In the process, it became normalized into a predictable kind of aesthetic, one that is inherently cultural in that it came to be normal, expected, and desirable. A lawn, distinct simply from a grassy yard, was established specifically as smooth, unbroken, and homogeneous ecology.

Returning to a critical assessment of apolitical approaches to the lawn then, while lawns are cultural (in the sense that they are meaning-laden), they are not the product of some pre-existing "culture," and are instead the meaningful expression of political and economic forces. The meaning of the lawn and its position in urban and suburban political economy are inextricable. Lawns are propelled into the landscape both by economic imperatives (e.g., real estate growth) and also by intentional and thoughtful efforts to produce certain kinds of subjects. Lawns are a strategy, therefore, both for capital accumulation and for making docile and responsible citizens.

But simply because lawns are part of a classed economy and are part of an economic vision of consumer citizens, does not mean such landscapes need be input-demanding or intensively managed by necessity. Given that lawns take the specific contemporary form they do, must they necessarily require high levels of inputs, including the chemical inputs that make lawn people so anxious?

CHAPTER 3

Does the Lawn Necessarily
Require Inputs?

A N APOLITICAL VISION OF TURFGRASS LAWNS suggests that lawn
choices are the products of aesthetics. Even allowing a more critical view
that these aesthetics are historically economic phenomena and vehicles
for producing a specific kind of citizenry, there is no reason to assume that lawns
are designed to *demand* the inputs that are so much a part of their contemporary management. A political ecological assessment, however, might raise sus-
picions that the specific characteristics of the lawn aesthetic as it exists actually
require and enforce ecological subsidies. To answer this question–do lawns need
the chemicals and labor they receive?–requires that we understand something
about turfgrass itself.

What is Turfgrass and How Does it Grow?

Plants, as a rule, tend to grow upwards towards the light, transforming available
moisture and solar energy into complex sugars that build tissue. While the range
of plant adaptations to meet this bottom-line need is vast, those of turfgrasses
are specific and notable.

Turfgrasses are perennial grass species that have evolved to withstand and
thrive under conditions of grazing. For most plants, as well as some other grasses,
such grazing represents a terrific challenge, since reproduction and growth typically occurs at the top and the outmost vertical extension. Being eaten from the
top down, as is typical in grazing, means for most plants enduring retarded
growth and reproduction.

Countless generations of grazing by wild and domesticated animals resulted
in the survival and reproduction of the specialized qualities of grasses, especially
turfgrasses. The evolutionary advantages of grasses, most clearly developed in

turfgrasses, are threefold. First, grasses are one of a class of plants called mono-cotyledons. This class differs from many other plants (dicotyledons), in that turf-grasses have growth tissue at the *base* of the leaf or shoot, versus at the tip. This allows turfgrasses to be clipped or grazed and still grow, survive, and reproduce. Second, their ability to send out side shoots (or tillers) is also unusual, as are the horizontal stems of perennial grasses, which can grow either above or below ground. Finally, the extraordinary root systems of Poaceae–as much as 90% of the whole plant in dry weight–allows the species to thrive where it is extremely cold, hot, or dry above the ground.[1]

Turfgrasses moreover–having adapted to generations of gnawing, pulling, and biting by grazers–have honed these advantages, maintaining their growing point especially close to the soil surface. This makes them not only resilient in the face of grazing, but also dependent on it to thrive. Such grasses form a dense, even mat, and continue to grow as they are clipped back; new growth occurs at the base, and actually benefits from being cut back, which clears the shady overgrowth above.

For the designers and proselytizers of the lawn in the eighteenth, nine-teenth, and twentieth centuries, turfgrasses were a logical choice. They grew best when clipped short, formed a dense, cushy mat when healthy, and were in a con-stant state of green regrowth after every "ecological disturbance" (e.g., mowing). The specific way in which these adaptations work, evidenced in the shape and growth patterns of turfgrass, tell us a great deal about their peculiar require-ments and demands.

Turfgrass Structure and Growth

Figure 3.1 shows the idealized structure and shape (morphology) of turfgrass plants. The belowground parts of the plant, its *roots*, capture soil moisture and nutrients required for photosynthesis. Turfgrass roots are actually shallower than those of other plants, especially the weed species with which they often com-pete, but are commonly more dense or extensive. The aboveground part of the plant, called the *shoot*, is the location of photosynthetic activity and a conduit for resources from below ground, taking the form of either leaves or stems.[2]

The *crown* is where the roots and shoot meet, near the soil surface. This is a dense area consisting of *internodes* and the meristem, the actual growing point of the plant, where cells divide and enlarge. As grass grows, it is literally push-ing upwards from this point, with new leaves emerging from the level of the soil. Constantly growing outwards from the crown are stems, which can expand either vertically or horizontally. Horizontal shoots that extend underground are called *rhizomes;* those that grow aboveground are called *stolons*. Vertical stems are cylindrical and compact, except during seeding, when they rise upwards to form seedstalks and seedheads. Leaves form from the meristem, grow upwards in sets, and fan outwards as blades to collect sunlight. New growth continues from the

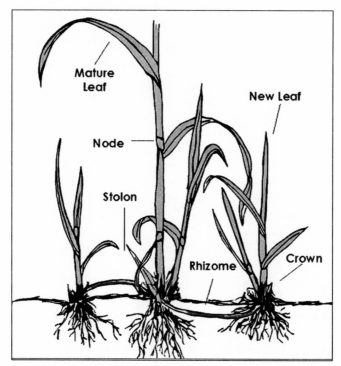

FIGURE 3.1   Turfgrass morphology.

base of the leaf blade. Leaves tend to live from three to six weeks, being replaced by new leaves pushing upwards from the crown. As long as the crown remains alive the grass survives, sending up new tillers (separate leaf/stem groups) from the meristematic tissue near the soil. What this means is that grazing, clipping, scything, or lawn mowing, no matter how much old growth it removes from the plant leaves, does not interfere with plant growth.[3]

Seeding versus clonal reproduction

This growth, outwards and upwards, is directed at doing what all plants are adapted to do: reproduce. For grasses, reproductive options are multiple and highly flexible. Unrestricted vertical growth of stem tissue, under the right conditions, will lead to seeding of the grass. Flowers and seeds emerge at the top of a stem as a cluster of spikelets, which are smaller and more inconspicuous than those of other flowering plants. Seeds, carried on the wind, can establish new plants and colonize new areas. The emergence of the seed head, however, tends to shorten the life of the tiller from which it emerges, since much of the plant's energy is invested into seeding.[4]

More commonly, owing to continual grazing or mowing of the seedstalk before it reaches the inflorescence stage, turfgrasses grow asexually through horizontal clonal growth. Horizontal stems (rhizomes or stolons) are constantly snaking outwards. Periodically, they form new nodes, from which roots are dropped, new tillers formed, and new surface shoots emerge. These daughter plants are genetically identical to the parent plant, unlike those reproduced sexually by seed.

Because growth comes from the base and because disturbance (grazing or mowing) encourages horizontal growth and new leaf production, mowing and cutting is *essential* to produce the kind of greenness and density typical of the lawn as it came to be understood in North America in the last two centuries. This is in part because mowing reduces the height, producing a carpet-like appearance. In addition, however, since the most green and vigorous growth is in the *new* leaves, growing from the base of the crown, the removal of the higher and older browning plant structure reveals this green growth and allows it to receive light. Once the lawn is "established" and extended horizontally, it continues to live in place, producing new leaves and shoots as the old ones die and decay to become organic matter in the soil.

This makes the turfgrass lawn one of the most dynamic ecosystems known. It is in a perpetual state of change, with tillers, leaves, and stems disappearing every few weeks, replaced by new ones from below. Maintaining vigorous, monocultural, and emerald green grass is therefore about constantly rejuvenating (literally–"making young again") a constantly aging and dying population. Fertilizing a lawn (unlike, for example, a tree) is not about greening the existing leaves or growth, but instead about causing a burst of new tillers, which are greener than the aging leaves. Super-green color only occurs when young leaves are produced at a rate as fast or faster than old leaves are dying.[5]

To sum up, turfgrass, even if not expected to look like a monocultural "lawn," minimally requires some kind of labor input to survive, in the form of grazing or mowing. Should a green color be required, it further demands regular fertilization for the process of encouraging new growth from the base. Since leaf tips die back in all grasses every six weeks, lawn managers are in a constant scramble to encourage growth; without it, the lawn inevitably turns gray/brown.

Turfgrass Growth Cycles
Of course, as noted previously, grasses have evolved to deal with harsh and uneven conditions. Living in some of the most extreme temperature and precipitation zones in the world, Poaceae are prepared to live periodically without water or nutrients. Indeed, each species of grass is uniquely adapted to the periodic scarcities of water, sunlight, and nutrients typical of the area to which they are indigenous.

Grasses that have adapted to, or been bred by plant breeders to be adapted to cool humid climates take advantage of the lengthening days of the spring. During their first six weeks of growth, these grasses maximize their vertical growth,

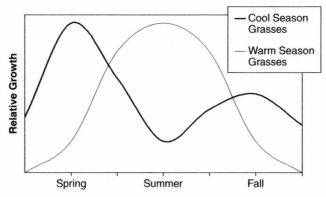

FIGURE 3.2 Turfgrass growth rates.

and produce as much as half of their annual vegetation. During the summer the rate of growth is minimal, and should dry conditions prevail for more than a few weeks, the turf inevitably turns dull and brown, with aging leaves most apparent. With the arrival of fall, growth resumes, but typically in a more horizontal direction, although often less vigorously than during the spring. Inversely, warm-season grasses perform most of their vigorous growth in the summer, with the amount of growth determined largely by moisture availability and angle/amount of solar radiation, rather than day length. Figure 3.2 shows the general pattern of growth for cool and warm season grasses.

A central lesson from the preceding discussion is that there are inevitably long periods of dormancy built into turfgrasses, just as there are periods of high vertical and horizontal growth. It is expected that the thickness and greenness of even the healthiest lawns will vary over the course of the year, under any climate or rainfall conditions. It also means that, should one desire a lawn that appears to withstand seasons, time, and rainfall at every stage in its lifecycle, it is *necessary* to constantly cope with, prepare for, and facilitate new growth, vegetative senescence (death), dormancy, and reproduction. This means continuous and changing demands; continuous and ongoing labor; continuous and ongoing inputs.

Why Lawns Need So Much Care

For all the reasons outlined above, grasses are tough survivors. They are considered weeds in agriculture and are found in the most extreme conditions. They are opportunists, whose aggressive lateral growth means they can pop up in all sorts of places. Indeed, the successful sales of the chemical glyphosate (Chapter 4) in recent years are ironically driven in part by the attempt to control runaway yard turfgrasses as they invade sidewalks, gardens, driveways, and every other place outside the yard. In other words, left alone, grass will do just fine. Assuming that dull-colored areas can be tolerated; that dandelions, plantains, clover, ground ivy, and other weeds can be ignored; that high growth and seeding can be disregarded; that occasional dead spots and openings can go unnoticed; and that whole areas altogether devoid of grass species can be overlooked; a yard requires little or no care, short of periodic mowing. Moreover, once these conditions can be tolerated, the lawn ecosystem will in many ways become self-regulating. Such conditions, however, do not in any way resemble the American Lawn as we have come to understand it.

The American Lawn is a Demanding Ecosystem

The American Lawn, on the other hand, that velvety swath described by Downing as essential to moral citizenship, is a weed-free, clean monoculture, which is emerald green throughout the growing season, does not go to seed, and is even and uniform across its surface. As the standard textbook for training turfgrass management professionals still insists: "An attractive lawn has a uniform consistent appearance. The color, texture, and density are similar throughout the turf area. All of the grass looks the same . . ."[6] On the road to achieving such a specific aesthetic, a huge range of things can go wrong. This is true for a number of reasons.

Firstly, polyculture is inevitable. No ecological system develops towards monoculture over the medium term. Even areas that have experienced the invasion of aggressive non-native species (lantana, mesquite, kudzu, and a host of other notorious invaders) are commonly broken up by opportunistic local plants, which are either taller, shorter, less thirsty, or adapted to disturbance in a way that the invader is not. Indeed, it is biodiversity in grassland environments that has been demonstrated to provide the best resistance to noxious species invasion.[7] The struggle against polyculture in maintaining the American Lawn requires extraordinary and exhaustive efforts to remove and control weeds, reinforce areas of weak grass development, and police seed dispersals and edge invasions: an uphill battle.

Secondly, grasses naturally go dull or brown, even during their growing season. In the off-cycle of growth for both warm and cool season grasses, dormancy is an adaptation. This extremely normal and natural phenomenon in grass, however, is anathema to the lawn. To maintain growth during the off-cycle requires massive nutrient and water subsidies, much of which are usually lost during application, leading to fertilizer runoff and water waste.

Thirdly, insects are the most abundant creatures on Earth. Outnumbering all other animals in total numbers, the number of known insect species is also larger than all other animals and plants combined. Insects are diversely adapted, reproduce quickly, and are at times ravenous. Their arrival in a monocultural lawn in significant numbers is a periodic inevitability unless constant vigilance, labor, and inputs are used.

Fourthly, lawn grasses inevitably go to seed. While rhizomatic growth is excellent for turfgrasses and preferred by lawn owners, left alone for a little while (a very little while during high growth periods), turfgrass will attempt to reproduce by seed. The resulting "prairie look" may be disdained by homeowner associations, and indeed may be illegal in some communities, but it is all very normal.

Finally, organic materials decay. If decomposition is retarded for any reason, dead material can build up as thatch on the surface of the soil, crowding around the lawn's crown. Mowing is of course essential for avoiding this, but so are other cultural techniques like de-thatching the turf by vertically mowing with specialized equipment, topdressing it with sand, and rolling the surface with a heavy machine to push roots back into contact with soil. These sorts of painstaking efforts are somewhat unusual on the typical lawn, but are essential for producing idealized lawns that resemble putting greens.

Soils, Competitors, and Predators

The overarching picture is one of a struggle against some very basic material tendencies that come from well-established ecological principles. Several other features of urban ecology make the task of American Lawn management even harder, however, and compound these ecological realities, including especially the quality of urban soils, the choice of lawn cultivars (selected grasses), weeds, and bugs.

Suburban Development, Soil Poverty, and Poor Cultivars

The development of new housing in the United States and Canada depends on a process of land conversion that is inherently bad for plant growth, and which leads to high and increasing demands on homeowners. Specifically, new home developers act to create soil conditions that are hard, impoverished, and unsustainable. This is especially ironic since much of the land converted to housing in North America in the last thirty years, and the accompanying areas with the largest ratio of lawn cover, have been on the exurban fringe of cities, where formerly agricultural soils are thick, nutrient-rich, and well prepared to support the growth of grasses, shrubs, and ornamental trees. The destruction of this soil resource is a result of standardized development practices that turn, invert, and remove essential nutrients and structure during the process of construction.

To understand this, something must first be said about the typical characteristics and profile of soil. Soil is made of mineral particles including sand, silt, and clay, as well as living and dead plants and animals (organic matter), air, and water. But differing layers of soil, at differing depths, have different mixes and densities of these materials. Soils are layered with differing "Horizons" stacked on top of one another, usually identified from the so-called A Horizon (near the surface) through the B and C Horizons down to bedrock. The A Horizon is the dark soil layer at or near the surface. It tends to be loose, crumbly, and loaded with organic material. Water runs into the A Horizon, and a range of living organisms cycle and recycle nutrients there. These are preferable planting soils, and agricultural soils usually have well developed A Horizons. Below this, the B Horizon, or subsoil begins. These are lighter colored and dense, containing little or no organic matter. When water runs through the A Horizon, it carries heavier mineral materials with it, and these collect in the B Horizon, which tends to be heavy in clay, iron, and other compounds. Below this, the C Horizon contains rock and clay, and little else.[8]

This profile becomes relevant as agricultural lands are converted. Because A Horizon soils from productive farms are valuable and nutrient-rich, land buyers usually treat them as a mineable resource for resale. Prior tc construction, therefore, tractors and land moving equipment scrape the many tons of valuable soil off the surface and cart it away (consider: a 100 square yard site scraped to the depth of just a few feet will produce around ten tons of soil; at retail, 40-pound bags sell for $6 each). This leaves a far thinner layer of good soil near the surface. Even where intentional removal of topsoil is not conducted, construction typically leads to large-scale erosion of this valuable topsoil layer that, coupled with compaction from heavy equipment and machinery, later makes for a poor growing environment.[9]

During the next phase of construction, the basement and sub-basement of the house are dug. This excavation draws tens of thousands of tons of B (and sometimes C) Horizon soils to the surface. With little or no resale value, these soils are simply spread around the surface of the site to serve as the basis for landscaping after construction is complete. Starved of organic material and loaded with minerals (not to mention plaster, cement, lumber, and other debris), these soils are a prohibitively poor base for planting. It is little wonder mulch is an increasingly popular ground cover in the suburbs.[10]

Adding to the problem of once farm-quality soils being made worse during development is the fact that most of the mixes of species found on lawns are not selected by the person who has to manage the lawn–the homeowner. As noted previously, the range of possible turfgrass cultivars is large, and each behaves in a different way, has a differing tolerance for drought and cold, and grows and develops with differing levels of care. The selection of grasses, however, is rarely made with these questions in mind. "Contractor seed mixes" tend to be a blend of cultivars that sprout and grow quickly, leaving a good-looking site soon after construction. As a result, however, the wrong grass is typically in the wrong place most of the time. This problem is sometimes even more acute in older homes, built and landscaped in a time when only a few cultivars were popular. So even where homeowners may be willing to tolerate less than ideal lawn aesthetics, the poor combination of impoverished soils and inappropriate cultivars makes inputs of some kind a typical necessity.

Weeds and Bugs

The problem of poor conditions and species is coupled with the fact that turf-grasses, whether appropriate cultivars or not, are rarely alone in the yard, and have a huge range of weeds and bugs as their neighbors. "Weed" is not a biological term, but is rather a geographic one. Generally it refers to any plant species that is out of place. When the Kentucky Bluegrass from your back lawn grows through the cracks of your front sidewalk and you deem it necessary to pull it or use herbicide on it, the grass has become a "weed."

The concept must be at least as old as the practice of agriculture, therefore, although the English term has an obscure etymology, deriving from the Old English/Anglo Saxon *wéod* or old Saxon *wiod*, specifically referring to undesirable vegetation that hampers the growth of something else. Potential lawn weeds are as countless, therefore, as there are species other than the ones desired. When Tall Fescue, a turfgrass planted in some parts of the country as an appealing yard cover, appears in a Bluegrass lawn, it suddenly becomes a weed and is doused with chlorosulfuron, a potent agricultural chemical.

Having said this, there are species that exhibit especially "weedy" properties in their inherent ability to occupy and thrive in areas where soil is barren, disturbed, or low in nutrients. Such species usually have at least one of the following "invasive" characteristics relative to competing species: adaptability,[11] aggressive reproduction,[12] and vigorous growth.[13]

Adaptability refers to the range of environmental conditions under which a species can survive and reproduce. Invasive weedy species tend to survive in a higher range of environments than others, including highly arid/humid conditions, areas of highly direct/indirect radiation, and varying edaphic (soil) conditions. Many weeds can also survive varying rainfall and solar radiation conditions over the course of the year, during which other species may go dormant. During stress periods, some weeds are active, grow, or reproduce precisely when potential competitors do not.

Weedy plants can seed quickly and have good mechanisms for seed distribution. Think here of the remarkable air-sailing seeds of the dandelion, some 12,000 of them produced by a single plant.[14] They can also quickly colonize new areas in this way, especially after some event or disturbance has displaced competing species.

The vigor of growth in weeds is also important, since fast-growing species seize sunlight and precipitation from slower-growing competitors. This general profile has allowed biologists and ecologists to create a generic picture of weeds as hardy and capable of setting roots where other species simply cannot make it.[15] Kudzu, a well-known example, was introduced from Japan and extolled as a ground cover to stop Dust Bowl era erosion on bare areas; it did this so successfully as to become the bane of Southern U.S. forestry and a nasty weed decades later.[16]

In this sense, weeds are desirable and inevitable plants that colonize barren areas allowing for later overgrowth and succession. The appearance of patches of clover in the lawn, therefore, is not a problem of the weed per se, but rather a sign that these areas are low in nutrients; as a nitrogen fixing plant, clover can enter and thrive where lawn grass has trouble establishing and reproducing, making way for future grass growth.

"Pest" insects are an equally subjective order of things. Whereas some small range of bugs are a health nuisance to humans, including ticks that may carry Lyme disease, most yard insects are nontroublesome except insofar as they make it hard for grasses to maintain an emerald green color and reproduce consistently and effectively. Some species like grubs (the larvae form of beetles) emerge from deep in the ground to feed on the roots of grasses, develop into adults that feed on surface foliage, and then return to the soil to lay eggs. Other insects, such as chinch bugs, sod webworms, and cutworms, feed on the surface foliage and lay eggs directly on grasses. All prefer turf environments.

Weeds and insects also interact in complex ways. If an insect invasion occurs, it may lead to minor die-back in grasses, which allows the incursion of some other species. Billbug infestations, for example, have been shown to have some enhancing influence on weed growth.[17]

A bug's life is hard, of course. A huge number of animals, birds, and other predator insects feed on even the most persistent of lawn insects, making a sustained invasion extremely difficult. For the most part, these species and their infestations might be easily ignored, and they tend to dissipate over long cycles, with growing populations tempered by predator species and other influences. Even so, bugs are inevitable and tend to create spotty, uneven growth and greenness, which although not irreconcilable with the growth of grasses, are incompatible with the perfection associated with the lawn. They require some form of control.

The Lawn's Needs Become Those of the Turfgrass Subject

In sum, the development conditions of urban and suburban ecosystems, coupled with the inherent characteristics of turfgrasses, makes it nearly impossible to maintain the American Lawn ideal without subsidies to the system of some kind or another. These subsidies take the form of water, fertilizer, and a range of chemicals, but also mean cutting, raking, and otherwise constantly tending to the system—a system of labor that must be carried out either by the homeowner or by someone hired to manage the grass. In this sense, lawn people have remarkably little "choice" in the matter of labor and inputs, except insofar as they might choose not to have a lawn and instead plant a garden or tolerate a mixed and mottled coverage of a range of species, including "weeds," among their turf. Alternatively, other systems of inputs, including Integrated Pest Management, and other cultural techniques are also potentially available (Chapter 7).

Barring these, lawn people have a number of specific obligations that allow them surprisingly little discretion. Mowing, watering, fertilizing, and applying

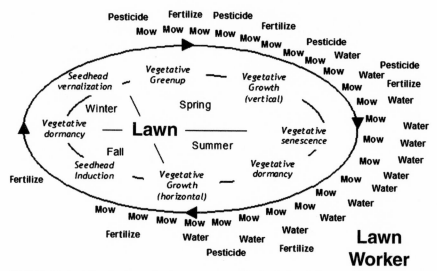

FIGURE 3.3   The rhythm of subjects–an annual schedule of observed behaviors of grass and people.

pesticides must be done at appropriate intervals, determined entirely by the internal ecological clock of the grass. Figure 3.3 shows the way lawn work follows the specific needs of turfgrass: in this case a cool season grass, and based on observations of my own neighborhood in Ohio versus the ecological habits of the grass described in a turfgrass management textbook. As the grass emerges from vegetative dormancy in the spring and begins to "green up," pesticides and herbicides are judiciously applied and a period of aggressive mowing begins. With the late spring, more cutting becomes essential to maintain vertical growth and control seeding. With the dryness of summer and a period of natural vegetative senescence, the aging of top growth and slowing of production is countered by more aggressive watering. After summer dormancy ends, fertilizers and pesticide treatments begin again, including late fall treatments in anticipation of winter dormancy and conditions in the following spring.

Day after day then, across the seasons, lawn people emerge from their houses, observe the conditions of the turf, and act. If we consider these actions are repeated from household to household, block to block, across the densely yarded regions of suburban areas, we can begin to imagine the rhythm of whole neighborhoods, indeed whole cities, synchronized with the habits of grass. The chorus of mowers can be heard in near unison during dry daylight weekend afternoons, syncopated with the clicking of the Rainbird sprinkler sounds in the early morning hours.

This description captures some of the regularity in the lives of lawn people, but it is also true that once it is expected that a lawn can and should maintained as an invariable bright green turf monoculture, a series of complex,

ever-changing puzzles are continuously placed before the manager. The unre-
liable seasonal demands for nutrients and the periodic outbreaks and returns of
weeds and insects all require judicious applications of inputs at key points in
time, and call upon a highly specialized form of technical knowledge. Do these
inputs represent a risk of any kind? Has their evolution over the last century led
to increased or decreased hazards for lawn people? To this we turn next.

CHAPTER 4

Are Lawn Inputs a Hazard?

I F LAWNS WERE LEFT ALONE and just periodically mowed–interspecies interactions in turfgrass, along with predator and prey relationships in the insect world, and the patterns of succession–would lead to diverse, nonpathological yards. These yards would be uneven in their species composition, however, and would have mossy, clover-covered areas, bare spots, brown seasons, and other expressions of the normal complexity of grassland ecology. On the other hand, assuming there is an aesthetic demand for a monocultural American Lawn (purified, uniform, weed-free, atemporal) means inputs are inevitable and nutrient supplements and pest controls are *necessary*, precisely for the reasons stated in preceding chapters, including natural variability, the inevitability of weeds and pests, and poor soils and cultivars. Assuming these conditions prevail–and they typically do–a range of inputs become essential, each of which is targeted at one of the inevitable problems that rise in matching landscape ideals to actual landscapes. Are these inputs a hazard? If they are, to what degree is this risk communicated or translated into consumer information and government control over their production and use? Has the risk associated with inputs increased or decreased over the past century as the lawn chemical economy has matured and environmentalism has bloomed?

The Dawn and Maturing of Lawn Chemistry

As lawn historian Virginia Scott Jenkins concludes, "front lawns are the product of two elements: the ability and the desire to grow and tend lawn grasses."[1] To say that a coherent lawn aesthetic had been established in the late 1900s and that the land economics of the mid-twentieth century made available the space for its creation and the condition for its desire (Chapter 2) by no means assures

FIGURE 4.1   The earliest lawn care machinery was ungainly, expensive, and viewed as a luxury in its time. The original caption for this figure reads, "Lawn Mowing A Luxury!" The motor lawn mower with rotary knives is invaluable on large estates in its economy of labour. Its service as a roller is no less important, the machine weighing from one thousand pounds up. Reprinted from Barron, L. 1923. *Lawn Making: Together with the Proper Keeping of Putting Greens*. New York: Doubleday, Plate 26.

that the ability to grow a lawn was available to the general public. At its point of inception, the demands that this aesthetic placed on a late nineteenth century homeowner far outstripped the capital available for installation and maintenance–including management of bugs, removal of weeds, control of fungus, cutting, fertilizing and watering–despite the arrival of expensive and ungainly lawnmowers in the 1860s (Figure 4.1). These necessary investments made realizing the monocultural lawn almost impossible throughout the early years of the twentieth century. Only by offsetting labor with other inputs (petrochemicals, in particular) could the lawn of Parson's imagination achieve ubiquity. To attain the aesthetic advocated by lawn enthusiasts and mimic the lawns of Downing's elites and Olmsted's parks (Chapter 2), significant shifts in the system of cultivation would have to occur. The long bridge between those moral landscapes of grass advocated in the nineteenth century and the lawns of the late twentieth century was crossed consciously, aggressively, and intentionally by the lawn industry.

This shift to aggressive lawn management began to take place in the 1930s and 1940s. At this time, a new mode of land management was instituted, one that depended on periodic inputs of fertilizers and pesticides to achieve and maintain the lawn. In an accelerating cycle, the availability of new kinds of inputs raised the standards for lawn aesthetics, making closer-cropped, and increasingly weed- and bug-free landscapes more possible, and yet more elusive. With each new innovation came an incentive for the production of more powerful and effective inputs. An examination of lawn care practices advocated by professionals across the century will provide some sense of this transition.

Managing the Prewar Lawn

Table 4.1 and Table 4.2 show a summary of the weed and insect treatments advocated by several popular lawn care guides that we reviewed from the years 1891 through 1973. Several things are apparent. First, lawn care practices were relatively uniform before 1945, and depended on familiar strategies that changed little during this early period. In particular, all guides from the pre-World War

TABLE 4.1 Recommended Herbicidal Treatments from 1891 to 1973

	Parsons 1891	Barron 1923	Rockwell 1929	Dickinson 1930	Sprague 1940	Dawson 1954	Plants & Gardens 1956	Schery 1961	Schery 1973
Hand weeding	✗	✗	✗	✗	✗		✗		
Chicken manure		✗							
Iron sulphate	✗	✗				✗			
Ammonium sulphate				✗	✗	✗			
Sodium chlorate					✗	✗			
Sodium Arsenate					✗	✗	✗		
Arsenic acid					✗	✗	✗		
Calcium Arsenate					✗	✗			
2,4-D						✗	✗	✗	✗
MCPA/MCPP						✗			✗
Dicamba									✗
Methyl Arsenate								✗	✗
DCPA (Dacthal)									✗

2,4-D = dichlorophenoxyacetic acid; MCPA/MCPP = meta-chlorophenylpiperazine 2-methyl-4-chlorophenoxy-acetic acid

Sources: Barron, Leonard. (1923). *Lawn making: Together with the proper keeping of putting greens.* New York: Doubleday, Page and Co.; Dawson, R. B. (1954). *Practical lawn craft.* London: Crosby Lockwood and Son. Dickinson, L. S. (1931). *The lawn: The culture of turf in park, golfing, and home Areas.* New York, Orange Judd Publishing. Parsons, S. (1891). *Landscape gardening.* New York: G.T. Putnam and Sons.

Plants and Gardens. (1956). Handbook on lawns. Special Issue of *Plants and Gardens* 12(2). Rockwell, Frederick Frye. (1929). *Lawns.* New York: The Macmillan Company.

Schery, Robert. (1961). *The lawn book.* New York: Macmillan Company. Schery, R. W. (1973). A perfect lawn: The easy way. New York: Macmillan. Sprague, H. B. (1940). *Better lawns for homes and parks.* New York: McGraw Hill Book Company.

TABLE 4.2 Recommended Insecticidal Treatments from 1891 to 1973

	Parsons 1891	Barron 1923	Rockwell 1929	Dickinson 1930	Sprague 1940	Dawson 1954	Plants & Gardens 1956	Schery 1961	Schery 1973
Carbon bisulphide		✗	✗	✗					
Kerosene		✗							
Chickens		✗							
Carbon tetrachloride			✗						
Mercury bichloride			✗	✗					
Lead arsenate			✗	✗	✗	✗			
Nicotine			✗	✗	✗				
Thallium sulphate					✗				
DDT						✗	✗	✗	
Dieldrin							✗	✗	
Malathion								✗	
Lindane								✗	
Chlordane							✗	✗	✗
Heptachlor							✗	✗	✗
Aldrin							✗	✗	✗
Carbaryl									✗
Diazinon									✗
Pyrethrum									✗
Carbaryl (Sevin®)									✗

DDT = dichlorodiphenyl-trichloroethane.

Sources: Barron, Leonard. (1923). *Lawn making: Together with the proper keeping of putting greens.* New York: Doubleday, Page and Co.

Dawson, R. B. (1954). *Practical lawn craft.* London: Crosby Lockwood and Son; Dickinson, L. S. (1931). *The lawn: The culture of turf in park, golfing, and home Areas.* New York:, Orange Judd Publishing; Parsons, Samuel. (1891). *Landscape gardening.* New York: G.T. Putnam and Sons. Plants and Gardens. (1956). Handbook on lawns. Special Issue of *Plants and Gardens* 12(2); Rockwell Frederick Frye. (1929). *Lawns.* New York: The Macmillan Company; Schery, Robert. (1961). *The lawn book.* New York: Macmillan Company; Schery, R. W. (1973). *A perfect lawn: The easy Way.* New York: Macmillan. Sprague, H. B. (1940). *Better Lawns for Homes and Parks.* New York: McGraw Hill Book Company.

II period emphasize hand weeding and immediate reseeding of all areas of weed growth.

   In this sense, Leonard Barron's volume *Lawn Making* (from 1923), gives a good sense of what might have been required to manage turfgrass in the early twentieth century. Lawns needed a good deal of human energy in the form of constant management and intervention. Barron insists, however, as do other early turf guides, this labor can be avoided if turf health is maintained. Hand

FIGURE 4.2   Early lawn care guides instructed homeowners in the mechanics of hand picking weeds. The original caption for this figure reads, Digging Dandelions. Before they flower is the proper time to attach the weeds. Cut out as much of the root as possible; fill any large hole with soil and scatter a pinch of seed on the surface. In ordinary cases "make good" by tramping the edge. Reprinted from Barron, L. 1923. *Lawn Making: Together with the Proper Keeping of Putting Greens.* New York: Doubleday, Plate 17.

labor was the norm, especially when considering the primitive, expensive, and ungainly character of the behemoth lawn mower during this period. As a result, many plant species that would later be considered weeds are tolerated entirely in the early lawn care literature (Figure 4.2). As Barron notes, "Clover is not generally regarded as undesirable on the lawn (indeed it is usually seeded over to get a quick green effect), and many people advocate its presence because its low growing foliage leaves the newly cut lawn with a fresh green color . . ."[2]

These manual remedies are paralleled by calls for the use of livestock, including the common hen. Not only could barnyard fowl be brought onto the lawn to peck out insect pests, their manure was touted as the best spring fertilizer available, which "can be put on as thickly as convenient and will have a very stimulating effect upon the grass in the spring; so strong will the growth be that the weeds will be crowded out of existence."[3] This approach to the problem reveals a more general view of weeds in the prewar lawn largely as an *effect* of poor lawn condition, not a *cause*.

Within the next decade, however, this philosophy was reversed, with a range of new chemicals arriving to transform the expectations and demands of lawn owners, including mercury bichloride, a highly toxic corrosive sublimate, and lead arsenate. Even so, during this transition to the modern chemical lawn, early advocates were cautious. As late as 1940 Sprague's *Better Lawns for Homes and Parks* is explicit in this regard, "although the use of chemicals to kill weeds, without serious injury to turf grasses, is a fascinating proposition, homeowners should be warned that such "miracles" cannot be accomplished without considerable knowledge of the process and full application of the factors involved in lawn management . . ."[4]

In part, this insistence was linked to a growing understanding of just how dangerous many early herbicides and insecticides were. Lead arsenate is typical in this sense. As a chemical widely advocated for lawn use, despite a growing acknowledgment of its associated health risks, it would set the precedent for the ambivalence associated with lawn care inputs, those inputs we use and desire despite anxieties and concerns.

Lead arsenate was introduced to America in 1892, specifically for control of Gypsy moth outbreaks in New England. Sprayed on foliage, it stuck fast, was long-acting, and was highly toxic to a range of bugs. The chemical became more widely available in convenient paste and powder forms in the early twentieth century, which made its application to home lawns convenient and relatively inexpensive. In the 1930s lead arsenate production soared from 37 million pounds to 63 million; though most of this was for use in agriculture, it is readily apparent that this was one of the few effective and therefore ubiquitous lawn chemicals of the time.[5] Use of the chemical reduced somewhat during World War II as lead prices became prohibitive, but overall it remained one of the most popular chemical controls for the lawn during the period (Figure 4.3).

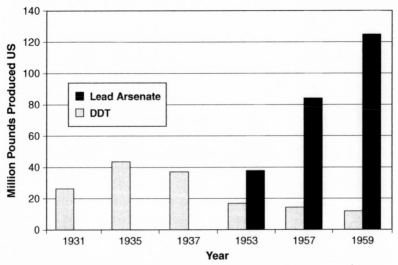

FIGURE 4.3   Lead arsenate and DDT before and after WWII.
Data adapted from Dunlap, T. R. (1981). *DDT: Scientists, citizens, and public policy.*
Princeton: Princeton University Press.

As early as 1919, however, it was determined that residues of lead arsenate persisted on crops and other surfaces. The human health risks associated with the compound began to be discerned during the period as well.[6] Even with this knowledge, the absence of alternatives made lead arsenate the chemical of choice for decades, prior to and even after, the appearance of dichlorodiphenyl-trichloroethane (DDT) in 1947. Unknown at the time–though later discovered with dismay–lead and arsenic in agricultural fields, orchards, and backyard soils were accumulating rapidly. In addition, the associated risks have more recently been determined to include carcinogenicity, reproductive and developmental toxicity, neurotoxicity, and acute toxicity. The case of lead arsenate reminds us that many of the compounds and substances used in the early twentieth century were every bit as dangerous as those we use today, or more so. It also emphasizes that the long-term effects of chemicals that appear benign often takes decades to discover. Most importantly, it demonstrates the way chemical use persists despite knowledge of its associated risks. This remains as true today as in the prewar era.

Pesticides and the Second World War

When chemist Paul Müller first developed his synthetic insect control chemical Gesarol in the late 1930s (for the Swiss-based company J.R. Giegy), the chemical entered a highly competitive market with a large range of arsenic-based insecticides already available. As a result, the chemical–made from chlorine, hydrogen, and carbon and later called by its more technical name dichlorodiphenyl-trichloroethane, or DDT–remained largely unknown in the United States.

As Edmund Russell explains in his book *War and Nature*, the Second World War changed the status and profile of this chemical dramatically. DDT proved to be an incredibly powerful insecticide, easily wiping out lice, mosquitoes, and a range of other pests more effectively than the best organic compounds. As it began to be manufactured in the United States, it became more easily available. More importantly, it persisted in the environment long enough to make one spraying effective for months afterwards. DDT was viewed as a wonder chemical.[7]

The exigencies of this war, moreover, made the use of the chemical all the more pressing. Along with the normal insect problems that emerged from military conflict, including lice outbreaks on an international scale, the logistics of combat were mosquito-friendly. Moving vast numbers of men and equipment across a north/south gradient, coupled with large-scale landscape transformations that resulted in standing water, mobilized malaria to leave its largely tropical jungle confinement, resulting in epidemic outbreaks across North Africa and the Mediterranean region. The war further encouraged the malarial outbreak in North Africa by nutritionally weakening populations and making them more vulnerable, by diverting resources away from treatment and prevention, and by providing mosquitoes long-range transport on planes and boats.[8]

As a result, the timely arrival of the chemical made it a war hero. Combined with a strategy of eradication (rather than control) of pest insects, DDT was used on a massive scale, received international press, and was incorporated into the propaganda machine of the late war period. This provided it an easy launching platform into civilian markets upon the cessation of hostilities.

The chemical's heroic status, moreover, caused its more unsavory characteristics to remain uncommunicated. Some experts within the U.S. government warned of the dangers that the chemical posed, especially the breadth of its effects and its persistence. As a broad-spectrum insecticide, it was known to affect a relatively wider range of species and so was potentially more harmful for nontarget insects (and people). The chemical's persistence meant that it could remain active for long periods. Even while long-term exposure effects were so far untested and unknown, this quality was troubling even at the dawn of the DDT era. In 1946, it was noted that: "DDT fed to lactating animals appears in their milk and can poison animals consuming the milk which poses another question of residues. It might conceivably be shown that, for instance, cows eating silage on which DDT had been deposited would pass it along in their milk to human subjects."[9]

Experiments with DDT during the war (specifically on soldier test subjects), revealed no apparent short-term harm, however, despite previous animal tests that suggested the chemical was dangerous. The merits of the chemical were compared to the potentially higher danger of existing compounds, especially arsenicals, and it was deemed exceptional and relatively safe. DDT came to replace lead arsenate and other materials (as shown in Figure 4.3 above),[10] and Müller won the Nobel Prize for Medicine in 1948.[11]

Managing the Postwar Lawn

DDT's uses for the lawn were immediately extolled in the postwar period. The chemical began to appear in lawn management guides and came to quickly replace almost all prewar insecticide formulations, becoming an all-in-one treatment for a range of insect problems. As early as 1946, DDT was described as "destined to take a place as the best weapon yet discovered in man's ages-long war with a hitherto unconquerable enemy, the insects."[12] The chemical was used liberally and often in multiple doses per year in the United States and Europe as a standard treatment for cutworms, sod webworms, and chinch bugs. As a British lawn guide noted in 1954, it had become typical to apply DDT "as a routine treatment in the autumn and the cost of such wise treatment may be regarded as a reasonable insurance premium" against leather jacket grubs and other pests.[13]

The subsequent invention of dichlorophenoxyacetic acid (2,4-D), a selective herbicide, further revolutionized lawn care, replacing prewar herbicides just as

DDT had prewar insecticides. Coupled with new organophosphate treatments, for a brief window in the 1940s the range of treatments recommended for lawn problems actually became more narrow, with these few chemicals topping the list for all lawn-related problems. At the same time, use of these chemicals became far more widespread and common, and even universal, in the population at large.

In part this change was simply a product of technological development that allowed ease of use. By 1975, it was no longer true that one needed "considerable knowledge of the process and full application of the factors involved in lawn management" (as Sprague had insisted three decades before) in order to control weeds and insects. These lawn chemicals were easy to use and could be applied with rolling spreaders, backpack sprayers, and other innovations. Chemicals had also become more widely marketed, with large, easily recognized petrochemical companies entering the market, utilizing their name brand recognition and larger advertising budgets to make chemicals seem desirable, simple, and safe. Lawn care had become democratic, at least insofar as knowledge was concerned; anyone could apply chemicals.

In particular, the use of DDT on lawns expanded in the 1940s and 1950s. The steady supply of the chemical–due to increased production and long-term stockpiles–drove the price downwards dramatically over the period, from $1 per pound in 1945 to $0.25 per pound in the mid-1950s. [14] The preference of DDT over lead arsenate for homeowners, rather than being a matter of safety, was largely a matter of costs; where grub-proofing with lead arsenate, for example, required some 20 pounds of active ingredient per thousand square feet, DDT could do the job with less than half a pound,[15] or less than a dollar in chemical costs. Its burgeoning use in and around the home is clear from the expansion of consumer sales and marketing.

The same period saw the rise of industrial fertilizers and the expansion of commercial sale of nitrogen, potassium, and phosphorus inputs for lawns. Early fertilizers included ammonium "sulphate"; dried blood; bone meal; cottonseed meal; guano; wood ashes; and a range of manures, including horse, poultry, and sheep.[16] Soluble inorganic commercial fertilizers manufactured from petroleum came to prominence around 1940 and were advocated for landscaping especially because they released more slowly into the lawn and so enhanced grass growth and hindered weed growth over longer periods.[17] By the end of the twentieth century fertilizer use had become widespread: 49 million U.S. households, or 73% of the total, used outdoor fertilizers in 1999.

After DDT: Better Knowledge Means . . . More Chemicals
The decline and fall of DDT is a piece of environmental history well documented elsewhere. Concerns about the chemical had in fact been pronounced by military scientists who had animal tested the compound during the Second World War. This was followed by a far greater concern about the impact of the

chemical on the ambient ecosystem. Since the chemical is persistent and stored in body tissues (especially fat), DDT tends to accumulate biologically, with high concentrations found in the bodies of predator species at the top of the food chain. Toxic to freshwater and marine microorganisms, fish, amphibians, and birds, DDT was blamed for the decrease or disappearance of a range of species. DDT residues, along with its metabolite (1,1-dichloro-2,2-bis(p-chlorophenyl) ethylene, or DDE), have such a long half-life (on the order of a decade or more) and have been used so extensively worldwide, that they have been found in birds and fish living in remote desert areas and the depths of the ocean.[18]

These concerns, along with those concerning human health–DDT was found in mother's milk, was a suspected carcinogen, and has since been shown to be an endocrine disruptor–led Rachel Carson to pen her classic book *Silent Spring* in 1962. Carson argued persuasively against DDT's pervasive usage, along with that of other formulations, including arsenic compounds, 2,4-D, and chlordane. Chlordane, a widely available insecticide, was equally celebrated by lawn care providers and chemical manufacturing companies for its persistence, and so began to eclipse DDT in the early 1960s. In particular, Carson targeted lawn usage of these chemicals:

> suburbanites–advised by nurserymen who in turn have been advised by the chemical manufacturers–continue to apply truly astonishing amounts of crabgrass killers to their lawns each year. Marketed under trade names, which give no hint to their nature, many of these preparations contain such poisons as mercury, arsenic, and chlordane. Application at recommended rates leaves tremendous amounts of these chemicals on the lawn.[19]

The more general backlash against DDT began in the decade after Sweden and the USSR banned the chemical in 1970, and most uses of the chemical were prohibited in many countries, including the United States in 1972.[20] Estimated total production of the chemical has recently fallen to roughly 15 thousand tons annually from a high of 400 thousand tons in the early 1960s.

The shift in public consciousness would change the nature of lawn chemical sales and usage for good, but without derailing the engine of their advocacy and growth in any way. As a prominent example, between the 1961 and 1973 editions of his popular guide *The Perfect Lawn*,[21] Robert Schery removed DDT, which had been banned for all uses by the U.S. Environmental Protection Agency (EPA) the year prior, from his list of recommended chemicals. More specifically, Schery, the executive director in the 1980s of the Lawn Institute (a lawn care trade association), dropped references to DDT altogether. While admitting that insecticides can be dangerous for nontarget insects and birds and urging caution in their use, he makes absolutely no mention of the fact that this much-vaunted home insect control chemical, which his previous guide had extolled, had been banned nationwide and that its effects on the ecosystem had been demonstrated to be devastating.

At the same time, however, new guides departed from previous ones, with the inclusion of strong ecological statements. In his 1973 guide, Schery admitted from the outset that:

> it is something of a paradox that almost everything man wants in his lawn and garden requires contesting natural ecological trends, to favor productivity rather than maturity and stability. Fortunately, a homeowner can have the beautiful lawn he desires because he has at his ready command modern tools which permit him to maintain the particular ecological stages he cherishes.[22]

These "modern tools," exhaustively detailed in guides of the post-DDT era, included complex agricultural chemicals, concentrated fertilizers, and a range of cultural practices (aeration, repair, seeding, etc.). The lawn was acknowledged as unnatural, but the number and range of tools to manage it grew rather than shrank as a result.

This shift is characteristic of a more general change in the tone and content of lawn care information in the industry. By the 1970s ecological consciousness about chemicals had expanded greatly. Moreover, the degree to which the lawn (monocultural and consistent) represented a struggle against the grain of ecological reality (diverse and variable) became increasingly and explicitly acknowledged.

Enthusiasm for chemicals by the industry and the public, however, went largely unabated, and indeed the number and range of available and recommended chemicals began to multiply in this period, with specialized formulations targeted at specific weed and insect problems. Aldrin, carbaryl, diazinon, Dicamba, meta-chlorophenylpiperazine (MCPP), chlorpyrifos, Carbaryl, Pyrethrum, and Dacthal (DCPA) all found their way to consumer markets in the next few years, capped by the arrival of glyphosate (known most commonly by its trade name Roundup®). Despite setbacks (as in the case of DDT), the chemical approach to lawn care has become normal and widespread, with more households using these chemicals every year.

It would seem that in the last quarter of the twentieth century, therefore, a new and contradictory quality had emerged in lawn care. Experts and lay people alike had begun to establish a more ecological sensibility. At the same time however, more people held themselves to higher management expectations than ever before. Negotiating this complex mental landscape, where conscientiousness about ecology and environmental problems parallels a general increase in chemical use, becomes the central problem for lawn people in the early twenty-first century, and one not as easily dismissed as in the era of DDT and before, when the risks were less well known and practices less widespread. This contradictory pattern of consciousness and behavior has been coupled with an overall increase in the amount of lawn coverage, and a concomitant rise in the overall quantity of chemicals applied across North America.

More Lawns Means . . . More Chemicals
Predicting growth based on past history, total lawn cover relative to residential lots will continue to grow on the order of hundreds of square feet of lawn per household into the twenty-first century, with new housing construction driving this expansive trend. That growth may eventually be limited by the decreasing size of residential lots (even in low-density housing zones), and by increasing house size, but there is every reason to expect a long period of turfgrass expansion. Lawn grass likely increased by more than 155,000 hectares (ha) in the United States between 1982 and 1997. [23]

These predictions portend serious implications for chemical hazards. Specifically, increase in lawn coverage tends to offset chemical reduction benefits that the United States and Canada have experienced through recent decreased usage in the agricultural sector. Table 4.3 shows calculated estimates of the per-hectare, proportional, gross, and net input in chemical deposition on residential land. [24] These numbers suggest that lawn chemical users apply far higher quantities of inputs to lawns than their agricultural counterparts. They also suggest that while agricultural chemical deposition and its concomitant risks are decreasing, [25] lawn applications are increasing both as more consumers adopt high input options and as the total coverage of lawn continues to expand. In particular, insecticide usage

TABLE 4.3   Estimated Chemical Deposition Change in Agriculture versus Lawn Care.

	Agriculture Deposition 1997 (kg/ha)[1]	Lawn Care Deposition 1997 (kg/ha)	Lawn Care Change 1982–1997 (kg)[2]
Herbicides	1.397	2.430	5,656,871
Insecticides	0.244	0.843	1,962,588
Fungicide	0.158	0.397	923,571
Other pesticides	0.491	0.099	230,893
Other chemicals[3]	0.517	2.976	6,926,781
Total	2.807	6.745	15,700,704

1. Calculated from total usage (U.S. Environmental Protection Agency [EPA] 1996) by land cover (Natural Resources Conservation Service 2000). Figures are given in kilograms of *active ingredient*. Lawn calculated as 23% developed cover.

2. Calculated from cover change and deposition per hectare.

3. Chemicals registered as pesticides but often marketed for other purposes, i.e., multi-use chemicals, including sulfur, salt, sulfuric acid and petroleum products (e.g., kerosene, oils and distillates).

Reprinted from Robbins, P., and T. Birkenholtz. (2003). Turfgrass revolution: measuring the expansion of the American lawn. *Land Use Policy* 20:181–194, with permission from Elsevier.

on lawns–though currently representing 17% of the total U.S. input–expands dramatically with increase in lawn coverage, since residential users apply more than three times the quantity per hectare than agricultural producers do. The figures are similar for other inputs as well, including fungicides and other chemicals. This increase in deposition has occurred simultaneously with an explosion in the diversity and complexity of lawn chemical inputs. A bewildering new suite of inputs is available as any trip to a big-box retailer will reveal.

The Contemporary Chemical Suite

Following the decline of DDT, starting in the early 1970s, a range of new chemicals began to appear on the market, each aimed at slightly different problems facing the lawn manager. Table 4.4 shows the dominant inputs into lawns and gardens at the end of the twentieth century. The following brief survey

TABLE 4.4   Pesticides Used on U.S. Lawns and Gardens

Pesticide	Metric tns Active*	Type**	Toxicity (EPA)**	Environ Toxicity**
2,4-D	3150–4050	Systemic phenoxy herbicide	Slight to high	Birds Fish Insects
Glyphosate	2250–3600	Nonselective systemic herbicide	Moderate	Birds Fish Insects
Dicamba	1350–2250	Systemic acid herbicide	Slight	Aquatic
MCPP	1350–2250	Selective phenoxy herbicide	Slight	NA
Diazinon	900–1800	Nonsystemic organophosphate insecticide	Moderate	Birds Fish Insects
Chlorpyrifos	900–1800	Broad-spectrum organophosphate insecticide	Moderate	Birds Fish
Carbaryl	900–1800	Broad-spectrum carbamate insecticide	Moderate to high	Fish Insects
DCPA	450–1350	Phthalate preemergence herbicide	Low	Birds Fish

2,4-D = dichlorophenoxyacetic acid; DCPA = Dacthal; NA = not available.

*Millions of metric tonnes of active ingredient used in the United States (United States Environmental Protection Agency 2000).

**(Extension Toxicology Network 2000).

Reprinted from Robbins, P., and T. Birkenholtz. (2003). Turfgrass revolution: measuring the expansion of the American lawn. *Land Use Policy* 20: 181–194, with permission from Elsevier.

of these chemicals shows the diversity of applications, suggesting the ever-increasing complexity of lawn maintenance. Each compound is directed at a different purpose, each functions in a different fashion, and each has its own risks.

2,4-D and the Debate Over Carcinogenesis

2,4-D is one of the earliest of the modern herbicides. Replacing arsenic compounds of the preWWII era, 2,4-D arrived for lawn usage in the mid 1940s. The chemical's attraction is its remarkable ability to be used on weeds (e.g., dandelions and plantains) that had already emerged on lawns, while not adversely affecting perennial growth of desired grasses. The chemical enters the weedy plant through leaves, stems, and roots; moves throughout the plant's system; and disrupts its metabolic processes by stimulating nucleic acid and protein synthesis that affect enzyme activity, respiration, and cell division. To do its job fully, however, 2,4-D must sit on the leaf surface for between several hours to a full day to allow lethal dosage of the chemical to penetrate leaves.[26] The chemical is therefore vulnerable to rainfall, mowing, and foot traffic, which wash away or dissipate the chemical.

When used commercially, 2,4-D has produced serious eye and skin irritation among agricultural workers. The direct risks of the chemical to humans makes it an EPA toxicity class III–slightly toxic when ingested orally, but toxicity class I–highly toxic, for eye exposure. Immediate, direct, acute, and high-level exposure can injure liver, kidney, muscle, and brain tissues.[27]

Even so, 2,4-D is advertised as being safe to humans when used as directed, and there is no evidence that the chemical bioaccumulates like DDT does, or that it has any immediate effects on human reproduction or human organs. Although 2,4-D made up nearly half of the active ingredient of Agent Orange, the controversial defoliant used in the Vietnam War, the stated problems with that compound were associated with the contaminant component, dioxin, not 2,4-D itself. As a result, 2,4-D is designated as a General Use Pesticide by the EPA, requires no specific training or licensing to use on the home lawn, and is available in a number of formulations.[28]

Toxicity of 2,4-D to animals and nontarget plant species is far less clear-cut. It is slightly toxic to wildfowl (e.g., quail and mallard ducks) and moderately toxic to some other bird species. The toxicity of the chemical to aquatic life varies both by chemical formulation and by animal species, though it is clearly toxic to many species, including stream trout, earthworms, and beneficial insects.[29] 2,4-D has been shown to cause genetic damage in crops including barley, wheat, rice, and onions and can also increase the severity of some plant diseases.[30]

As with almost all lawn chemicals, the long-term human effects of exposure to 2,4-D remain entirely unclear. Laboratory animal studies have shown that the chemical can migrate into nerve tissues and accumulate in the brain, with resulting behavioral changes in test rats.[31] Whether the chemical is a potential carcinogen for other species, including humans, is also the source of long-standing controversy.[32] One well-known study established a linkage between 2,4-D usage and malignant lymphoma in dogs. Although the methodology of that study has been disputed by the lawn care industry, more recent studies have further reinforced the association between canine cancer and phenoxy herbicides including 2,4-D.[33] The growing body of research raises questions about 2,4-D's status as a Group D chemical–one with inadequate evidence of carcinogenicity to be regulated. With around 4 million metric tons of the active ingredient applied around the United States annually, the stakes in this debate remain extremely high.

Glyphosate and the Roundup® Ready World

Probably the fastest growing herbicide on the North American market is glyphosate. Introduced in the late 1970s by Monsanato under its trade name Roundup®, this chemical is now known by a range of other evocative names, such as Rattler®, Rodeo®, Shackle®, and Sting®. Glyphosate is a nonselective systemic herbicide, which kills plants whether monocots or dicots, including grasses, broad leaf weeds, and even woody plants. The chemical enters the plant, and disrupts an enzyme required for the production of amino acids that are essential to plant growth. The plant dies within a day or two, down to its roots, inhibiting regrowth or further reproduction.

Because the enzyme targeted by glyphosate is not present in humans or other animals, the product is advertised as entirely safe by the industry. The EPA rates glyphosate as toxicity class II–practically nontoxic even by direct ingestion. Industry advocates celebrate glyphosate as an international ecological success.[34]

Again, however, while toxicity from lengthy exposure to glyphosate appears to have minimal effects[35] and the chemical is only slightly toxic to wildfowl and fish, the long-term effects on ecological systems are less than fully clear. It remains a suspected carcinogen and mutagen in animal, plant, and human populations.[36]

The largest environmental concerns surrounding glyphosate, however, come in the concomitant introduction of "Roundup-ready" plants, genetically altered to withstand and survive applications of the chemical. The obvious reason for the development of such plants is to ensure that "desirable" plants–crops or lawn grasses–can survive Roundup® use, whereas a general application will kill off all other competing plant species. Advocates for such innovations, moreover, argue that such a configuration will serve to decrease herbicide usage overall, including and especially more controversial chemicals such as 2,4-D. Roundup Ready® Creeping Bentgrass, co-developed by Scotts Company and Monsanto, is already in test trials for golf courses.[37] Being resistant to a "common weedkilling chemical" (probably glyphosate), the grass is not only a product in itself, but further increases the ability to spray herbicides indiscriminately with no risk to the grass, resulting in increased demand for those herbicides specifically.

Reasonable concerns, however, have been raised by ecological and conservation communities. Long the source of worry for organizations such as the Union of Concerned Scientists, pesticide-tolerant crop species (e.g., soy and rice) could very conceivably become nuisances, by escaping farm fields and entering sensitive environments, such as wetlands or forests, where traditional controls would be less than fully effective. As "superweeds," such new species might become a serious ecological problem, given genetic advantages over indigenous species, and so invading other ecosystems with impunity.[38]

Extending this logic to turfgrasses, which are already aggressive, fast-growing, and often weedy species (owing to their many adaptive qualities), raises further questions. By genetically producing grasses that are immune to the effects of the currently more effective and most useful herbicide(s) available, the likelihood of future weediness of these species is nearly assured. Beyond the potential harm that such an unchecked species might cause for local ecologies, the promulgation of such grasses assures the demand for continued innovation, production, and sale of *new chemical formulations* to control the species rendered uncontrollable through genetic engineering. This circle of ecological adaptation and ecological intervention is a familiar one in the history of the agro-chemical industry.

Herbicidal Cocktail: Dicamba, MCPA, and DCPA

The remaining popular herbicides vary greatly in chemical formulation and effect. Dicamba (3,6-dichloro-O-anisic acid) is a benzoic acid postemergence herbicide used for control of broadleaf weeds, applied both to the leaves of weeds or directly to the soil. MCPA (4-chloro-2-methylphenoxy acetic acid) is a systemic postemergence herbicide, related to 2,4-D and other phenoxy compounds. DCPA (dimethyl-2,3,5,6-tetrachlorobenzene-1,4-dicarboxylic acid) is the most popular preemergence herbicide, used to thwart the growth of annual grasses and annual broadleaf weed species in the lawn. It is applied broadly to the grass and soil, where it forms a barrier to seed and plant growth.[39]

These three chemicals are all deemed practically safe by the EPA, although long-term exposure effects are unknown. Dicamba is listed on the EPA's Toxics Release Inventory, and is commonly detected in ground and surface water. Its immediate toxicity to wildlife is slight, although there is some evidence of toxicity to aquatic life in particular. MCPA shows a medium toxicity for bees but is more notable for its effects on reproductive capacities of test animals, impacted reproductive function in rats and adverse sperm and testes effects in dogs.[40] DCPA is listed as practically nontoxic by the EPA in terms of immediate exposure, but remains a suspected carcinogen, suspected mutagen, and suspected teratogen (an agent that can cause malformations of an embryo or fetus).[41]

These three chemicals are commonly used in combination either across the year, or are bundled together in combination products, likely making the triumvirate the largest single group of pesticides used around the home for weed control. As a result, the sheer quantity of these chemicals (perhaps 5800 metric tones [or 12 million pounds] applied annually in the United States) raises questions about hidden risks, not only to users, but also to ambient ecosystems, including the rivers and streams into which urban drainages pour.

Twilight of the Organophosphates: Diazinon and Chlorpyrifos

As of 1999, the most popular insecticides used on home lawns remained diazinon and chlorpyrifos (commonly known by its trade name Dursban®), both of which are organophosphates. These chemicals interfere with the nervous system by blocking the breakdown of the messenger chemical of the nervous system, acetylcholine. As acetylcholine builds up in the system, nerve transmissions are interrupted, the system is overwhelmed, and the insect dies.[42] During and after World War II, organophosphate based products were developed to control mosquitoes and became commonly used in and around the home. As more controversial chlorinated hydrocarbon insecticides fell by the wayside (e.g., DDT and chlordane in the 1970s), organophosphates rose as a "safe" alternative to take their place. For the lawn, these chemicals can be broadly used to control infestations by grubs and a number of other pest species.

Whereas many insecticides were the outgrowth of chemical warfare experimentation, organophosphates were actually the reverse. Developed by chemist Gerhard Schrader in Germany during the 1930s, this class of chemicals proved immediately effective in aphid and mosquito control, especially when combined with cyanide. Unlike DDT, however, it became immediately apparent that organophosphates were just as effective on people as insects, since acetylcholine (the target of organophosphate action) is the central messenger chemical for the nervous systems of both creatures. Research on the chemical shifted to the chemical warfare office of the German army, and some of the earliest nerve agents were born.[43]

Diazinon began to come under scrutiny when birds began to die off in large numbers around golf courses and sod farms where they congregated. As a result, the EPA canceled registration of the chemical for use in these commercial environments in 1988.[44] Chlorpyrifos began to draw attention in the late 1990s with studies increasingly showing schoolchildren being exposed to the chemical.[45] Unlike many other pesticides, the major concern in the case of organophosphates were residues present immediately after application and their fate in enclosed environments such as homes and schools, rather than the effects of long-term exposure to small quantities.

Most recent research continues to point to the immediate toxicity of these chemicals, the presence of their metabolites in the urine of the general population (especially children), and their potential long-term impact on reproduction.[46] More generally, the potential neural damage organophosphates may cause, and their influence on learning, attention, and behavior–especially in children. This harkens back to the slow, but eventual, consensus that arose regarding learning of lead's poisonous quality decades earlier.

The EPA's investigation of the chemicals and review of poison control center data eventually concluded in the late 1990s that organophosphate pesticides pose a greater exposure hazard than do other pesticides, especially for children, who were more likely to be hospitalized, admitted for critical care, and have experienced a major medical negative outcome or death than if exposed to some other pesticide.[47] Coupled with the mounting evidence of acute pesticide poisonings, the EPA moved to eliminate the chemicals altogether, despite a steady barrage of criticism from the industry (Chapter 5). The EPA did not actually ban the use of diazinon and chlorpyrifos, but in June of 2000 it reached an agreement with producer Dow AgroSciences to stop the sale of most home, lawn, and garden forms of these products. In the years since, a blizzard of new products have appeared on the market to replace them, however, and the lawn chemical economy shows no sign of slackening in sales or innovation.

Carbaryl: Inaction Amidst Evidence

A nonorganophosphate pesticide alternative is carbaryl, also known by its trade name Sevin®, which was introduced to the world in 1957 by Union Carbide, when insect pests were beginning to show some signs of resistance and immunity to other existing chemical compounds.[48] A broad-spectrum pesticide that kills dozens of insect species on contact or through ingestion, carbaryl is a carbamate nerve toxin that works by inhibiting the enzyme cholinesterase and so disrupting nerve impulse transmissions.

Depending on the formulation, carbaryl can vary from slightly toxic to highly toxic to humans. Direct exposure causes burns, nerve damage, nausea, and other immediate effects. Lethal to many nontarget bugs, including bees and other beneficial insects, the chemical also bioaccumulates (as did DDT) in the tissues of aquatic creatures (e.g., catfish, crawfish, and snails).[49]

Carbaryl is perhaps one of the best studied of the major lawn chemicals, and evidence of health-related risks related to its use date as early as the late 1960s, when studies of the chemical revealed both its toxicity and its potential impact on animal (and potentially human) reproduction. In 1969 the U.S. Department of Health Education and Welfare recommended restrictions on the use of the chemical, owing to mounting evidence that it may be tetragenic (causing birth defects).[50] Later research in the 1980s pointed towards the possible implication of carbaryl in neurotoxicity, brain function, and aggressive behavior.[51]

The mounting evidence, however, did not lead to the kind of significant regulatory action it did for DDT and later for organophosphates. Despite evidence that carbaryl causes birth defects in lab animals, the EPA ruled it to be insignificantly tetragenic, using the logic that the levels of dosage required to induce the effect were usually toxic to the pregnant animal in any case. Regulators, moreover, have discounted evidence of possible carcinogenicity for decades. Carbaryl retains a current status as a General Use Pesticide available over-the-counter in unlimited quantities.[52] This remains a test case of a chemical known to be dangerous in a range of settings remaining publicly used, industrially defended, and under-regulated based on complex risk assessment by regulators, firms, and individual users. The other shoe may yet drop for Carbaryl, but it may be much too late.

Fertilizers: How Much is Too Much?

Fertilizers provide plant food subsidies to encourage fresh tiller and root production by supplying nutrients that are otherwise a limiting factor on grass growth. Of the thirteen nutrients that are essential to lawn grasses, most are contained in sufficient abundance for turfgrass plants. However, nitrogen, phosphorus and potassium are often somewhat scarce in most urban and suburban soils (see Chapter 3). Nitrogen influences shoot and root density; and disease, heat, cold and drought susceptibility. Potassium influences turfgrass rooting as well as heat and cold hardiness. Phosphorus is important in establishment and rooting of young plants.[53]

Nevertheless, most of these functions are managed fairly well by the unsubsidized lawn itself. Especially where the grasses are growing amidst leguminous species such as clover, lawns are hardy enough to grow and reproduce even on some of the most impoverished urban soils. Indeed, deficiencies in soil nutrients usually only show in the yellowing of older leaves and some reduced shoot growth, rather than leading to death of turfgrass. Ongoing nutrient loss usually results from removing grass clippings after mowing, which is entirely avoidable.[54]

The stubborn requirement of the American Lawn aesthetic requires that the grass remains green throughout the season, (even at times when it is naturally dormant), and that it remain an even and emerald shade. This invariably means some form of nutrient input is necessary.

It is difficult to say with any accuracy the total quantity of fertilizers put on lawns in the United States. Since the home lawn market accounts for only approximately 5% of domestic fertilizer consumption overall, this means roughly 2.9 million tons of total fertilizer were applied to lawns in 2004.[55] While this amount is nowhere near the quantity of fertilizer applied by the entire nation of India (an oft-touted and inaccurate statistic), it is comparable to or exceeds the nutrient inputs into almost any major U.S. food crop, including wheat, soy, or cotton. Locally, nutrient loads vary highly but can be quite intense. With user inputs ranging anywhere from 24 to 151 kilograms per hectare,[56] the intensity of individual homeowner applications can be as high as three or four times the rates used on nutrient-demanding commercial crops like corn. Such high intensity use usually leads to overfertilization, which is both bad for the lawn itself and also leads to runoff and the spread of nutrients into waterways.

Fertilizers pose a largely environmental, rather than human toxicological, threat. By running off of farm fields, lawns, and other application areas, excess nitrogen and phosphorus eventually find their way to waterways (ponds, rivers, and lakes). With these increasing levels of available dissolved nutrients, there tends to be a short-term, excessive growth of algae and other aquatic organisms. After their short and vigorous life spans, these plants quickly die and decay–this process robs the waterway of oxygen; fish die and the system fails. The lake or pond is said to have "turned over," or eutrophied.[57]

The large-scale, agglomerated, downstream effects of nitrogen and phosphorus deposition can be devastating. Along the Mississippi River basin–which drains all of the Midwest or some 41% of the land area of the lower 48 United States–nitrate and phosphorous concentrations constantly exceed their statutory limit, and affected waters are rated as severely impaired. Deposited in the Gulf of Mexico, such nutrients are suspected to contribute to the 20,000 square mile low-oxygen zone off the coast, a region that has only recently shifted from a rich fishing area to a dead zone.[58] These chemicals also transport above ground or through soils to watercourses, where they affect ambient water quality and biodiversity.[59]

Most certainly the greatest culprit in excess nutrients is agriculture. Nevertheless, urban areas contribute a grossly disproportionate share of these chemicals (Table 4.5),[60] creating acute local stream problems. Lawn fertilization contributes to this effect, though to a degree not yet fully determined.

And indeed, working from the assumption than more is better, consumer overuse of fertilizers has been observed across the United States. A survey of lawn care around Washington, D.C., and Baltimore in 1998, for example, concluded that hundreds of thousands of homeowners across the area apply

TABLE 4.5   Total phosphorus and nitrate yields in runoff by dominant land use in the United States for 1980–1989 (kilograms per square kilometer)

Land Use	Phosphorus (kg/km2)	Nitrate (kg/km2)
Wheat	3.5	11.2
Rangeland	6.0	10.9
Forest	22.1	89.3
Urban	41.7	192.0
Mixed crops and soybeans	57.1	326.0

Source: Smith, R. A., R. B. Alexander, et al. (1996). United States Geological Survey Water Supply Paper no. 2400—*Stream water quality in the coterminous United States: Status and trends of selected indicators during the 1980s*, Reston, VA: United States Geological Survey (http://water.usgs.gov/nwsum/sal/intro.html)

twice as much fertilizer to lawns as state extension services recommend. These behaviors are by no means exclusive to "ignorant" homeowners: TruGreen-ChemLawn® and Lawn Doctor®, the largest lawn care providers in the United States, were found to exceed recommendations by this same margin.[61]

The short list of chemicals represents only a small fraction of the inputs applied throughout North America. Lindane, malathion, MCPP, metolachlor, metribuzin, oryzalin, pendimethalin, and pronamide are just a few other of the dozens of formulations for insect and weed control available at any hardware or home maintenance store. All of them are toxic to some degree or another, and question marks hang over many of them as to the risk they may pose for people and the ambient environment. The potential hazards of each of the chemicals described above hints at the range of contemporary hazards associated with lawn care.

Analytical Chemistry: Drift, Runoff, Volatilization, and Accumulation

Some of the problems associated with lawn inputs, whether pesticides or fertilizers, can be downplayed if we operate under the assumption that what is put on the lawn stays on the lawn, and that it disappears from the lawn after it does its job. With no diffusion either in space (by finding its way inside a house for example), or over time (by persisting in the ecosystem for a long period), chemicals would be less of a problem. The turf industry has naturally suggested for many years that, owning to the unique dense growth of turf, chemicals tend to stay on lawns. There is certainly *theory* in support of this argument. Turfgrasses and their dense and continuous biotic mats tend to trap the flow of materials across their surface, even during rain events, which in theory keeps runoff of chemicals (or anything else for that matter) to a minimum.[62]

Regrettably, lawns are highly heterogeneous environments: some are steep, others are flat; some get rained on a lot, others very little; some have deep loamy soils, others are shallow clays. Coupled with differences in size and shape of each lawn, this heterogeneity makes proving such an optimistic assertion more difficult. For this reason researchers have tended either to study golf courses or to use abstract mathematical models—instead of directly measuring flows of chemicals off of lawns—to evaluate and model the downstream effects of intensively managed turf in comparison to other land covers, including crops or trees. Initial results from golf course case studies and modeling efforts of this kind suggest that runoff of pesticides and other inputs from turfgrass is less than that for agriculture, though more than for a forest.[63] Even where chemicals stay in place, they tend to be broken down by sunlight, photodecomposed into harmless nontoxic substances, giving each chemical a limited half-life out in the open.[64] The chemical industry insists that because turf absorbs water and inputs it is a relatively safe surface for chemical application.

This might be conceivable, although not beyond questioning, if the only way for chemicals to travel was by water flowing over them and if all chemicals stuck fast to the lawn until they were gone. As it turns out, however, chemicals can be carried away by drifting on the wind, leaching downwards into the groundwater, volatilizing into gas, or clinging fast to human hosts or animals to be transported to locations where they become a greater risk. Herbicides have been shown to volatilize, for example, and drift to adjacent plots, harming vegetable gardens and flowers.[65] Whereas this is a minor nuisance in and of itself, it might be useful to ask where else chemicals might move and how else they might travel. On a high-traffic surface like the lawn, exposed to innumerable complex outside forces, it seems essential to directly measure the path and fate of potentially toxic substances.

The investigation of such problems is the business of analytical chemists who practice a highly technical applied science, where practitioners apply complex instrumentation (with techniques such as nuclear magnetic resonance [NMR] spectroscopy) in order to identify what things are, what things are made of, and whether there are undesirable things in air, water, or dust. In particular, analytical chemists are interested in providing better means for detecting smaller and smaller quantities of chemicals, since for many substances we do not even know the minimum hazardous quantity.

These researchers have revealed a range of pathways through which people (especially children) and pets become exposed to lawn chemicals. One of the unexpected means of exposure is the persistence of chemicals on the clothing of people who are either applying the materials or just walking across or near a treated lawn. A minority of estimates in this field suggests that typical contact with treated lawns (simply walking over them) leaves minimal residues of chemicals in human urine.[66] But the weight of evidence shows that such chemicals accumulate on clothing, which become a persistent source of contamination.[67]

Measurements of actual house dust in sampled residences where people use lawn chemicals is more disturbing. Even if the immediate exposure to these chemicals–now clinging to boots, shirtsleeves, and socks–did not prove a risk, the chemicals that hitchhike with us indoors have a more complex fate. Now released from clothing and accumulating in the home, chemicals with purportedly short half-lives begin to become more persistent. By settling in house dust, and therefore on carpets, the highest level of exposure falls on those close to the floor, which includes pets, but more importantly, toddlers, infants, and small children, who are disproportionately sensitive to the possible effects of these chemicals.[68]

These chemicals, as noted previously, are likely far more dangerous to children (especially neurotoxins such as chlorpyrifos) than has been generally suggested to date.[69] Family pesticide use, including lawn herbicide application, has been shown to be related to childhood brain cancer. Malignancies for children linked to pesticides in case reports or case-control studies include leukemia, neuroblastoma, Wilms' tumor, soft-tissue sarcoma, Ewing's sarcoma, non-Hodgkin's lymphoma, and cancers of the brain, colorectum, and testes.[70]

In addition to pesticide drift, the percolation of nutrients down through soil and into groundwater (called leaching) after lawn fertilization has been shown to cause nitrogen to increase in groundwater under subdivisions where it is applied, causing the nitrate-nitrogen value to significantly exceed the legal drinking water standard of 10 mg/L.[71] Other studies have revealed that intensively managed turfgrass environments contribute increased nitrogen and phosphorus loads to adjacent streams.[72] Since fertilizer compounds contain a range of nonmicronutrient substances that remain unused in plant metabolism, overuse can also lead to the increase in toxic elements (including thorium, cobalt, chromium, selenium, and antimony, among many others) in the underground water supply.[73]

In sum, these chemicals by no means simply stay where they are put and vanish when they are done. Nor should we be surprised. This is the first rule of ecology: nothing goes away.

Turfgrass Ecology and the Chemical Treadmill

Even to the degree that chemicals stay put in lawn environments, however, their usage tends to exacerbate and encourage problems that ironically require further chemical solutions. For example, certain pesticides, even when applied at recommended rates and dosages, can reduce nontarget earthworm populations. By decreasing earthworm activity, that can accumulate, leading to an unhealthy lawn, which then requires greater inputs and care to maintain. [74]

This kind of impact is complicated by the possible influence of these chemicals on the process of evolution itself. When a chemical comes into widespread use, especially an insecticide, it is only a matter of time before the target insects develop resistance. That is, those individual insects with natural resistance (as a result of natural variation and mutation) survive successive assaults of a given chemical and reproduce broods with similar immunity, which come to be common in the whole population. In a short period of time (because insects reproduce quickly), the species becomes resistant altogether (Table 4.6).[75]

There is evidence, moreover, that higher population densities and increased survival of some insect pests follow chemical treatments designed to control them. This is because such treatments result in the destruction of predator insects that naturally control pest populations. Killing the predators only increases the needs for future insecticide treatments. [76]

In this sense, pesticide and fertilizer use can undermine the goals of lawn care itself, impoverishing the soil and plant health required to maintain turf. This effect, known as the "chemical treadmill," emerged with the dawn of the green revolution in agriculture in the 1960s. The term was coined to capture the frustrating cycle where increased use of inputs leads to increased demand of the

TABLE 4.6   Resistance of insects to insecticides over time (number of resistant species by year)

Chemical	1938	1948	1954	1970	1975	1980	1984	1989
DDT	0	3	13	98	203	229	233	263
Lindane	0	1	5	140	225	269	276	291
Organophosphates	0	0	3	54	147	200	212	260
Carbamates	0	0	0	3	36	51	64	85

DDT = dichlorodiphenyl-trichloroethane.

Source: Muller, Franz. (2000). *Agrochemicals: Composition, production, toxicology, applications.* Weinheim, Wiley-VCH.

ecosystem for inputs. In this sense, the use of herbicides, insecticides, and fertilizers–because of their negative effects on beneficial nontarget insects, on soil structure, and on soil health–lead to conditions where only more chemicals can increase or restore productivity. Once an agro-ecosystem is in this way "addicted" to such inputs, the habit becomes hard to break, without having a lawn worse off than one that had received no such inputs to begin with.

Consider the case of nematodes, tiny entomopathogenic (insect parasite) roundworms. These represent a nonchemical and natural biological insecticide. By forming symbiotic associations with bacteria, which they deposit inside pest insect hosts, the nematode usually kills the pest within 48 hours. Nematodes are self-generating animals, typical in the soils of the non-chemical lawn.[77] They were, however, actually viewed as a lawn hazard for many years, and gardening guides from the 1960s and 1970s advocated chemical controls to reduce their number.[78] After decades of treatment, the density and productivity of nematode communities have declined around domestic landscapes. Lawn treatment companies are now ironically *selling* them, however, as a purchasable input alternative.

Taking Needless Risks: What We Do Not Know

With all of these many treatments being applied around the home, there remains a startling range of things we do not really know about chemicals and their long-terms effects. Firstly, little or nothing is known about the emergent effects that come from combining chemicals, either intentionally or incidentally over time through multiple treatments. Most testing of chemicals–which provides regulatory agencies like the EPA with the data and results from which they make their ratings, warnings, and restrictions–is performed on each active ingredient separately. While it is possible to anticipate the combined effects of chemicals by simply adding them together, it is also common for combinations of chemicals to have troubling synergistic effects.[79] Contact with the pesticide malathion after exposure to parathion, for example, can be far more dangerous than exposure to each alone; the first chemical exhausts the body of detoxifying enzymes, making someone extremely vulnerable to a dose of the latter one. Lawn care can become, therefore, something of a chemistry experiment.[80]

Secondly, the impacts of these chemicals are highly variable throughout the diverse human population. Some people, either high-risk populations–such as children or those with varying genetic vulnerability to such chemicals, complex allergies, or syndromes that make them especially sensitive to certain chemicals–may feel the effects of exposure far earlier and more strongly than others around them, including their neighbors. Since toxicology is a specialized field, and since many of these synthetic chemicals are so new to medical science, the effects of this exposure may be confusing to or misdiagnosed by consulting physicians or may go untreated for long periods, compounding exposure risks.[81]

Thirdly, owing again to their novelty, our understanding of the effects of long-term exposure to most all synthetic chemicals is still underdeveloped. Long-term problems stem either from long-lasting but hidden damage from a single-exposure event, or from continued small-exposure events, or from the cumulative buildup of the toxin in the body. In any of these cases, the long period of time often required to understand such effects, document evidence of their affects, and isolate causes, means that many exposure effects (as for DDT and diazinon previously), may be occurring but totally unknown to us today.

Finally, the "downstream" or secondary effects of many of these chemicals on the broader ecosystem also remain unclear. By removing both target (e.g., aphids) and nontarget (e.g., honeybees) insect and plant species (e.g., dandelions) from the environment, lawn inputs may over time increase vulnerabilities of regional ecologies to infestation, invasion, or other adverse ecological effects. A dandelion or other nuisance species may not be an "essential" ecosystem component in and of itself, however the generalization and simplification of ecosystems in pursuit of their elimination may make them more problematic over time. Load these chemical risks on top of other problems of conventional lawn management–including water demands, air quality problems,[82] and the influence of lawns on overall ecosystem structure,[83]–and a picture of needless costs and risks emerges, but one not that is easily regulated.

Lawn Risks Defy Regulation

Just as in the early history of lawn chemicals, when only a handful of toxic substances dominated the market, known risks concerning these substances has never stood in the way of their use and marketing. As in the case of both lead arsenate and DDT, as long as any level of uncertainty concerning the exact risks associated with a chemical persisted, aggressive marketing of the product continued. Only with either direct bans of these products or their replacement by something cheaper and more potent have sales ceased, usually with little or no acknowledgment of their previous risk by the industry after the fact.

The spread of the lawn is, moreover, creating new locally specific exposure problems in urban areas that may be unknown to us; while agricultural chemicals exposed people to risks through unwashed food and downstream contact, lawn chemicals are deposited right under the noses of urban residents. This represents a class of ecological policy problem previously unseen. And people who use these chemicals, as noted previously, are more likely to acknowledge the associated risks, at least vaguely, than people who do not. It is unlikely that people will immediately cease application even with more and better information concerning chemical risks.

Deposited by countless private citizens, moreover, lawn care toxins have also proven far more difficult to measure and far more resistant to traditional techniques of pollution control. The political momentum for water quality regulation lags far behind this changing land-use reality. The shift in the last few years to decentralized decision-making that allowed for the implementation of the Clean Water Act, for example, has not come to terms with this change. In this case, the Clean Water Act mandates the creation of total maximum daily load (TMDL) criteria, standards for cleaning up nonpoint sources such as farms, suburban developments, and other nonindustrial sites. These standards are drawn up by water quality management committees.

But these committees remain heavily loaded with suburban interests (e.g., developers) and traditional point-source industries (e.g., factories). These interests are eager to make agriculture "pay its fair share," while paying less attention to other important non-point sources.[84] So while agriculture remains an important target for nonpoint source pollution control, an immediate and proximate toxic risk to suburban dwellers is located in the under-examined areas right around their around homes, and this landscape is expanding while agriculture land use contracts.

Such apparent contradictions in regulatory trends are not lost on farmers. In the state of Maryland, for example, increased scrutiny of farm field fertilizers was instituted in 1998 to reduce nonpoint source runoff. This was done with the explicit intention of protecting and recovering the waters of the Chesapeake Bay, where fertilizers have washed over the last few decades, fueling oxygen-choking algae blooms and spread of the toxic microbe *Pfiesteria piscicida*. The law, however, only applies to properties of three acres or larger, leaving most all lawns untouched by regulation. The local Farm Bureau president griped in response "You know they're not going to come down on the suburbs . . . that's where [the governor's] votes are."[85] As the lawn expands, therefore, the geography of nonpoint source pollution is changing faster than the political forces of regulation and control.

Lawn People, Hazards, Knowledge, and Risk

In sum, intensive lawn management has evolved over the century to include inputs that are increasingly necessary and ubiquitous. The development of increased lawn input usage has occurred simultaneously with a reevaluation of the serious hazards that such chemicals present, moreover, and a concomitant increase in environmental values in the United States and Canada. Evidence of the potential serious risks associated with many of these material is mounting. Where uncertainty prevails, well-documented historical precedent shows the value of precaution (consider DDT, lead arsenate, and organophosphates). Yet lawn care remains a source of a human and environmental hazards that is resistant to increased environmental knowledge. They are acknowledged by the consumers who use them. They are largely overlooked in any meaningful way by regulators, except where it is often too late. This is a risk calculation, one with some serious environmental implications.

Turfgrass chemicals are by no means the only toxic hazard faced by average people, nor indeed the most unjust or egregiously unfair one, of course. Consider, for example, the disproportionately high exposure of inner city residents to propoxur, chlorpyrifos, diazinon, and permethrin used to treat the insects and pests that are an everyday part of life in poorly maintained structures, rented by absent and indifferent landlords.[86] The use of such chemicals in lawn management is far less directly utilitarian than in inner city homes, however; such urban residents face a health hazard where lawn managers face a mere nuisance, if that.

Thus, the American Lawn is a political and economic (and not solely cultural) object that by its design (and not by any form of ecological accident) demands inputs. Many of these inputs are hazardous, and knowledge of these hazards is easily available to lawn people.

This does not necessarily mean, however, that the risks of lawn care are *necessary or inherent* to the larger lawn economy. The continued innovation of treatments, after all, is generally hailed by industry as a victory for chemistry that has led to decreased risk. DDT is arguably less hazardous than lead arsenate, or at least more efficient. Discovery of the hazards of DDT led to less persistent chemicals. Glyphosate is likely more benign than 2,4-D, and so on.

But a political ecology approach must draw into question the industrial logics of the lawn industry. What are the economic incentives that direct chemical marketing? What constraints in the larger economy act on firms that produce and supply chemicals? Do the necessities of shedding costs and declining margins impinge on the decision-making of even well-intentioned manufacturers and investors, with implications for either consumers or workers? Does the industry meet or instead create demand?

CHAPTER 5

Does the Industry Meet or
Produce Demand?*

WHEN ORGANOPHOSPHATE CHEMICALS came under fire in the late 1990s as a potential source of immediate and acute toxicity as well as a long-term neural hazard, especially for children, few complaints about potential regulation came from homeowners or other private citizens. While the U.S. Environmental Protection Agency (EPA) considered the evidence available that the chemical washazardous and awareness increased of exposure to the chemical among children both at home and in school,[1] the industry protested against the methods and data being used, defending the chemical as safe.[2] Some media, moreover, searching for fair and balanced coverage of the issue, began to express another side of the story, as reflected in this Letter to the Editor published in the Tampa Tribune that stated flatly:

> Chlorpyrifos has generated fewer health complaints than have the insects that it is designed to control. . . . Nevertheless, activists are trying to build a case against the vast body of existing science showing chlorpyrifos is safe.[3]
> –Dr. Ronald Gots, International Center for Toxicology and Medicine

How do we reconcile the EPA's decision to pursue a ban on chlorpyrifos (after one of the most extensive scientific reviews of a pesticide ever conducted) with the scientific accounts of an expert like Doctor Gots (from an International Center, no less?). We would of course be required to weigh some immensely

*Reprinted with modifications from Robbins, P., and J. T Sharp. (2003). Producing and consuming chemicals: the moral exonomy of the American lawn. Economic Georgarphy 79(4):425–451; with permission of Clark University.

complex toxicological data and seriously consider the uncertainties present in even the best science. The apparent contest between competing claims about pesticides appears to be one of honest disagreement over complex issues.[4]

Demand or Supply?

It would be no shortcut, however, to ask what is Doctor Gots' International Center for Toxicology and Medicine (ICTM) and what are its research goals? As it turns out, ICTM is a company whose stated goal is to assist attorneys, corporations, insurers, and facilities managers to develop strategies and tactics to support defense counsel in chemical liability cases, including preparing jury presentations and motions to exclude experts. The organization specializes in defending against claims of illness allegedly arising from toxic exposure.

According the watchdog group Integrity in Science, the ICTM includes among its member associations, the Chemical Manufacturers Associations, the Chemical Specialty Manufacturers Association, and the National Association of Manufacturers. Moreover, ICTM can count amongst its clients Allied Chemical, Dupont Chemical Co., Halliburton Corp., Industrial Petrochemical, and many others. And amongst these many corporate clients and trade associations comes most notably Dow Chemical Co., whose subsidiary, Dow AgroSciences, produced the chlorpyrifos lawn product Dursban®, until its removal from the market following EPA pressure in late 2000.

The reason the product did not go down without a fight, therefore, is not because chemical-using citizens could not manage their home environments without it, but instead because companies were defending their markets. It was not consumers that created controversy, but rather corporate entities and their allies. More than this, the conduits of consumer information and corporate advocacy for these products were many and subtle (letters to the editor for example), and did not simply take the form of direct advertising.

Similarly, in 1991, the Montreal suburb of Hudson became the first of many Canadian municipalities to entirely outlaw the use of cosmetic pesticides on lawns. Since that time, dozens of other towns have enacted similar bans, including some of that country's largest cities. A decade later, the Canadian Supreme Court upheld the Hudson restriction, giving local authorities across Canada the right to follow suit.[5]

This legal decision did not go unopposed by any means, either. Landscape contractors Spraytech and Chemlawn (now named Greenspace Services in Canada) brought the case to the Canadian Supreme Court, insisting that the ban was discriminatory against the lawn care industry and that, moreover, the ban should not be generalized to other provinces, as it is an entirely local matter. Organized under action groups with euphemistic names such as "Ontario Environmental Coalition," landscape and chemical company trade groups formed coalitions attempting to stall efforts to enact similar laws elsewhere.[6]

These high-profile conflicts reemphasize a question raised in Chapter 1. If in some places the public is struggling to ban chemical applications that the industry is fighting to maintain, is it demand or rather supply that drives the behaviors of lawn people, especially their application of insecticides, herbicides, and fertilizers, throughout the United States and Canada? More fundamentally, are the risks outlined in Chapter 4 essential to this economy, or incidental to it, an unfortunate market inefficiency that will soon be fixed through more and better competition? Can the industry produce alternatives? How does it communicate and manage risk?

The Lawn Commodity Chain

The range of economic products necessary for managing the contemporary lawn is mind-boggling. The economy includes, but is by no means restricted to, power and nonpower tool makers, seed growers, turf farms, raw chemical producers and chemical formulators, the retail outlets that supply many of these goods, the global workshops that produce them, and the offices that imagine, execute, and advertise their diverse forms.

The threads of this massive chain spread across the globe. While the leading wholesaler and formulator of lawn inputs, Scotts Company (with its headquarters in Marysville, Ohio), reporting net sales of $2.0 billion in fiscal 2004, the company's long reach includes processing facilities around the country and overseas. The raw chemical producers who provide the input components for these formulations, especially multinational firms such as Dow AgroSciences, have operations on every continent but Antarctica. Within each such operation, machines are operating, water and petroleum are consumed, and large numbers of workers are employed. Bayer, a company rapidly emerging to compete in lawn chemical sales, has agrochemical research centers in Germany, Japan, and the United States. Its production sites are spread across Europe, the United States, Brazil, India, Japan, and Turkey.

The vastness of the lawn maintenance equipment market is even more far-reaching. A typical mower, for example, includes a huge range of parts (blades, bags, handles, axles/wheels, gear systems, and an increasingly intricate engine system), each of which is manufactured at differing sites around the world, transported and assembled in pieces, and finally assembled and shipped to the retail store in which they are sold. These parts are cast from plastics and metals formulated elsewhere, themselves assembled from petroleum and raw minerals, mined and drilled from the four corners of the earth.

The grasses that make up the lawn are themselves commodities, sourced from distant locations. Each seed type is typically grown in a different environment (e.g., Oregon Ryegrasses or Florida Bahiagrasses), leading to a national and sometimes international seed and breeding business. Whole turf is also grown, on sprawling farms that themselves are supported by high levels of chemical and water inputs, all prior to their being rolled out across any individual homeowner's yard.

This is to say nothing of the enormous technical systems necessary to get raw water–sometimes partially recycled "grey water" but most often fresh–from its aquifer, river, or stream, through an urban and suburban distribution network, to the backyard lawn. If watering from a treated source, a huge amount of energy is hidden in this process of delivery, since the same water used on the lawn is provided to the kitchen sink and must therefore be suitable for drinking. These inputs include chlorine, fluoride, and ammonia, along with host of other trace chemicals provided for coagulation of contaminants, all of which must be brought to treatment centers from elsewhere. Beyond this lies the hidden costs of downstream water treatment, which the water that runs off of lawns and into storm sewers later receives when it is redrawn from the streams or rivers into which it is dumped.

Including chemicals, equipment, seed, and water necessary for turfgrass growth–each with multiple links in its own chain between raw materials and home use–every lawn represents the crowded environmental convergence of an enormous economic system. Indeed, a true cost accounting of what goes into the lawn maintenance would be a work of phenomenal scope. Of course, *all* consumer products reflect equally dense and lengthy chains, but the lawn is remarkable for the diversity and extent of its required inputs. Few other home features require both biotic and nonbiotic inputs and ongoing high levels of sustained energy in the way turfgrass does.

In considering the problems faced by lawn people, however, specifically bearing in mind the ambivalences surrounding lawn care that so closely couple with lawn activity, no more revealing economy exists than that of the chemical input industry. This is primarily because the supply side the chemical economy is simultaneously far larger than its lawn segment, but also uniquely dependent on the perpetuation of high-input care; individual lawn owners are a crucial link in the survival of global firms. Simultaneously, on the demand side, unlike other inputs such as water or fuel, chemicals make lawn people nervous; as we have seen, internal struggles within households and communities attempt to balance between pesticide use and pesticide anxiety. Strategies for getting around this "chemophobia," as the industry describes it, are central features of the chemical commodity chain, as are the unusual demands that lawn grasses themselves place upon firms who provide inputs.

The Chemical Commodity Chain

As with most consumer products circulating through the economy today, the chemicals that people use in lawn care travel through many hands prior to their final fate. This vast commodity chain is international in scope, diverse in players, and intricate in connections. Figure 5.1 maps out the multiple parties who

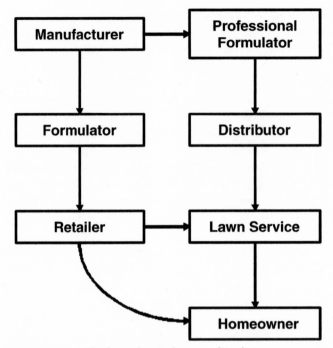

FIGURE 5.1   The lawn chemical commodity chain.

exchange both chemicals and information about chemicals, including advertising and advice.

At the bottom of the chain is the user: a home or property owner. This is the decision-maker who decides when, where, and how many inputs to apply, and also decides whether to apply the chemicals or to hire an applicator company to do it. In either case, the user pays the highest mark-up, purchasing small quantities and bearing the costs of the many other players in the chain, who each take a small surplus for playing their part. Prior to the consumer come retail outlets and applicator companies. The retail link includes a range of small hardware and garden stores, but for the most part means "big box" retailers such as Home Depot. Lawn service applicator companies are a diverse group of firms that range from small one-person enterprises to large corporations and huge franchises. Although the total number of such firms is difficult to estimate, the main professional organization representing them–the Professional Lawn Care Association of America–reports more than a thousand member companies, probably just a fraction of the total. The dominant firm, TruGreen Chemlawn–a franchise that serves around four million customers worldwide–is itself a subsidiary of ServiceMaster, a conglomerate of companies ranging from insect extermination chains to domestic cleaning services.

Next in the chain, supplying retail outlets, come formulators. These relatively few companies purchase raw chemical inputs for lawn care, combine and brand them, and supply them to retail outlets. ' These large firms are increasingly well known to homeowners, and have extended their reach and familiarity through direct marketing and careful branding. One prominent example of a formulator company is Scotts, the pioneering firm in the industry, which converted from agricultural seed sales in the late 1800s to specialize in lawn care products in the 1930s. This leviathan, which employs thousands of people worldwide, has been joined by recent competitors, including multinational giant Bayer.

Professional applicators, especially those companies or franchises of any size, rely on their own independent distribution and formulator companies. One such firm, Lesco, distributes lawn care products to applicators, golf course managers, and other professionals. Their products reach 130,000 such companies and clients worldwide, using innovative distribution networks, including not only traditional service centers but mobile sales and service units.

Feeding these formulators with raw materials, agrochemical firms–large, diversified, general chemical companies who manufacture the active ingredients in agricultural and lawn care products–sit at the far end of the commodity chain from the consumer. With familiar names like DowElanco, DuPont, and Ciba-Geigy, these companies together manufacture millions of metric tons of active ingredients annually, an industry worth more than thirty billion dollars every year.

Each of the key links in the chain–especially applicator services, formulators, and manufacturers–operates by its own logic and each has its own imperatives. By considering each in turn, we get a better picture of the latitude, choices, and strategies of each. We also come to better understand the profound influence that suppliers have over consumers, even while we see the pressures and contradictions that these firms face, and the way the ecology of turfgrass itself impinges on global capital investment and trade.

Producers: Searching for Buyers

The largest and most powerful players in lawn chemical commodity production, who sit at the farthest end of the chain, in many ways face the most serious immediate problems and so act as one of the central engines for growth in chemical use. These agrochemical firms, who produce the raw inputs for lawn care, have faced increasing competition and ongoing challenges in a fickle market. This has led to new strategies and adaptations, with implications for lawn people in distant suburbs, far down the chain.

Declining Markets

As described in Chapter 4, pesticide and fertilizer manufacturing is largely an outgrowth of military technology developed during World War II. Discoveries in this field showed that pesticide production could be cost-effective, and postwar conditions made pesticides very profitable. American agricultural land prices were rising, farming was profitable (but farm labor was scarce), and growing middle class affluence meant people were willing to pay for more kinds of foods, demanding those with no signs of pest damage or disease. In addition, the post-World War II baby boom in North America and Western Europe encouraged increases in food production.[7] Farmers in North America and Europe, encouraged by the invention of cheap and reliable tractor-drawn spray equipment, quickly adopted inexpensive, easy to use farm chemicals.[8] The new petroleum industry was also creating a variety of organic chemical byproducts, and petrochemical companies entered pesticide manufacturing as a way to market their byproducts. Use of farm chemicals also increased through active promotion by academic researchers as well as extension agents,[9] resulting in the steady growth of pesticide and fertilizer production through 1975.[10]

Following the energy crisis of the 1970s and the U.S. farm crisis of the mid-1980s (with its concurrent economic recession), however, a contraction of farm chemical markets began. After 1985, there were fewer acres planted in crops, and economically strapped farmers became more discerning customers of farm chemicals. By the 1980s, pesticides had already been developed and marketed for all major pests and crops in North America and Europe. By 1985, over 90% of all U.S. cropland was already treated with pesticides.[11] Demand for farm chemicals began to drop as the market became saturated.[12] Demand continued to remain low throughout the 1980s and into the 1990s.[13] In the spring of 2000 analysts predicted that continued depression in commodity prices would mean a continued reduction in the market for and drop in the price of agricultural chemicals.[14]

Some chemical manufacturers began to seek new farm chemical markets in the global "South," particularly in rapidly developing countries such as Brazil and India. However, marketers have had difficulty breaking into the world of unfamiliar crops, cultivation patterns, and knowledge systems of "Southern" producers.[15] So far, attempts to sell pesticides to the developing world have been profitable but not a panacea for industry woes, despite hopes that population growth would increase the demand for food and that rapid urbanization would decrease available farm labor and so create chemical demand.[16]

Rising Costs, Regulations, and Consolidations

In addition to a contracting market, manufacturers currently face several challenges specific to pesticides. The costs of raw materials, solvents, and other chemicals needed for the reactions and purification processes have climbed in recent years. This pattern is a part of the more general rise in costs of materials associated with chemical manufacturing as a whole.[17]

Perhaps the largest cost associated with pesticide production is the cost of research and development, which has risen dramatically over the last few decades. About 15,000 new compounds must be tested to yield one marketable pesticide, and it takes eight to ten years to bring a pesticide from the stage of initial synthesis to the commercial market. There are various estimates of the cost to develop a single new pesticide, ranging from $20 million to $50 million.[18] Research and development costs as a percentage of sales are much higher in the pesticide industry than in manufacturing as a whole.[19]

The rising costs of research and development come from several sources. Most pesticides are developed using the so-called "empirical method," in which multitudes of miscellaneous chemicals are reacted together, with the resulting compounds applied to plants and insects to determine their impact. This method requires propagating vast colonies of insect and weed pests. Companies must also invest considerable time testing a pesticide for effectiveness under a bewildering variety of situations. Even the most generic pesticide will work quite differently under the vagaries of disparate soil, climate, weather, and cultivation systems around the world. Finally, applying for new patents requires extensive toxicological and environmental safety trials. The extent and cost of these trials have risen in recent years as regulation of pesticides has increased.[20]

All pesticides sold in the United States must be registered with the EPA under the Federal Insecticide, Fungicide, and Rodenticide Act (FIFRA), as well as with a local environmental or agricultural agency in the state in which they are sold.[21] In addition, pesticides must pass U.S. Food and Drug Administration (FDA) tests for the amount of residue allowed on food by the Federal Food, Drug, and Cosmetic Act (FFDCA). Meeting regulatory conditions for new pesticide approval became more difficult in 1996 with the passage of the Food Quality Protection Act (FQPA). Under FQPA, all pesticides that had previously been declared safe were subject to review by EPA.[22] Industry analysts say FQPA makes registration for new pesticides more difficult to obtain.[23] The 2000 FQPA ban on the production of chlorpyrifos, a common pesticide for farm and household use, raised an outcry from the chemical and agricultural industries precisely because it had long been considered safe by regulators.[24]

To protect intellectual property, a new patent must be applied for before EPA and FDA tests begin. Because the research and application process takes so long, a new pesticide will not show profit until about ten years after application and most patents in the North America and Europe last for about twenty years. Therefore, the manufacturer must absorb a decade of loss from pesticide development and then gain only ten years of profit before the patent expires. Pesticide makers must constantly have new pesticides in the development stage to take over the role of profit-maker when older pesticides lose their patents.[25] The rising costs of research and the restrictions of patent law have fueled an increasing consolidation in the pesticide manufacturing industry. In the mid-1980s, the patents on several major herbicides expired, inspiring a series of mergers and acquisitions.[26] Pesticide makers must be quite large companies to afford the costs of research and development and diversified enough to absorb a decade of negative cash flow during years of regulatory testing.[27] As a result, pesticide manufacturing is now dominated by a few large companies,[28] in increasingly direct competition.[29]

Lawns as a Solution to Agrochemical Stagnation

The picture of global manufacturing that emerges is one of remarkably limited room for maneuvering. The agrochemical industry of the early twenty-first century must deal with saturated agricultural markets, rising costs of materials, the expenses and lengthy time requirements of research and development, extensive and retroactive regulatory requirements, patent expirations, growing problems of pest resistance, and the intense competition of a highly concentrated industry. Profits from agricultural pesticides have been low for years as a result of these pressures, and agrochemical manufacturers are increasingly turning away from conventional agriculture and now seek new markets.[30]

To a great degree, this is because consolidation and competition are working as they are supposed to, and increasing efficiencies in production, which leads to lower prices. Chemicals are cheaper now than ever before. While this poses a problem for the manufacturers, it presents an opportunity for new users and marketers of chemicals, especially for formulators and applicators. What *has* proven successful, therefore, is the cultivation of the North American yard as a site for pesticide and fertilizer use. Agrochemical companies are increasingly finding that yard chemical formulators are their most reliable customers. Formulator companies have developed agreements with chemical manufacturers to secure exclusive access to pesticide and fertilizer active ingredients.[31] Shrinking profit margins in the industry mean that manufacturers will continue to seek out relationships like these, which in turn strengthen the ability of formulators to develop new marketing plans and increase the ranks of chemical-using lawn managers. Changes in the broader economy of agricultural chemical manufacturing have paved the way for increases in the sales of lawn chemicals.

As a result, raw *nonagricultural* pesticides represent a worldwide market currently worth $7 billion, which is growing at 4% per year, a rapid increase relative to contraction in the agricultural sector. Forty percent of these sales represent U.S. household consumption. Proportions committed to lawn care are difficult to determine, but the turf care market for raw chemicals is itself about a billion dollars, and is also increasing annually.[32] Total chemical sales of turf care products dedicated to lawn care also vary regionally, the turf care sector dominates as a sales outlet in urban areas. State-level studies are illustrative. According to the Human Health Technical Work Group (HHTWG) of the New Jersey Comparative Risk Project, over 500,000 pounds of lawn care chemicals are applied annually in New Jersey, as compared with 63,000 pounds for mosquito control and 200,000 pounds for golf course.[33]

To summarize, an increasingly constricted industry is an engine for the expansion of chemical commodity markets and the invention of new arenas for the consumption of chemicals. It is in part the *supply* of pesticides, herbicides, and fertilizers that sets the conditions for chemical demand. Internalizing the costs associated with chemical risks, especially under these constrictive economic conditions, is essentially unthinkable. As such, the risks and hazards associated with the industry are largely shunted downwards along the commodity chain to other players, including applicator service providers.

Applicators: Tending the Weed Business

During an applicator certification seminar at Ohio State University Extension in 2004, when an ecologist running a training session asked rhetorically: "Are weeds really bad?" one lawn service owner answered glibly, "No, they keep us in business!" To be sure, applicators are an immediate beneficiary of purified lawn aesthetics, and they know it.

Applicators are familiar to most Americans who see them driving in their vans or trucks through neighborhoods, spraying lawns and landscaping, or going door-to-door selling their services. For many lawn people, applicators are the most direct contact to the larger industry described above and serve as the most important interpreters of turfgrass conditions and ecology. As such, applicators depend heavily on communicating a specific vision of the lawn to find and maintain markets for the glut of chemicals flowing through the global system. Some companies charge a flat fee–where customers pay for an end result regardless of the number or types of applications–and a very few charge by the amount of product applied, but most companies charge by the visit. This means, quite simply, that the more care, attention, and inputs consumers and communities think they require, the higher a company's receipts. This leads to a situation where it is in the vested interest of applicators to recognize, identify, and communicate to consumers that they have a problem.

Incentives in the Lawn Service Industry

Having said this, when surveyed and interviewed (see Appendix B) most applicators are quick to point out that their preference would be a "results-oriented" approach to lawn management. In their opinion, homeowners have a poor understanding of ecological dynamics of lawns, appropriate care, and the limited usefulness of chemicals. Instead, they commonly explain, customers evaluate only what they can see, *people at work*, and often complain not about the condition of the lawn, but the apparent labor of the operator. One owner-operator explained: "It would be great to get a flat fee and just take care of the problem, but then people don't think you're doing your job. . . . If I mow too high [in an effort to maintain a healthy lawn] the customer thinks I'm not working hard enough. It takes as much time to [mow short as to] mow long!"

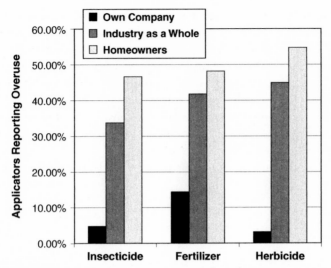

FIGURE 5.2   Who uses too many inputs? Applicator perceptions of over-use.

This leads to a business model in which the main goal of the applicator is to look busy to the consumer and to appear to be providing services regularly and effectively. As a result, when asked whether either professionals or homeowners overuse chemicals, many applicators feel that the industry as a whole tends to use too many inputs of fertilizer, herbicide, and pesticide. An even greater proportion of operators feel that homeowners, when left to their own devices, tend to over-apply as well. Notably, of course, few lawn service providers perceives that their own firm over-applies chemical inputs. (Figure 5.2).

Whereas it is extremely difficult to evaluate whether applicators get better results than homeowners, some preliminary findings are instructive. An intensive study of thirty-one home lawns conducted in the summer of 2003 in the Wayne and Holmes Counties of Ohio sought to compare the characteristics of lawns that were left untreated, relative to those treated by homeowners and those managed by professional applicator firms. Onsite evaluations of these lawns measured weed, insect, and disease infestations. The results suggest that homeowners applying their own high-input suite of chemicals–a vigorous, calendar-driven program including herbicides and fertilizer as recommended by formulator companies–produced results of *no significant difference* than those who applied no chemicals at all, with comparable levels of dandelions, ground ivy, and buckhorn. Professional applicators fared somewhat better, with some reduced infestation levels in all categories.[34] To a degree, this vindicates the positions of professional applicators who, it can be said, at least get results from applying potentially toxic substances to home lawns.

In any case, the logic of professional applicator companies holds that homeowners are poor or inefficient managers of turfgrass, that they have a poor understanding of lawn ecology, and that they often have a problem with their lawns that they do not even recognize. Most lawn services, therefore, devote significant resources to door-to-door marketing and lawn "evaluations" to communicate to potential customers that their lawns have problems caused by weeds and hidden bugs, or are vulnerable to future problems. These "evaluations" are a central device for creating and maintaining sales.

These marketing strategies also require carefully nuanced risk communication to build new customers and maintain old ones. Sales pitches reflect many of the difficult conceptual negotiations that occupy lawn people. For example, TruGreen Chemlawn conducts extensive sales representative trainings for their door-to-door service providers, making sure that, on the one hand, they do not make any legally prohibited claims (e.g., that their products are less toxic than common consumer products) while on the other hand seeing to it that consumer objections are overcome by emphasizing the importance and necessity of a "healthy" (i.e., monocultural) lawn. Applicators–who are some of the most immediate information sources and contacts that lawn people have to the chemical industry–approach and communicate with customers with the view that consumers are inefficient in their chemical use, unnecessarily chemophobic, and ignorant concerning the value and importance of input-based lawn care. Driven by the conditions of the economy applicators encourage chemical use by touting their expertise and appealing to lawn people's worrisome feeling that something is terribly wrong with the untended lawn.

Applicators Face Opposition

Although it is likely that applicators produce better results than homeowners, especially per unit input (with results being a monocultural, evenly shaded, emerald, crew-cut lawn), the industry remains mired in controversy, including questions about health and safety standards and about dubious business practices. The first problem involves a growing string of lawsuits concerning false advertising about the hazards associated with intensive lawn care. The second challenge comes from consumers who report unnecessary and unrequested services, especially from large franchise outfits.

Regulation of the lawn care industry has historically been somewhat ad hoc. This leads to frustration on the part of applicator companies, especially national firms who find themselves sorting through literally thousands of local statutes and laws when organizing, preparing, and franchising chemical sales.[35] It also means, however, that these firms were somewhat ill-prepared for the upsurge in concern surrounding chemical use and the organized legal challenge to applicator products in the last two decades.

The hazards of chemicals, as noted previously, are well-documented, and even the dominant formulator companies in the industry have been forced to acknowledge to their shareholders that there are inevitable risks inherent in the use of such products (see below). Expressing, describing, and explaining those risks is especially difficult for an applicator industry that needs not only to meet stringent homeowner demands, but to convince nonusers that they need more chemicals. The results of this tension are, as noted previously, direct advertising campaigns and door-to-door sales pitches that, to some degree, inevitably muddle some of the complex risk issues associated with chemical use.

This has been further complicated by a rapid acceleration of direct advertising by the applicator industry beginning in the early 1980s. For example, the promotion budget at Chemlawn (now Trugreen Chemlawn), (currently the largest applicator firm), grew by 40% in 1982 and 48% in 1983 (to around $11.7 million annually). With campaigns mounted by advertising giants such as Ogilvy & Mather Direct, direct mailing and newspaper inserts have since become familiar tactics in the industry. The results were boom years in the industry in which sales grew by as much as 25% annually.[36]

Such aggressive advertising led in the decades following, however, to a series of complicated legal imbroglios, fomented by the contradictory necessity of advertising products as family-friendly, while acknowledging the inherent risk associated with them. In 1988, the Attorney General for the State of New York filed a suit against Chemlawn to permanently enjoin the company from engaging in what was described as "false advertising." Specifically, the company's brochures, which claimed, "only those materials proven to be safe as well as effective at these concentrations are used by Chemlawn . . ." came under scrutiny.[37] The lawsuit was settled a few years later, with Chemlawn agreeing to refrain from making broad safety claims. In the wake of the settlement, however, the company maintained that it had never made misleading statements and that the increased scrutiny was part of an irrational backlash against chemicals: "*chemophobia.*" Even so, other lawn-care firms followed suit proactively in the months after, changing assertions in their brochures concerning nontoxicity of these chemicals to humans, pets, and the environment.[38]

A U.S. Federal Trade Commission (FTC) complaint was similarly filed against Orkin lawn care, which had claimed that "under the most accepted product rating scale, our applications are rated 'practically nontoxic;' the lowest toxicity rating," that "they have a lower toxicity rating than many common household products like suntan lotion or shaving cream;" and that "we'll keep weeds and harmful bugs out, using environmentally safe, biodegradable products that are neither harmful to you nor your soil." The lawsuit, which was successfully resolved in 1993, forced Orkin to temper these claims.[39]

This was followed by a more recent case where TruGreen agreed to pay $600,000 to settle alleged violations of pesticide laws in New York. The complaint charged that the company had applied pesticides on thirty-five occasions without informing property owners. As part of the settlement, the company agreed to implement more extensive notifications, including both lawn postings and contract specifications with property owners. Additionally, TruGreen agreed to a reduction in the use of pesticides throughout the state, which they intend to accomplish by using more detailed and frequent inspections of lawns and by devising alternative nonchemical pest controls. The pesticide notification requirements to which the company is responding grew from consumer action in the years prior to this case.[40] Other more direct lawsuits against applicators followed in the years after, including one filed against Chemlawn by a man who had developed malignant melanoma on his feet.[41]

These lawsuits and settlements have been joined by more recent allegations of unfair and deceptive trade practices and violations of other codes. Applicators have been found in violation of do-not-call phone advertising restrictions, for example. TruGreen Chemlawn also recently settled with the State of Pennsylvania over allegations that the company added unnecessary surcharges for lawn care services, jacking up prices surreptitiously over time.[42]

Such difficulties and problems, which are arguably inherent in an industry selling chemicals that even (and especially) their customers claim to be hazardous, do not decrease the sales pressures of applicators, but instead *increase* them. Despite the growth in the number of lawns nationally, with a more difficult-to-maintain customer base, more resources must be dedicated to increasing communication, advertising, and sales, to redirect consumer attention from chemical risks.

Divergent Experiences of Health and Safety

But how do lawn service providers themselves view such risks? Applicators continue to claim publicly, of course, that their products are safe, including making the often-circulated and unverified claim that customers eating 300 cups of treated grass clippings would have consumed the equivalent toxicity of one cup of coffee. The structure of the applicator industry allows a tremendous diversity of firms, however, and differentially placed participants in the lawn chemical economy are differentially sanguine about health and safety claims made by the industry's public relations machine.

The industry includes a large proportion of owner-operators, usually made up of one self-employed, year-round worker who hires seasonal help when the number of customers exceeds a few dozen clients. At the other end of the scale are vast franchises employing thousands of people and serving hundreds of thousands of households. In between are any number of small regional firms. For any operation of more than one owner/worker, moreover, the division of labor is spread between owners, managers, sales staff, and "technicians" (people who spray the chemicals).

Our survey results suggest that perceptions of pesticide hazards vary dramatically by respondent's position within a company (Table 5.1). Notably, owner-operators–entrepreneurs who both work and run small applicator businesses–show the least concern regarding the dangers of chemicals leaching

TABLE 5.1   Differences in Risk Perception in the Applicator Industry (percent of respondents)

	Technicians & Sales Reps	Managers, Vice-Presidents & Superintendents	Owner Operators
Do you feel that elements of your job threaten your health and safety? (% some or a lot)	44	23	18
Does lawn chemical application affect water quality in lakes, streams, or rivers? (% some or a lot)	70	85	35
Are you concerned about pesticides and nutrients in your drinking water? (% some or a lot)	59	54	41
Lower income (% <$30,000 per year)	48	0	6

into ambient water systems and drinking water. These businessmen also express a lack of concern regarding threats to their personal safety and health posed by applying chemicals. Certainly this is a product of self-selection in the industry. Those with life-long experiences with chemicals and who make their living both selling and applying these chemicals appear largely confident about their safety and are unconcerned about any possible association between chemicals and water degradation.

Managers and administrative personnel in larger companies are more ambivalent about the safety of chemicals, with a far higher number of respondents expressing concern both about environmental and risks of lawn chemicals, and a proportion even asserting risks to health and safety. To a great degree, this view reflects the professional and educated demographic of people more generally; as seen previously, more-educated professional people more commonly acknowledge the hazards of chemicals they apply. This view is tempered somewhat by their professional position, and their exposure to literature asserting the safety of chemicals. The concerns of "technicians" and sales representatives—the field personnel of applicator companies—are of greater interest. A large proportion of this group (almost half) believes that elements of their job threaten their health and safety. Respondents in this group specifically list as the hazards they face as: "exposure to chemicals; long-term exposure; mixing, spray drift; being around concentrates; herbicide use; 'chem' application; breathing chemicals during spray application; weed control application; leaching; pesticide and chemical inhalation; and eye contamination."

More tellingly, these workers are often less-skilled and of lower income, and are sometimes made up of from ranks of young workers. In particular, lawn chemical applicator is a common job for young men under the age of eighteen, topping cashier, dishwasher, and store clerk as the most commonly reported under-age job in many places. A study performed by the North Carolina Injury Prevention Research Center, the East Carolina School of Medicine, and the University of North Carolina School of Public Health reveals, for example, that 57% of males and 11% of females between the ages of fourteen and seventeen who have worked outside the home, have done so in lawn care labor. More than this, 27% of male, and 9% of female, workers in this same age bracket have been exposed to pesticides and other chemicals in their work.[43]

It is no wonder then that despite the confident safety assertions of lawn care application companies, hands on chemical workers remain less than fully convinced. The army of young people in the applicator industry, handling potentially toxic substances, is doing so during key years of physiological development, with ramifications that may last for the rest of their lives. Many of them, it would seem, are fully aware that the hidden costs of lawn chemical application (which take the form of chemical externalities) are borne by them at an age where they cannot legally vote or otherwise forcefully participate in the democratic mechanisms that might institute regulation.

In short, the lawn applicator industry is one in which pressures by homeowners for monocultural lawns, coupled with aggressive sales and marketing, has led to a booming business fraught with communication and public relations crises and contradictory views by both consumers and workers. This murky part of the chemical economy is also the one aspect most immediately familiar to lawn people, and remains one of the most prevalent sources of their information, whether through direct door-to-door sales or through flyers and direct advertising. This information is painstakingly crafted to produce and maintain demand for services and inputs.

For this industry then, is risk necessary? The short answer must be yes, but the flow of that risk is unevenly realized. The hidden costs of chemical hazards are borne primarily by those who apply chemicals. Unsurprisingly then, while some (owner-operators) deny personal or environmental threats from these chemicals, others (wage laborers) are more likely to acknowledge ecological and personal peril.

Formulators: Producing Green Desire

Long before the advent of professional applicators and the formation of a youth chemical work force, most homeowners dealt directly with local retailers. Perceiving a problem with their lawn, homeowners might approach a garden supply or hardware store owner or employee, describe the conditions they see, and leave the store with the product recommended by the local expert. The companies that supplied chemical formulations to these retailers–the formulator firms who buy, mix, and brand chemical combinations–were largely hidden from the view of average consumers, who may or may not have been familiar with specific brands.

The relationship of formulators to consumers has changed dramatically in the last twenty years, however, as pressures on production and marketing have created new constraints. These pressures take several forms—including declines in retail outlets, difficulties in financing, rising raw materials costs, as well as regulatory problems—but all result in narrowing profit margins in the industry and an increasing imperative to expand the number of chemical users and the intensity of chemical use per lawn. Like agrochemical production companies, then, the recent economic strategies and adaptations of formulator companies in response to economic crises have dramatically altered their relationship to lawn people.

From Mom-and-Pop to Big Box

First, the formulator industry has come to be increasingly reliant on mass discounting stores and home improvement warehouses.[44] This is primarily because small hardware stores and other traditional retailers shun the standing warehouse stock required for seasonal industries such as lawn care.[45] As in many seasonal industries, given the risks in variable weather conditions and consumer demands, retailers increasingly prefer not to stock spring merchandise the previous fall. As Scotts executive Charles Berger explains, "nobody wants March merchandise in November."[46] At the same time, there is an increasing shift in retail sales toward the cheap prices of mass discount and home improvement stores, which have become the new centers of lawn and garden retailing.[47]

As a result, hardware stores and nurseries—the traditional outlets for lawn care products have lost market share in chemical sales—and formulators have come to rely more heavily on a relatively smaller number of larger-scale customers: home improvement and mass market retailers. A handful of North American retailers now account for most formulator pesticide sales, and mass sales and bulk wholesaling reduces formulator industry receipts as a result.[48] Ten North American retailers account for 70% of sales from the Scotts Company, for example. Home Depot, Wal-Mart, Lowe's, and the recently troubled Kmart provide 60% of sales, with Home Depot alone accounting for 28%.[49] In fact, in 2003 Home Depot declared Scotts "partner of the year."[50] Competition among these retailers is intense, however. If any of these customers should falter, formulators will lose important outlets.

Consolidation, Rising Costs, Regulation, and Debt

Consolidation has also created a pattern of aggressive and capital-intensive product acquisitions in recent years.[51] These have, in turn, resulted in reduced credit ratings for many firms, stock share price declines, and most importantly, significant standing debts.[52] This debt is further aggravated by plant closures and severance packages, along with product recalls. The Scotts Company, in a prominent example, spent $94 million on interest payments in fiscal year 2000, a figure inflated by the high interest rates of that year, placing tremendous pressure on cash flow.[53]

Formulators must also deal with increasing costs of raw materials. Urea, the principal ingredient in most yard fertilizers, has risen in cost.[54] Scotts sold their professional golf turf business partly because of the increased cost of raw materials such as urea and fuel.[55]

These kinds of increased expenses and reduced receipts have been coupled with the rising costs associated with the difficult patenting systems associated with developing pesticides. As for chemical producers, the relatively short patent life for these products requires ongoing and increasing research and development costs for pesticide production, since many keystone product chemicals can be quickly lost to generic competitors.[56] For example, the patent for glyphosate–the active ingredient in one of Scott's best selling herbicides–expired in September of 2000, opening production opportunities and tight competition for market share.

Regulation increases other costs. Environmental violations arising from waste disposal, asbestos, or other hazards at production facilities have become an increasing fact of life for formulator firms.[57] Scotts Company recently paid fines and cleanup costs for unlicensed waste disposal and asbestos contamination at several sites in the U.K. and Ohio.[58] Federal, state, and local environmental regulators strictly regulate waste disposal from fertilizer- and pesticide-formulating plants. Companies also must be prepared for the potential costs of remediation or liability if any pesticide causes harm.[59]

At the same time, many formulators face increasingly difficult financial situations. Scotts' leveraged buyout in 1986, as a prominent example, cost $211 million (of which an investment-banking firm financed $190 million). This debt was blamed for the 11% fall in Scotts' stock share price from June 1999 to June 2000.[60]

In an attempt to increase sales through acquisition, formulator firms have assumed even more debt with the purchase of new product lines, resulting in declines in credit ratings.[61] Other expenses in the industry–including developing company software, closing facilities operating at a loss, severance pay for redundant employees, and costs associated with product recalls–also drive significant debt. In fiscal year 2000, Scotts Company spent $94 million on interest payments alone, a figure inflated by the high interest rates of that year, requiring the company to increase sales to generate sufficient cash flow.[62]

Ecological Challenges

Moreover, the lifecycles of turfgrass pose problems for formulators. The seasonal nature of grass and garden growth means cash flow is cyclical. Early spring and summer bring the highest sales of lawn and garden products. To meet this demand, fall and winter are the highest production times at formulation plants. Yet fall is the time of lowest cash flow because receipts from spring and summer sales have not yet been received. As a result, formulators must maintain their highest production at a time when cash flow is lowest. This cash flow "crunch" has implications for financial integrity. The ability to make even minimal debt service payments presents an annual challenge. Because debt service is so crucial, companies must boost sales enough to provide adequate capital even in the fall and winter "crunch."[63]

Changing weather affects formulators, as well. A wet spring slows fertilizer sales, but increases pesticide sales. Conversely, a dry spring can increase fertilizer sales but decrease pesticide sales. Worse, a very cold spring can slow all lawn and garden sales. This is one reason formulators seek an international market, hedging against a cold spring in the United States with sunny weather in Europe, and vice versa.[64]

The development of resistance to pesticides by insects and herbicides by weeds poses a further ecological barrier for the industry. Industry analysts estimate that pests usually develop effective resistance to any new pesticide in less than ten years.[65] This means new compounds must constantly be researched and run through the EPA registration process to replace those active ingredients that become useless, in addition to those that lose their patents or are banned by the FQPA.

The Drive for Markets: From "Push" to "Pull" Representations

Taken together, the picture that emerges of the formulator industry is one of tight and decreasing margins, constant consolidation, and debt. To overcome the rising costs of raw materials, to deal with the possibility of losing an important retail customer to ensure sufficient funds to acquire new active ingredients, to manage environmental liabilities, to meet winter debt service obligations, and to compensate for weather fluctuations, formulators of the early twenty-first century must increase sales of lawn chemicals, and do so at an increasing rate.

Fortunately for firms, changes in the retailing environment have led the industry into a new era of consumer advertising to generate sales. These direct-marketing systems depend on clearly representing the lawn aesthetic to the potential consumer. Although some direct-marketing has been a hallmark of major formulators since the mid-twentieth century, the perfection and expansion of this approach is a relatively recent phenomenon, representing an expensive revolution in industry strategy which is of fundamental importance for maintaining and expanding the monocultural lawn aesthetic. Specifically, formulator firms have turned to aggressive techniques of "pull" marketing.

In the traditional "push" marketing typical of the twentieth century industry, formulators made bulk seasonal sales to small retail stores who, in turn marketed to consumers on an informal basis.[66] Like most formulators, the dominant firm, Scotts Company, sold yard chemicals prior to the mid-1980s using a "push" strategy, where incentives were provided to a close network of retailers—usually independent hardware stores, nurseries, and specialty garden stores—who ordered large shipments of merchandise. Products were shipped to stores in the fall, held by retailers until spring sales, and then sold to consumers, relying heavily on a knowledgeable, motivated sales staff.[67]

But in 1986, following a leveraged buyout from their parent company ITT, Scotts proceeded with an innovative marketing tactic: "pull marketing."[68] Based on direct advertising to the consumer by formulators themselves (via television, radio, and print advertising), a "pull" approach concentrates on creating demand at the customer level. Rather than relying on a retailer to sell a specific brand, the formulator presents its products directly to the consumer using carefully crafted imagery.[69] "Pull" marketing involves the branding of chemical products and direct marketing through mass mailing, company representatives placed in stores, and door-to-door sales. The consumer is made aware of chemicals (and the *need* for chemicals) prior to recognizing any specific lawn care problem, and is directed to approach retailers to ask for the products they see on television or circulars by brand name, hence "pulling" the product towards them rather than having it "pushed" at them.[70] The approach is in no way unique to lawn chemicals. Consider the explosion of pharmaceutical advertising on television, which encourages consumers to "ask their doctor" if a brand name product is "right for you," rather than wait for an ailment, describe it to a physician, and take their suggestion of treatment.

The "pull" strategy, moreover, seeks to increase applications per user. Addressing the industry press and potential shareholders, Scotts representatives speculated on potential areas of growth: "Consider the $900 million lawns category: almost 30% of homeowners are do-nothings! The average do-it-yourselfer still makes fewer than half the recommended product applications each season. If every homeowner made just four applications a year, lawns could be a $2.8 billion market!"[71]

This change in approach is relatively recent. Since it was first practiced in the late 1980s by the Scotts Company, the "pull" strategy has been received by the trade as revolutionary, innovative, and crucial for industry survival, although not without significant cost increases and changes in firm structure and priorities. For formulators, the difference in strategy has a two implication. First, it means devoting significant budgets towards market research and the investigation of household chemical habits, with the specific goal of changing them. Second it requires, as it does for the applicator industry, massive increases in direct advertising costs: television, radio, and print advertising, aimed at creating consumer demand.[72] In addition to traditional advertising venues, purchasing and application advice is made available through toll-free help lines, in-store counselors, web pages, and e-mail reminder services.[73]

This emphasis on marketing is also capital-intensive. Formulators now spend millions of dollars on television advertising where traditionally retailers shouldered such expenses.[74]After purchasing a new pesticide line, Scotts Company spent twice as much as its former owner to advertise it.[75] In 1998, with only about half the market share in yard care supplies, the company spent 75% of all the advertising dollars in the sector, and purchased $8 million of television airtime in 2002.[76]

This marketing revolution has proven successful by all accounts. Consumer spending on lawn chemicals has increased in many markets, and has remained steady despite declines in other areas of herbicide and insecticide sales.[77]

But "pull" marketing does not simply represent an increase in direct advertising costs. Rather, it suggests a total reinvention of the way the industry interprets the lawn for homeowners. Specifically, the formulator industry has reinvented itself as the producer of a directly marketed aesthetic tied to a way of being a "good person" through ecological community values: family, nature, and collective good.

Traditional advertising imagery generally shows manicured yards, menacing magnified pests, and specific branded compounds that provide solutions. This approach implicitly assumes that the viewer already desires a green lawn, but needs to know how to go about getting one. The emphasis is traditionally on the lawn manager, the ease of application, the threats to the lawn, and occasionally a glimpse of what a perfect lawn might look like.

The more recent images born of "pull" marketing depart from this approach to a great degree by presenting not only a new landscape, but a new kind of person as well. Specifically, the lawn is represented as something that transcends personal value to home lawn managers, with collective activities and pride among neighbors in increasing prominence (Figure 5.3). In most of these ads, the lawn is a place for community and family activity, especially the traditional nuclear family. Advertising typically depicts young, heterosexual couples working and relaxing amid a healthy sward of monoculture lawn, and portrays the lawn as a place where children learn to play and share, and where turfgrass bonds foster and enhance relationships between parents and offspring.

At the same time, "pull" advertising builds upon and reinforces a sense of lawn management as a bridge to the biotic, nonhuman, natural world, showing the yard as a place in which the urban homeowner can engage in the timeless human activity of planting growing things in the soil. By sowing and nurturing living green plants, these ads suggest, modern people can reconnect with the soil, sun, and water. Other advertisements emphasize lawn care (presumably including chemical inputs being advertised) as a way for homeowners to care for their small part of "Planet Earth."

FIGURE 5.3   "Pull" advertisements representing the lawn as family and community space
Copyright © 2001 The Scotts Company, Marysville, Ohio; reprinted from Robbins, P., and J. T. Sharp.2003. Producing and consuming chemicals: the moral economy of the American lawn. *Economic Geography* 79(4): 425–451; with permission of Clark University.

Chemical Economies: Ecology, Risk, and Representation

In sum, the industries that manufacture, process, and sell inputs for the lawn find themselves under increasing pressure to find and produce markets. Global chemical producers, with rising costs and constrained markets, require consumer outlets to move a glut of chemicals under conditions of falling prices.

Applicator companies, coping with a range of legal liabilities aggressively sell services door-to-door. The formulator industry, undergoing a consumer retail revolution, is under increasing pressure to find new markets in an increasingly constricted sales environment, leading to new representational strategies.

Three additional conclusions can be drawn from the preceding, with implications for the lives and fates of lawn people. First, the latitude for innovation in the industry that might reduce potential risk from chemicals is extremely limited. Absorbing the potential costs of such innovation or structural change, if it was ever possible, is entirely unfeasible in a contemporary globalizing market. At each link in the chemical commodity chain, producers must constantly instead seek to *shed* and *shift* risk onto either workers (as in the case of the applicator industry) or consumers. This is in line with political ecological explanation discussed in Chapter 1. The accumulated hazard of chemical production and consumption is not a conspiracy dreamed up in a cigar smoke-filled back room. Rather, it is one of countless unintended but logical outcomes of larger forces, consolidations, and negotiations of global industries in early twenty-first century capitalism.

Second, it is also clear that the pressures and opportunities acting on these industries are not exclusively socioeconomic but also fundamentally ecological. Seasonality, inter-annual variability, and insect adaptations over time pose serious and ongoing problems for chemical producers and formulators; these problems have led to increased debt, consolidation, and the pressure for markets in diversified environmental contexts. Nor is the lawn unique in this sense. Indeed, its features parallel those of capitalist agriculture more generally.

Environmental variability and adaptation, including highly variable precipitation and temperature regimes as well as adaptive insects and diseases, have long been recognized to represent a serious *barrier* to capital accumulation in agriculture.[78] This is certainly true for turf and chemical firms, whose profits rise and fall intra-annually and whose expansion is checked by scarcities of water and variable soil conditions. It should be noted, however, that the strategies used by lawn chemical firms–including international diversification of lawns and the chemicals that support them, credit and sales efforts to overcome seasonal shortfalls, and marketing strategies to overcome patent rotations–all also represent *opportunities* for investment capital, whose goals include finding new borrowers and new lending products. The fact that seasonality plagues lawn production, for example, actually becomes a driver for new types of credit, marketing, and finance. As George Henderson adroitly observes for agriculture: "nature shapes opportunities for the investment of money capital for precisely the reasons that industrial capital may shy away from the farm."[79] Investment in toxins today and biotechnologically advanced lawns tomorrow in this way become an economic solution as much as a cause of an environmental problem. Finally, this analysis of the industry suggests that at the points of contact between industry and consumer, a blizzard of representational strategies are at work to portray potential hazards in a way that is both palatable and desirable. The conditions required for economic survival require representational strategies–both in the form of risk communication and product advertising–that not only emphasize the input products or even the lawn itself, but also the identity of input users: lawn people. Although this is not unique to turfgrass economies–sexy car commercials and manly beer ads obviously draw upon, define, and reproduce identity as well–the character of the lawn input user is specific, and it stresses family, community, and environment.

Herbicides that flow off of lawns and represent a hazard to the collective good are represented as fundamental to "proper" community behavior. Lawn chemicals that are potentially harmful to children and collect in carpet dust are viewed as "important" for the family. Lawn chemicals with potentially detrimental effects on the ambient environment are understood as "taking care" of the environment. The tension in such a configuration should be immediately recognizable in the profile of lawn people. Chemical input users, to the degree they behave in a way idealized in "pull" advertising are, by implication, those concerned about their neighbors' values and feelings. They are more likely to be motivated by their family. They are more likely to be concerned about the issue of environmental quality. The central contradiction of lawn people portrayed at the outset of this book, therefore, is reproduced in the representations pursued by the industry.

But do lawn people really resemble those "perfect" figures that occupy the frozen advertising images of the formulator industry? Do they embrace chemical inputs for lawn care warmly or with ambivalence? Are intensive lawns managed for one's self, community, family, or some more instrumental economic reasons? Put simply, how do lawn people see themselves?

CHAPTER 6

Do Lawn People Choose Lawns?*

W E HAVE SEEN THAT THE AMERICAN LAWN, while a cultural artifact, is one historically tied to the political economy of property and the creation of certain kinds of people. We have seen that as a green monoculture, the lawn absolutely requires certain repeated patterns of homeowner labor and the application of key inputs, which are by their nature hazardous. We have also seen that the promulgation of these inputs is increasingly required for a range of economic "actors"–all of whom are increasingly insinuated into the lives of consumers and who are concomitantly communicating specific messages not only about risk, but also about identity. Citizenship, ecological metabolism, chemical hazards, and economic imperatives come together every time someone practices intensive lawn care. For those people who participate in intensive lawn care practice–which is a majority of lawn owners–how are these several forces understood and reconciled? How do these people understand their behaviors in the context of their home, family, and community?

Chemical Communities

The survey results briefly outlined in Chapter 1 tell us something in this regard: lawn chemical users are wealthier urban and suburban people whose neighbors tend to use chemicals, and who tend to be more worried about chemical usagethan those who do not use them. This contradicts many of the most commonly used predictors of "green" conduct. Higher education, as an obvious

---

*This chapter was written with the assistance of Julie T. Sharpe.

TABLE 6.1   Survey Responses on Community and Chemicals: Direction of significant relationship, positive

Parameter	"Interested in Knowing What's Going on in Neighborhood"	Believe "Neighbors' Practices have a Negative Impact on Water Quality"
Lawn chemical use	+++	+
Neighbors known by name	+++	
Age		++
Education		+
Lawn care companies negative impact on local water quality		+++
Home owners negative impact on local water quality		+++

$(+++\ p<.01,\ ++\ p<.05,\ +\ p<.10)$

example, tends to coincide with higher use of lawn chemicals. As such, more careful examination of the survey results may be required, beyond the demographics of individuals, including responses that hint at the associations lawn people feel to a larger collective or community.

Considering people's commitment to community relative to their lawn care behavior presents a more detailed, if more complex, picture (Table 6.1). Specifically, people who claim an interest in what is going on around their neighborhood and who tend to be able to list a greater number of their neighbors by name are far more likely to use lawn chemicals. This suggests that intensive lawn care is "neighborly," in the sense that the more involved members of a community manage their lawns more intensively.

Assessing the relationship between people's chemical use and their views of their neighbors' impact on water quality complicates this picture (see Table 6.1). On the one hand, those who claim their neighbors' influence on water quality is negative (whatever their neighbors' specific behavior) tend to claim that homeowner practices are generally bad for water quality, especially the use of a lawn chemical applicator company. These people also tend to be older and better educated. Education and life experience indeed are reflected in environmental awareness, and a general feeling that what people do around the home influences the ecosystem. More importantly, chemical use is correlated with awareness of one's neighbors and cognizance of environmental impacts. This is the case even when using multi-variate regression to consider and hold constant all the previously mentioned variables (education, income, etc.). These results are revealing, if a little counterintuitive. They contribute to a profile of chemical users as not only more socially involved and concerned, but also more aware of environmental impacts. They are more communitarian, but again more anxious.

Lawn Neighborhoods

Add to this the fact that a majority of people (52%) surveyed *believe that their neighbors use lawn chemicals*. The effects of these uses, while considered deleterious for water quality, were also viewed as good for the community. While most reported that their neighbors' practices had no impact or negative impact on water quality, half also agreed that these practices had a positive impact on property values (Table 6.2).

As noted in Chapter 1, homeowners with higher incomes and higher property values are more likely to use lawn chemicals than homeowners with lower property values. The cost of lawn care chemicals certainly plays some role in differential use. According to the National Gardening Association, U.S. households spend $222 each on lawn care equipment and chemicals annually, the marginal cost of such an investment; this climbs considerably in households with incomes less than $30,000.[1]

The association of inputs with housing values (which accrue to the homeowner as well as the neighborhood more generally), suggests some obvious instrumental motivations not only for chemical application but for the positive association between such practices and community values. As most realtors will tell you, lawn upkeep is a relatively inexpensive investment for maintaining property values. In follow-up discussions, some lawn owners explicitly told us that their lawn care inputs were investments in their homes. Indeed, people with higher incomes and expensive homes have much more capital–in the form of an existing manicured lawn–to protect with chemical applications. Despite any expectation of social reward for environmentally protective behavior, homeowners are actually rewarded for environmentally detrimental behavior.

But instrumental thinking seems to only be a small part of this set of logics. Far more significant than the affect on property values, most respondents believed that their neighbors' lawn care behaviors had a positive influence on "neighborhood pride." This distinction implies something far beyond instrumental economic logic. The practice of lawn care is instead part of a normative communitarian practice. The unbroken, unfenced, openness of the front yard

TABLE 6.2 Perceived Impact of Neighbors Behaviors on Local Conditions (percent of sampled respondents)

Impact of neighbors' practices	Negative	None	Positive
Water quality	34	49	11
Property values	6	41	50
Neighborhood pride	5	18	73

parkland–connecting household to household with no borders–is ultimately a form of common property, the maintenance of which is part of normative institution of community care. Participation in maintenance is a practice of civic good. Disregard for lawn care is, by implication, a form of free-riding, civic neglect, and moral weakness. This is further reinforced by the ecological character of lawn problems, including mobile, invasive, and adaptive species such as grubs, dandelions, and ground ivy. These pests, if eliminated in one yard, can easily be harbored in another, only to return later, crossing property lines, blowing on the wind, and burrowing underground. Intensive care by one party merely moves problems around; only coordinated action can control "outbreaks" and achieve uniformity. In this sense, lawn care differs from other kinds of individual investment in community, such as Christmas lights, painting, or other efforts. It is a far greater problem, requiring coordinated collective action, at least where green monocultural results are desired.

As such, intensive lawn management tends to cluster. If your neighbor uses lawn chemicals, then you are more likely to engage in intensive lawn care, (e.g., the hiring of a lawn care company or the using of do-it-yourself fertilizers and pesticides). In addition, lawn management in general is associated with positive neighborhood relations. People who spend more hours each week working in the yard report greater enjoyment of lawn work, but also feel more attached to their local community. Yard management is not simply an individual activity but is instead carried out for social purposes: the production and protection of neighborhoods.

Taken together, the picture of intensive lawn practice is not one of individual people making individual choices on their personal property. Instead, the evidence points to the profile of a highly regulated community. Lawn people are residents of lawn neighborhoods, relatively well-educated, high-income communities with expensive homes. Of course, these communities also share a collective anxiety, since chemical users do perceive a link between their neighbors' behaviors (if not their own) and fouled drinking water. Since, however, ince more concern tends to coincide with more use, it would seem that lawn communities are reading the boxes and bags of the products they use, communicating or quietly acknowledging risks, and then proceeding with a collective ecological project.

This kind of behavior raises as many questions as it answers. How are such risks and benefits reconciled in real life? What does such a community feel like to live in? Are such obligations seen as a joy or a burden? Does participation in the lawn community provide satisfaction or pressure? What room for maneuvering or the lack of participation is there? Do people trust the information they receive regarding lawn care, either from chemical applicators or from the packages they purchase? What are we like, those of us with deep personal and community investments in our lawn? Impersonal national surveys can only get us so far in answering these kinds of questions.

The Lawns of Kingberry Court

To get some insight into how people actually reconcile individual benefits, community priorities, environmental hazards, and personal risks, we conducted intensive, face-to-face household interviews in a suburb of a large Midwestern metropolitan city. These eight resident families ring the cul-de-sac of Kingberry Court and were chosen both because of their relatively high socioeconomic status (matching the profile of the most likely chemical users) but also because they are all close neighbors, physically next to and across from one another in a nearly closed residential space. Their geographical proximity to one another meant they were more likely to know each other and that the lawn management activities of each would have a visual and environmental impact on each of the others. Treating this small group in a kind of "village study," we hoped to get a view of the way a face-to-face lawn community functions, in an environment where mutual expectations are set through simply living daily life in close proximity.

Kingberry Court is an example of upper-middle-class life in an fairly average American suburb. Like many other Midwestern suburban developments, the area was converted from corn and soybean fields to suburban tract development, built in response to rapid suburbanization from the nearby city in the mid-1980s. Developers built eight houses on the cul-de-sac in 1987–1988, marketing the homes to professionals who wanted to escape the city and raise children in the higher-rated, well-funded schools of the suburbs. Legally located within the central city limits, Kingberry Court is particularly attractive to urban professionals because it straddles the boundary between city and suburb. The residents of Kingberry Court gain three kinds of advantages that typically make such developments attractive: a short commute to work, lower tax rates, and the benefits of suburban schools (demographic details are described in Appendix B).

Although the houses on Kingberry Court are larger and more expensive than average for its metropolitan region or for the United States as a whole, they fall under rather typical restrictions, taking the form of a stringent development charter to protect the market value of homes. Outbuildings such as sheds or detached garages are not allowed in the development, compost piles are not permitted because they may produce odors or attract insects, and even vegetable gardening is prohibited (because the presence of food in the yard is thought to attract local pest animals such as raccoons and skunks). Most of the residents of Kingberry Court do have small vegetable patches surreptitiously hidden at the sides of garages or near back property lines, but they are all aware they are operating in defiance of the community charter in doing so. Such charters (see Chapter 7) are extremely common for subdevelopments established in the last twenty-five years.

The people of Kingberry Court are themselves typical examples of upper-middle-class Americans. Six of the eight respondents interviewed hold advanced degrees and all eight households earn more than $100,000 per year. Their occupations include professionals (two medical doctors, one lawyer, and three research scientists with doctoral degrees) and business ownership (one owns a manufacturing firm, the other a construction business).

Each of the eight respondents is white, married, and has children. Seven of the eight respondents were male. Four of the respondents have been living on the circle since it was first completed fifteen years ago, and the other four bought houses between five and eight years ago. Their ages range from early thirties (the newcomers) to late sixties (original residents).

All of the eight residents use lawn fertilizers and pesticides. Walter, Arthur, Suzanne, and Frank[2] hire lawn care companies to spray fertilizer and pesticides on their yards at regular intervals during the growing season. The number of treatments per year range from two (Walter) to six (Arthur). Tom and Patrick are do-it-yourselfers. They both purchase the same pre-packaged fertilization and pesticide program from a home improvement store and apply the chemicals themselves that requires four treatments a year. Michael and Jason are also do-it-yourselfers, but design their own programs by purchasing different combinations and brands of fertilizer, herbicides, and pesticides and applying them at their own rates, five or six times a year. Thus the residents of Kingberry Court also represent the more general profile outlined previously: socially elite homeowners who also tend to be lawn chemical users. With this in mind, we set out to determine whether these residents–lawn chemical users all–viewed the lawn as an environmental risk; whether they trusted the information they received regarding their yards; how their daily lives influenced their lawn care choices; and what responsibilities they felt to one another, to the environment, and to their yards.

Is the Lawn a Personal Risk or Environmental Hazard?

In talking with these residents about their environmental commitments and concerns, it became clear that "green values" are complex and uneven commitments. Homeowners described varying levels of allegiance to "environmentalism." Only three identified themselves as environmentalists, three were ambiguous about their concern for the environment, and two vocally declared no concern about environmental issues. Overall concern for and about the environment, however, was not a prerequisite for being concerned about the specific dangers of lawn chemicals or vice versa. Six of the eight residents described the potential risks of lawn chemicals, and expressed some uneasiness in using them.

Suzanne and Frank each identified themselves as "environmentalists" and discussed their general environmental ethic at length. They also identified themselves as recyclers and expressed concern about environmental issues especially including air pollution and hazardous waste. Frank explained,

We left our previous home because of a hazardous waste incinerator. We didn't want the kids around that. We try to do as much as we can naturally, without the [lawn] chemicals. We put coffee grounds in with the tomato plants. We used to do composting back in the old neighborhood.

Walter, Jason, Arthur, and Patrick expressed ambivalence over their concern for the environment and espoused a middle-of-the-road approach to environmentalism. Walter described the contradiction these four all felt between protecting the environment and maintaining the look of their yards:

I would call myself an environmentalist, but there are different kinds. I am not strict. If I had an outbreak of bugs that were going to kill the trees I've worked on for twenty years, there would be no question that I would spray to get rid of them. I would use lindane, even though it's illegal, because I have worked on those trees for decades. But I try to keep from doing any more spraying than I have to.

Arthur echoed these feelings with his statement,

Of course I am concerned about the environment. Of course there is always a little bit of a risk [when using lawn chemicals], but it is small enough that it is not going to stop me.

When we asked Patrick if he would call himself an environmentalist, he said,

I would be right in the middle. I'm surely not going to strap myself to a tree to save it. But I would vote for someone with a strong environmental record. You know, I try to recycle. But I don't do anything to extremes. I just try to do my part.

Michael and Tom flatly denied any concern over the environment. As Michael said,

I'm no environmentalist. I use all the chemicals I can. I don't care about chopping forests down. There's plenty of wood and everything. I'm not one of these organic farmer type guys.

Certainly, our conversations underlie the fact that that a direct relationship between socioeconomic status and environmental concern cannot be assumed. Michael and Tom, the least environmentally conscious residents of Kingberry Court, were the most highly educated (Michael) and had the highest income (Tom).

Even so, six of the eight residents, including four who would not accept the label of environmentalist, expressed concern over the dangers of lawn chemicals. Only Jason and Michael said they had no concerns at all about the chemicals they were using. Jason said he was using such a small volume that his chemicals posed no hazard, and Michael, a (medical) doctor, insisted that lawn chemicals simply were not harmful. The remaining six residents' anxieties centered around three more specific concerns: children, pets, and the wider environment.

Children, Pets, and Nature
Walter, Suzanne, Tom, Patrick, and Frank all expressed concern over the impact of their use of lawn chemicals as specifically being concerned about the children in the neighborhood. Frank does not let his children into the yard for several days after a treatment. Suzanne talked about some of her friends who have stopped their treatments because they have small children at home. Tom said,

> Certainly I've been responsible over the years when there were younger kids in the neighborhood. I made sure they weren't getting on the grass, and put those little flags up, keeping them off so that they don't walk through it and put it in their mouths.

Walter talked about his grandchildren:

> I try not to go out there and zap things all the time. I am particularly conscious about it because I have an autistic grandson. Nobody knows what triggers that. He's always smelling the roses, and I'm thinking, did I put something on there that's going to make him worse? I want a nice looking lawn, but I don't want to endanger my kids walking across it.

As noted in Chapter 1, Suzanne's anxieties extended to her dog, though not to the point of changing her lawn care behaviors. Similarly, Patrick, Walter, and Frank all expressed concern over the impact of their chemical use on their dogs. (Tom did not have any pets). Frank explained that his dog is not allowed outside for several days after a lawn treatment or until after it rains. Patrick said:

> Six or seven years ago there was a big debate in our paper about what some of the chemicals were doing to the animals. Dogs, lymphomas, things like that. That was an awareness thing for me: I'd never heard of that.

Patrick, Arthur, Walter, and Frank all expressed concern about the impact of their chemical use on wider ecological relationships in the region. Frank described the problem of runoff and drew a comparison between farmers

fertilizing their fields and homeowners fertilizing their lawns, both of them con-
tributing to water quality problems. As Patrick said:

> It all just runs off in the sewers. So you want to make sure you are put-
> ting as little as possible into the ecosystem . . . There is that considera-
> tion, where does all this go, potentially, eventually? Maybe it's washing
> off into the river system. I do a lot of water sports, so I am concerned
> about that.

Walter told a story about his son's job at a local golf club:

> My son worked at a country club north of here, and I saw what they did.
> They were putting diazinon on. It rained, and it killed all of the ducks
> at the country club. The country club didn't want anyone to know about
> it, so they hired him [Walter's son] to put them all in a dump truck and
> take them away. And I'm thinking, geez, you know there's some really
> horrible environmental effects here. Obviously, if it kills ducks, it kills
> fish too. It says that on the bag [of pesticide], but you know you don't
> pay much attention to that. Still, it goes down the drain. I want a nice
> looking lawn, but I don't want to endanger any [wildlife].

What do these stories tell us about the environmental awareness of lawn
chemical users? To begin with, there is a prevalent and apparently deep anxiety about the environment associated with lawn care, even amongst people without "environmental" concerns. These anxieties are most commonly expressed
and experienced at a personal level, especially concerning children and dogs.
Even so, these anxieties do little to curb behavior. The case of Suzanne, who
would rather tie booties on her dog's feet than change her lawn care practices,
is a somewhat extreme example.

These concerns, we have shown earlier, are specifically more pronounced
amongst people who use chemicals than people who don't. Most obviously, it is
because chemical users read (or at least glance at) the bags of chemicals they
apply, as Walter explained. But where does most chemical information come
from? Is it trustworthy? How is it reconciled with the pronounced anxieties of
lawn managers? Why use chemicals about which you are so anxious?

Trust in Experts

Our group of neighbors together told us three typical stories to explain their
use of lawn chemicals despite knowledge of their hazards. The first of these–
centering on trust in professional experts–was most common, since several residents employed other people to manage their lawns. Generally, residents
believed that because lawn chemical producers and the companies that apply

chemicals are acting in a professional capacity, environmental risks are reduced or eliminated. This trust in the expert status of members of the lawn chemical industry was used to transfer responsibility for lawn chemical dangers from individuals to the industry itself.

Trust in experts was an important factor for Frank, Arthur, Suzanne, and Tom. Frank, Arthur, and Suzanne all placed environmental responsibility for treatments with their lawn service companies. For Frank and Suzanne, this trust was facilitated by their own self-proclaimed lack of knowledge of the technical details of treatments. As Frank explained:

> I don't know their job, but they seem to know their job. We really don't know the impact of what they are doing. . . . We've had a variety of bugs eating something. I don't know what they were. I don't know what they spray with . . . When they come out they just look and see what they need to do.
>
> The guy that does our chemical treatments was a botany major at [local university]. That makes us feel better than if there were some teenage kid that doesn't know anything about anything doing our lawn . . . These guys seem pretty safe. They seem very professional. We trust the people we are paying to put it [the treatment] down. They know what they are doing.

Arthur echoed these sentiments:

> Of course, I am concerned [about the environmental impact of the treatments]. But I have had a discussion with the head of our fertilizing company and he pretty much assured me that the amounts and the way we are doing it, plus the professional manner in which they do it, that I am not worried. We are not overdoing it.

Suzanne reiterated her own lack of knowledge and her willingness to place technical responsibility on her service company's shoulders.

> [The company] comes out and does our fertilizing. When they find some bugs or something they just spray and leave us a note. We've used them for years, so they just go ahead and do whatever they need to do.

Tom placed environmental responsibility with the company that manufactured his four-step program.

> I rely on the fact that I buy [this brand of] products. They're a big company so they should be environmentally responsible. I rely upon their expertise to put these products on my lawn.

When asked if he would ever switch from his current treatment program, he replied:

> I guess I've just grown accustomed to using [this brand]. I've had good success with it, feel like it's a good product, it's worked well. So, I'd just stick with that out of brand loyalty.

Tom is the owner of a small manufacturing company himself. He spent a portion of the interview describing his company's recent efforts to reduce waste and increase recycling in production processes, viewing this effort as integral to the company's financial success. Tom's statements reflect an increasingly prevalent view that a successful business enterprise would by default also protect the environment. In this way, responsibility for the fate of lawn chemicals is tied to the manufacturer rather than the user, or perhaps more directly, to the free market economy. Environmentally unsound businesses cannot thrive or even exist in a complex and efficient economy.

Tom never asserted the possibility that he may be using the chemicals in the wrong way, at the wrong times, or in the wrong amounts. Tom also avoided discussing the possibility that the manufacturer itself may be causing environmental risk. Tom's story provides an interesting contrast to the liability claims of lawn chemical producers themselves, who assert that the environmental fate of lawn chemicals rests solely with the user.

For these four Kingberry Court residents (Frank, Arthur, Suzanne, and Tom), the professional status of lawn care service companies and chemical manufacturers goes a long way to ensure the safety of lawn chemical treatments. Whereas some scholars emphasize that modern Americans are increasingly skeptical of experts,[3] reconciling lawn chemical application with deep anxiety requires some measure of faith in the responsibility and knowledge of others. The importance that homeowners attach to the concept of trust in professional experts, moreover, is directly related to what this concept means in their lives. In this sense, the general tendency of applying lawn chemicals to be more likely among upper middle class professionals is linked to the professional character (and assumed legitimacy) of the professions such people occupy. Frank and Arthur hold advanced degrees. Tom, Frank, and Arthur all seemed to derive a strong sense of identity from their professions (business owner, chemist, and medical doctor, respectively). Suzanne also took pains during the interview to stress the career and status of her husband, a construction contractor. For these four at least, their sense of themselves as professionals is central. Because they are well-educated and successful in their own careers, they assume that other educated professionals must be good at their jobs, dedicated, honest, and forthcoming. This concept of skill in one's profession is understood to include taking care of any potential health or environmental dangers resulting from one's work. It is not clear if people doing other kinds of labor (e.g., waiting tables, washing dishes, or answering phones) would share such faith in the expertise of others. The professional status of chemical-using communities plays a key role in reconciling environmental anxieties through trust in the corporate management of risk.

Qualified Mistrust

Walter, who uses a lawn care company, and Patrick who is a do-it-yourself applicator, both openly distrusted lawn chemical companies. Walter explained his uneasy relationship with his lawn care company.

> Right now I'm hiring [this company] to do my lawn. I did it all myself
> up until a year ago when I hurt my back. . . . Now they offer this program
> where they claim you can regulate your own stuff. . . . I tell them what
> I want on it, and they claim they follow my instructions. Now, whether
> they are really doing that, I am suspicious that they probably aren't. . . .
> I think I'm living under an illusion [that the treatments applied are safe].
> They are using less of it than I would have myself, and I'm hoping they
> are putting on what I told them I want on there. . . . but I'm not 100%
> certain of that, nor am I certain that nothing at all might not be better
> than what I am doing now.

Despite his misgivings, Walter continues to employ the same company, however. And while Patrick and Tom both were do-it-yourself applicators and both used the same branded four-step program, Patrick further described some mistrust in the manufacturer, at least in terms of prescribed volumes. Patrick explained:

> I use [this brand's] four-step fertilizer system. And I cut it in half. So I
> use a very low level. My wife is concerned about, with all the little kids,
> through the years, having fertilizers back there of a high concentration.
> So we initially had [a lawn service company], then thought that that
> might not be environmentally the safest thing to do. Plus, the expense.
> And I thought, [this brand's] four-step program and I just cut it in half
> and it seems to work fine. Hopefully I'm not putting on more than I
> need. And I figure it might be a little bit safer for the animals.

What motivates Walter and Patrick to continue to apply lawn chemicals, despite their misgivings about the safety of their actions? If trust in experts is crucial, but by no means unqualified, what motivates intensive lawn care practice?

Hectic Lives

In explaining their use of chemicals, residents largely emphasize the pace of their lives. Four of the eight residents stated, with some degree of pride, how busy they and their families are with careers, hobbies, sports, and travel. This often translated into a feeling that they did not have time to worry about lawn chemicals. Although they knew that lawn chemicals might have some dangers, and that they themselves might in fact be responsible for these dangers, they felt that they did not have the time to educate themselves in the technical aspects of lawn treatment or weigh the health and environmental impacts. This feeling was sometimes related to another theme that emerged from the interviews: for some Kingberry Court residents, yard work is boring and distasteful. In addition, residents suggested that, on balance, the yard simply did not play a major role in the life of the neighborhood. Both the reluctance to do yard work and the yard's lack of explicit importance probably contributed to these a sense that chemical treatments simply are not worth much consideration.

Walter, Michael, Tom, and Suzanne all emphasized that they did not have time to worry about treatments. Michael spoke about the demands of his eighty to 100 hour work week. Walter explained:

> When I first moved here I was traveling a lot so I didn't have time to do much in my yard. I thought, my lawn must need something, so I was treating it . . . I think of yard work as a fun activity . . . But I just don't have the time anymore.

Tom had to cut his interview short because he was getting ready to go to his son's state championship soccer game. He commented:

> To be honest, we have a very busy household here. Our kids are very busy with soccer and we do a lot of traveling for their sports events and such.

Patrick, Michael, and Jason explained that they did not enjoy yard work, and so they tried to spend as little time and mental energy on the yard as possible. Patrick explained:

> I'm not as meticulous about the yard as maybe other people. I want the grass to be just barely alive in the summer so that I don't have to cut it . . . If I had to spend more than an hour a week [in the yard], it's getting to be too much. I like to do a little, just to spruce things up. But that is not how I . . . that is not my escape. I won't cut my grass twice a week and I won't edge unless I have to . . . [my wife] likes to go out and put in her hour or two a week. It works out real well. With both of us putting that kind of time in, it's not a burden . . . I like to put my hands in the dirt, *a little*. After a couple of hours, that's it, I'm done.

Jason said:

> Mowing the lawn is fine, but all the other stuff I could do without . . . We certainly like the way it looks, but we wish it took a little bit less time

to keep it that way . . . It's an obligation for me. I'd choose to do many things before I'd go out in the yard.

Michael explained:

Cutting the grass is work. I've tried to pay people to come and cut it but our yard is so small, it doesn't meet their minimum. I hate the cutting . . . if I could find someone to take care of it reasonably, I'd do it in a heartbeat.

Without question, the incidental and taken-for-granted character of the lawn puts it at a low priority, at least for daily concern or worry. Somewhat ironically, this tends to lead to a defaulting decision to apply chemicals(or hire a company to do it), largely indiscriminately. The hectic lives of residents make the submersion of anxiety easier to reconcile. For several of the residents, this taken-for-granted character of the lawn is reinforced by an insistence that the lawn has little to do with the life of the community. At the same time all agreed that they knew their neighbors fairly well, the residents explained that interactions with their neighbors were more likely to revolve around children, careers, and hobbies rather than the yard. Patrick explained:

We know the neighbors pretty well. We have cookouts and we know each other. We have kids the same age . . . the conversation is not about the yard. That's not my main motivation to go over and talk to someone. Mostly it is about common aspects of kids and sports.

Suzanne, one of the more senior residents of the Court, described the neighbors' relationships:

Our street is very friendly . . . Our street used to do little street carnivals at the end of the summer because the kids all played together and the parents all were very friendly. So we are lucky. I don't know if it's that way everywhere.

Tom echoed these thoughts:

[We talk] more about the kids, school events, sports, athletics they're involved in, that kind of thing. Not necessarily what our yards are doing! Occasionally, if someone is doing something, you'll take notice of it, which is kind of the polite thing to do: 'Hey, I like that new tree.'

Walter said:

We talk about our kids and jobs just as much [as we talk about our yards]. We are so much older than most of our neighbors, so that makes a big difference. A lot of my neighbors are in their forties and they are more or less interested in their kids, and that's it.

Jason described his interaction with his neighbors:

We more often talk about our kids or our jobs . . . We've never ever talked with Tom and his wife about the yard even though we talk quite a bit.

As Michael described it:

I never see them [the neighbors while I'm doing yard word]. We don't cut at the same time, don't do anything at the same time. If I'm out there in the yard, I gotta get it done.

Unsurprisingly, it would seem then that busy, professional, urban residents spend little conscious mental energy on the mundane arrangements of everyday life, especially something as trivial as the lawn. Despite misgivings and anxieties concerning lawn chemicals, therefore, the lawn is largely described as nominal and tangential to the pulse of the community. As economists have asserted, the use of lawn chemicals is a near unconscious trade-off for the return on increasingly scarce time in the harried lives of the leisure class: a nonchoice.[4] The lawn managers of Kingberry Court receive benefits from lawn chemical applications in the form of reduced mental energy and decreased time spent on the lawn. They have little reason to consider the potential negative consequences of the routine, every-day practice of chemical use. According to these lawn managers, the yard is seen as an incidental part of the taken-for-granted domestic scene. It is not worth discussing with the neighbors, and the work surrounding it should be minimized. Even if the yard was not so commonplace, any concerns about lawn chemical treatments would probably fall by the wayside, swallowed up in the hectic pace of professional and family life on Kingberry Court.

This may overstate, however, the degree to which the management of everyday life and its objects, like the lawn, is passive. The level of civic engagement embodied in the maintenance of the lawn in a face-to-face society like Kingberry Court suggests something else. Despite an insistence that the lawn is collectively trivial and tangential, there is a persistent moral responsibility tied to lawn care that no resident can deny.

A Moral Responsibility

Indeed, our discussions with residents suggested this sense of a "neighborhood norm" of lawn management is the most important driver lawn chemical use. Six of the eight homeowners explained their decisions about lawn chemical use in terms of something that they owed to their neighbors. Four lawn managers also described the ways in which the neighborhood itself actually forced certain kinds of lawn management onto individuals.

Patrick and Arthur described their lawn chemical use as something they felt they had to do to meet the expectations of their neighbors. Patrick explained:

> I know that this neighborhood has a certain status. A certain look. I surely wouldn't want to ruin it for anybody . . . [I don't enjoy yardwork] But I do want it to look–you know, I want to fit in. I won't cut my grass twice a week and I won't edge unless I have to. I'm not going to have the most meticulous yard and a water sprinkler system. I'll water by hand, if I have to, occasionally in the summer. So I'd say I'm more of a follower. I want to do just enough work to fit in.

In explaining whether there were any circumstances under which he would increase his lawn chemical treatments, Patrick described his system of monitoring, which relied heavily on a notion of the view of his lawn by the neighbors. When weeds grow prominent,

> I would feel really out of place. It's not only how the yard looks to me, but how it looks to the neighbors. If it's not in keeping with the neighborhood [then I'd have to spray more]. . . . I'm willing to go to the edge in this neighborhood [in terms of less mowing, letting a few weeds grow in], but I'm not willing to go to the other side and have big holes in the yard. It's funny you mention this, because my mom's yard [which is not sprayed] looks like that (big holes in the yard) right in the middle of [a nearby town], where if you don't cut twice a week you are a communist! It's like, oh man!

Arthur's wife, Helen, made an association between the value of her house, the number of weeds in her yard, and the character (and perhaps the ethnicity of the her next door neighbors:

> I respect the whole neighborhood. I would not let the house run down. I would not let it grow up to look unseemly. That's just out of common courtesy. You want to keep up what you paid a heck of a lot for. You start to let it go downhill and then the neighborhood changes. Not that I mean by kinds of people, because we have all kinds here, all . . . nationalities. I just mean things start to go downhill . . .

Arthur added:

> Everyone around here works very hard keeping up their homes. I wouldn't insult my neighbors by not keeping my house up.

Jason's wife, Karen, talked about a potential "backlash" from her neighbors if she failed to maintain the yard in a certain way. She said:

> I think we'd get a lot of complaints [if I didn't do yardwork]. Maybe you might not hear it, but everyone here keeps their lawn looking nice. If you were the only person who didn't mow . . .

Walter spoke about a neighborhood backlash from over-treatment of the lawn, as well:

> If something happens to your yard, the neighbors are on you. That's the reason I changed from [this lawn care company]. When they killed my yard and it went absolutely dead, I was ostracized around here. People wanted to know, what the hell are you doing? You are decreasing our property values!

Frank said he himself felt insulted by his neighbors' yard maintenance, or lack thereof:

> Everybody around here, they'll put out a few marigolds, a few impatiens, just enough to dot the landscape . . . We get kind of irritated when people don't do something with their yard. I get mad if people don't put plants out to make their front yard look nice.

It would seem that although Kingberry Court residents insist that lawns play little overt role in the neighborhood and are rarely the topic of discussion or serious consideration, front yards influence, and are heavily influenced by, an overarching sense of neighborhood monitoring. In fact, the actions and opinions of the neighbors suggest that residents have a comparatively small range of actual choice in the management of their lawns.

Moreover, the direct actions of neighbors is repeatedly reported to influence how others treat their lawns. Michael and Frank both talked about a neighborhood outbreak of grubs which forced them to start using grub-control chemicals. As Michael put it:

> We don't have a grub problem, but the neighbors all do the grub treatment and chase them all over here. So, we kind of have to do it.

Collectively, this arrangement of lawn care begins to assemble itself into a kind of community pattern, or an ordered neighborhood rhythm. In a prominent example, the decision to mow on a particular day emerges as a collective group nondecision. Suzanne explained:

> The neighbors have a lawn service and their guy comes out on Wednesdays. So, I try to cut my grass on Wednesdays also because our yards

kind of flow together. And the neighbor behind us, if they see us out they will also cut their grass on the same day, to keep it all looking nice at the same time. . . . So we kind of keep an eye on each other, thinking OK, this is grass cutting day. And also keeping an eye on the weather. This Wednesday it's supposed to rain, so Thursday will probably be grass-cutting day this week.

Several lawn managers spoke about the imperative to mow in time for the recent high school prom. Limousines came to the cul-de-sac to pick up several high school students, pictures were taken on front lawns, and everyone wanted their yards to look perfect. Frank described the scene:

We were out cutting our grass at 9 o'clock at night in the rain, because the next day was prom for the neighbors' kids. I was going to let the grass go for a couple of days, but after talking to Suzanne, whose daughter was going to prom, I thought I better cut it today. So if we know people are going to have parties, we try to cut the lawn [the day before] just so it will look nice.

Sometimes, the actual tasks of lawn management themselves are taken over by other residents. In these situations, not only decisions about lawn work but actual carrying out of tasks is out of the hands of the homeowner. Walter describes two experiences:

We recently had a hailstorm and one of my neighbor's said, 'I was going to come over and pick up your [fallen] branches.' He thought I was a little slow getting to it because I am too old.

My neighbor here [Frank] was having some problems with his job, so my son and I mowed his lawn for him. We didn't ask, we just mowed it. I knew he was under a lot of pressure and needed help.

Whereas the above described behaviors are concerned with planting and mowing, chemical treatments are also greatly influenced by the neighbors. When we asked Suzanne why she continued her lawn chemical treatments even though her dog's paws were bleeding, she replied:

I guess we didn't want the yard to look bad when everybody else's looked so nice . . . You try to make it look as nice as you can, without offending other people.

Walter, another long-time resident, described himself as a "trendsetter" on the Court. He used a lawn chemical company when he first moved to Kingberry Court, and he says that all the other residents were soon following suit. When he fired the service company a few years later, all the residents also dropped their lawn services. Walter explains:

> If all of the sudden I want back to spraying my yard, they probably would too. It's very much a group activity around here. People come around and they ask you information, they are worried about everything. They know I am from [local college]; they see me as kind of an authority.

Risk Citizens, Contradiction Reconcilers, Networked Actors

Taken together, the survey results and the stories of the people of Kingberry Court suggest a profile of people who apply chemicals despite anxiety, who are skeptical about chemical producers but have faith in those who produce and apply them, and who downplay the importance of the lawn in community life while setting their environmental schedules by the community lawn clock. Arguably, these urban residents together participate in a "lawn community."

The behaviors and feelings of these lawn people fundamentally contradict apolitical theories of green citizenship, which hold that people engage in environmentally protective behavior to receive social rewards from the community. In research on environmental consumerism, such green behaviors are often described as a "social dilemma" in which individuals must choose to make small individual sacrifices for the common good. In this line of thinking, convincing people that their sacrifice is worth the group's reward is the key to creating green behavior.[5]

The picture of lawn people and chemical-using communities suggests something else entirely, since individual sacrifices are made in the form of environmentally destructive behaviors that are rewarded by, or are at least in service of, community. Refraining from using chemicals on the lawn is a behavior that creates costs to the group, at least as perceived in chemical neighborhoods. The maintenance of a weed- and pest-free lawn requires some personal sacrifice and potential risk, but results in a shared good, enjoyed instrumentally (in housing values) and more abstractly (through social cohesion). Using lawn chemicals confers social rewards on the user. A well-maintained lawn is a sign of good character and social responsibility, a commonly expressed and central countervailing incentive for chemical lawn care, despite known and acknowledged risks. Input of labor and even the application of chemicals that people may regard as environmentally problematic are sustained as a form of collective action, driven both through an impulse towards collective good and an urge to avoid being noncooperative, lax, or antisocial. Three further things are also evident.

First, the inherent hazards of community maintenance through intensive lawn care are largely reconciled through qualified anxiety. Keeping in mind that people who do not worry about lawn chemicals are the ones that do not tend to use them, lawn people (such as those in Kingberry Court) are by their nature anxious. They acknowledge uncertainties and hazards, especially those rooted in their own behavior. Are their applications hurting their pets, their family, their neighbors? When ultimately this worry is externalized by a qualified faith in chemical capitalism, for most members of such communities, proper citizenship involves ongoing inner dialogue concerning the hazards that are inherent in the practice of everyday life.

In this way, lawn people are model citizens of Beck's "risk society." As risk is individuated–both by the reduced regulatory responsibilities of the state and the risks shed from corporate to consumer spheres–lawn people shoulder the burden of a range of new choices. They are reflexive about their decision making, however, constantly evaluating the complex choices that new technologies present, and reconciling them with the priorities of their community. It further underlies Beck's point that, since the modern individual is compelled to his individual responsibilities in a larger context, a community of individuals emerges: "individualization thus implies, paradoxically, a collective lifestyle."[6]

Second, people who practice intensive lawn care do, to some degree, resemble the rigid caricatures in advertising photos promulgated by the chemical industry. As suggested in "pull" marketing, these lawn people are dedicated to family and community and they feel obligations of stewardship to the landscape itself. Clearly advertising does not *produce* this effect, however, since the source of such behaviors is rooted in the social community and the landscape. Even so, the mutual mimicry of the social-communitarian subject and of the economic-consuming subject is relevant to our understanding of the lawn, which serves as a bridge between the two. Desire and community obligation cannot in themselves be marketed as commodities, after all, as deeply held "feelings" they provide no outlet in and of themselves for economic growth or accumulation. But as embodied in intensive lawn practices, such desires can be bought or sold to provide an industrial source of revenue and a sink for risk. To produce and maintain this link between consuming and participating, the lawn industry projects back to lawn people images of communities that can be actively achieved through hard work and the right commercial products.

Advertising neither actively creates turfgrass subjects nor passively represents them, but instead creates a discursive connection between people's image of themselves and the industrial image of the lawn, maintaining the flow of chemicals that is essential to the survival of beleaguered formulator and applicator firms.

In this sense, lawn people are the ultimate logical participants in O'Connor's ecological contradiction of capitalism.[7] As noted previously, O'Connor emphasizes the irreconcilability of accumulation and sustainability. The implications of this contradiction, it would seem, are not merely a series of ecological crises (though bear in mind that chemical production does produce acute site-specific problems that have drawn the attention of regulators [see Chapter 5]), but are also the constant shifting of responsibility for this contradiction to the point of consumption. Here, individual people–instead of firms or even states–become responsible not only for consuming surplus goods and services, but for experiencing and regulating the externalities that result.

The rhythms and behaviors of these neighborhoods, although enforced by human communities, are dictated by the pattern, pace, > and specific ecological needs of other species. Lawn grass has at its disposal not merely the labor of individual homeowners (who might at any time neglect to mow or spray for grubs on an ad hoc basis) but instead an entire social machine, organized to enforce and make regular all of the practices necessary for turfgrass growth.

Lawn people are, therefore, also perfectly enrolled participants in actor-networks. The turfgrasses to which they are linked (many of which are already evolutionary beneficiaries of grazing ecologies of previous imperial ecologies [see Chapter 2]), benefit from lawn chemicals and demand the labor of lawn people. Lawns, in this sense, are not simply plots of grass, but instead are a fixed cluster of grasses, chemicals, and people: a form of socioenvironmental monoculture.

But alternatives exist. A cottage industry for reform has emerged in recent decades to provide a menu of antilawn options for urban residents. Do these practices represent real alternatives? Are they realistic under the current legal regime? Or do alternatives simply reinstitute the position of lawn people as the lonely adjudicators of a larger socioeconomic machine?

CHAPTER 7

Can Lawn People Choose Alternatives?

A S THE CHEMICAL TAIL CONTINUES to wag the turfgrass dog, there are signs of organized opposition from individuals and communities at local, regional, and national levels. Movements by people and advocacy organizations have begun to collectively challenge the high-input lawn. Efforts to set new neighborhood and community standards are also gaining momentum. Most of these alternatives however, as we shall see, are born of the apolitical logics outlined previously, which insist lawns are consumer choices, that they are rooted in a "culture" that is malleable in the face of new and better information, and that the hazards they oppose are an incidental outcome of decisions, rather than a necessity of larger economic arrangement.

Landscape Alternatives

Even so, most of the practical options available to individuals are low-cost, simple, and based on widely available information and resources. At the individual level, alternatives are most commonly implemented by growing ground covers other than turfgrass–either by simply allowing secondary succession to establish whatever diverse herbaceous, shrub, and tree species grow on a neglected plot, or instead by actively planting new communities, especially of native species.[1]

Planting native species in the yard to replace turfgrass represents an effort to restore traditional and locally viable ecological communities on a small scale. Such species include not only historic and prehistoric forest species mixes (oak-hickory, and beech-maple for example), but also wildflower meadows, as well as tall and shortgrass prairie. The advantages of such landscapes are that they tend to be low-maintenance, resist weeds, and attract birds and other wildlife. Native landscaping also can be used to produce yards with fruit, nut and berry

trees, making literally "edible landscapes" that extend the garden into the traditional terrain of the lawn.

It might perhaps be a mistake to say that such "native" plant landscapes are
any more "natural" than lawns. While such native plant communities evolved
throughout North America in the era before extensive modern landscape modification, they were themselves influenced by Native American land management
practices in many places, including fire, planting, and harvesting. Maintaining
a "meadow" in the front yard may indeed require more time and energy than a
lawn monoculture. Having said this, the degree to which such plants and landscapes are better adapted to regional soil, moisture, and climate conditions is
undeniable. Oak-hickory forest for example, a landscape promoted by advocates of lawn replacement, originally dominated throughout many parts of Eastern North America. Its constituent species are fire-tolerant and produce hardy,
stable, and diverse environments.

Less "purist" (though equally viable) alternatives include a large array of
ground covers and herbaceous species that can carpet the ground like the lawn
but that require few or no inputs and often provide ancillary benefits. Among
the vast number of other ground covers, species of *Hosta, Bergenia,* and *Sedum*
are planted, along with wild ginger (*Asarum canadense*) and periwinkle (*Vinca*
species). Some of these ground covers can be edible and herbs and strawber-
ries, for example, make hardy alternatives to turfgrass since they tolerate shade
and poor soil conditions.

Similarly, clover, considered a bane for lawn managers since the mid-
century, is in actuality the perfect ground cover throughout much of North
America. Clover usually requires minimal watering and no mowing; it is cheap,
and comfortable underfoot, and evergreen. Unlike turfgrass, moreover, it
actually restores soil health through nitrogen fixation, rather than drawing constantly on soil nutrients, as is more typical of perennial grasses. In fact, early in
the twentieth century, clover was commonly included in grass seed mixes for its
value in supporting soil health. Where specific battles with lawn health are especially problematic–for example, where soils are acidic, compacted, or shady–a
"natural" problem sometimes also provides a solution. In such soil conditions,
moss growth is typical. This is another source of frustration for lawn managers,
but can actually be tolerated and encouraged to produce thick, soft, attractive
cover. Impervious to weeds and needing essentially no care, rock cap mosses,
fern mosses, and sphagnum moss are all available from growers and easily
planted.

Where dense, wet, standing water is a problem (as is typical in the Upper
U.S. Midwest and central Canada), rain gardens have provided another alternative. These landscape features are little more than shallow depressions that
allow rainwater and runoff from roofs and gutters to infiltrate into the ground,
recharging aquifers and providing for the growth of a range of diverse perennial plants. By fostering infiltration in areas with deep-rooted perennials and

native species, rain gardens require minimal maintenance after establishment, though not without the added nuisance and hazard of mosquito breeding.

Conversely, in areas where water is more scarce, homeowners have begun to experiment with xeriscape designs, where low water-input plants and rock gardens entirely come to displace turfgrass, an increasingly popular option in the West. Given that a proportion of municipal water is commonly dedicated to lawn maintenance, such landscapes have obvious ecological advantages. They also consist of native plant communities, and have the same advantages, both in terms of enhanced aesthetic and reduced labor, that native plants do.

Finally, some lawn owners have begun to pursue lawn management using cultural techniques from Integrated Pest Management (IPM). IPM utilizes management rather than inputs for control of problems. For example, where white grubs (larvae of scarab beetles) are typically treated with diazanon, IPM approaches recommend changes in fertilization, seeding, and watering. In IPM, moreover, the typical "zero-tolerance" approach is eschewed. Pests are tolerated to a point and actions are taken for control of insects or weeds only after their numbers and effects become unacceptable. In the case of the grub problem, a few years of tolerance typically leads to a decline in the insects that reproduce and migrate in long-term cycles. Less dramatically than formal IPM practices, many homeowners simply choose to allow clover, dandelions, and other plants to enter their lawns; to mow less often than their neighbors; and to tolerate dormancy (and browning) of grasses during the drought season.

The extent to which such alternatives are pursued throughout the United States is somewhat unclear. A large proportion of respondents to our national survey report attempts at some kind of alternative practices. Thirty-nine percent of respondents have used some form of nonchemical control, whether hand-weeding or more complex cultural methods, such as mixing new cultivars. Twenty-three percent have replaced at least some portion of their lawn with another ground cover altogether. Perhaps most striking, 11% nationally report that they have eaten wild species, especially dandelions, off their lawns. These tend to be nonchemical users coming from rural areas in the Midwest or Northeast, and who have a well as the source of their water. Although this last behavior is perhaps more unusual, it seems clear that there are "lawn dissidents" across the United States.

Although seemingly innocuous, such behaviors (as shown previously) violate rather widely held norms. While dandelion-eating is a rather traditional and unassuming practice, for example, formulators have explicitly advertised against the practice, and offer a alternative "recipe" to weed control: glyphosate and other postemergence chemicals (Figure 7.1).

Organized Activism
Lawn alternatives seem to represent opposition to larger system, one with significant momentum. Failure to adhere to local yard norms often represents an

Don't Eat 'Em
Defeat
'Em

You may or may not know that some people often turn to dandelions as a dietary supplement.

The early colonists came to America in their great ships with ample supplies of dandelions on board, for use as a food and medicine. Today, you can find recipe books devoted solely to different ways to enjoy dandelions.

While recipes can be a good use of dandelions, we at Scotts are not in the business of recipes.

Some people include dandelions in their diet

Instead, we can give you the right ingredients to rid your lawn of dandelions and other broadleaf weeds in late spring and summer.

Our "recipe" keeps them out of your lawn!

FIGURE 7.1   Don't Eat 'Em Defeat 'Em
Copyright © 2001 The Scotts Company, Marysville, Ohio; reprinted from Robbins, P., and J. Sharp (2003). Producing and consuming chemicals: The moral economy of the American lawn. *Economic Geography* 79(4):425–451; with permission from Clark University.

explicit struggle for homeowners who have alternative aesthetics. Alliances among individuals at a larger scale–within and among activist organizations–have therefore attempted to make inroads into unraveling the system through collective action. Formal organizations such as the Wild Ones and the National Wildlife Federation have become increasingly prominent in Canada and the United States, acting to encourage biodiverse home spaces and to provide and distribute information about low-input alternatives (see Appendix A).

The Wild Ones was founded by naturalist and teacher Lorrie Otto. She planted blue and white aster (*Aster azureus*), yellow goldenrod (*Solidago canadenis*), and fragrant bergamot (*Monarda fistulosa*) in her Milwaukee yard to displace the lawn and spruce trees she found upon moving there. Officials then invoked municipal weed laws against her, viewing the wild fern garden as "weeds" and cutting it down. Founded in the dispute that followed, the Wild Ones seeks to establish and extend biodiversity and sustainable landscaping in municipalities, with special attention to homeowners.[2]

Similarly, the National Wildlife Federation, through its Backyard Wildlife Habitat Program, has worked to encourage and protect homeowners who seek to attract wildlife to their yards through landscaping alternatives. This program not only provides information and education, it advocates and argues for the increased value of property and the improved character of community that come from implementing alternatives. In addition, these kinds of organizations are active in drafting model municipal ordinances and amending ordinances to encourage native plant communities in public (nonlawn) landscape design.[3]

Many organizations dedicated to "sustainable living"–whether through "greener" consumption, promoted by "Eartheasy," or more radically through more simple lifestyles, advocated by the "The Simple Living Network"–also present a range of information sources and ideas. These approaches put the lawn and lawn practices in a more holistic context, pointing out the way lawn care is connected to and a part of a range of consumer choices that are not only unsustainable but that also create harried lifestyles and personal unhappiness.

Much of the activity on this front has come from more broad-based organizations and coalitions. Targeted more directly at legal action, "Beyond Pesticides" is a coalition of nonprofit organizations founded in 1981 to connect advocates against both irresponsible pesticide use and sales. This network provides information about pesticide risks and alternatives, using a range of languages and formats from the more informal and informational to the more technical and scientific. The organization attempts to inform citizens and decision-makers and engage in local, state, and national policy debates that might otherwise come under inordinate pressure from the chemical industry. In this way, the organization is less directed specifically at landscape concerns (as the Wild Ones are) or personal fulfillment (as simplicity movements are), but instead toward general exposure and the regulatory context of lawn debates.

In a similar vein, the Toxics Action Center (TAC) provides information and activism resources. Focusing on local- and community-scale activities, their "Be Truly Green" campaign includes an informal boycott of chemical applicator companies and espouses a zero-tolerance approach to turfgrass pesticides. These efforts are tied to a wider agenda, however, simultaneously opposing hazardous waste sites, landfills, and incinerators. By uniting the traditional concerns of environmental justice movements (which seek to expose the way marginal populations, minorities, and the poor are more vulnerable to technological hazards and risks) with consumer consciousness, TAC goes beyond green consumerism to challenge the several economic and political conditions that make communities vulnerable.

These are just a small sample of players in the increasingly vocal and well-organized postlawn movement. These organizations all share a similar, somewhat volunteerist, approach to the problem of lawn chemicals. Working through voluntary boycotts, information dissemination, and press releases, these groups organize individuals to think differently about their communities while also uniting individual households and decision-makers for mutual support.

Elusiveness of Alternatives

All of this activity, no matter how promising, represents only a nibble at the fringes of a dominant, hegemonic, set of landscape practices and most homeowners continue to apply chemicals of some kind or another and to manage their landscapes for monoculture. While these groups are at work, municipal codes and property restrictions for homeowners are actually moving in the opposite direction, enforcing monoculture with increasing stringency. In virtually every municipality in the United States, homeowners are required by law to cut their grass on a regular basis and keep the property in a "neat and clean" manner, usually setting a maximum lawn height of six to eight inches. Cities will generally fine violators of such laws, cutting the grass of those who do not follow such rules and charging them for the time and expenditures.

As identified by Brett Rappaport, these "weed laws" include federal, state, county, and local statutes or ordinances that place limits on what sort of vegetation can be grown on private land within its jurisdiction, and at what height. Most commonly, these laws represent some extension of municipal health codes, which are targeted at the features of yards that might help harbor pests such as rats or mosquitoes or that might present a potential fire hazard."[4]

Owing to the poor and vague draftsmanship of these codes, however, and to their broad interpretation by enforcement authorities, the laws are commonly imposed where no threat to health and safety exist, but rather where aesthetic violations have occurred. As a result, several precedents exist limiting the enforcement of weed laws, usually on the basis of direct expert scientific testimony contradicting the notion that nontraditional land covers (e.g., anything that is not mowed perennial turfgrass) are hazardous, including *New Berlin v. Hagar* (1976); *Montgomery County, Maryland v. Stewart* (1987); and *Little Rock, Arkansas v. Allison* (1988).[5]

For the most part, however, the broad enforcement of these rules to control and extirpate alternative yard management has been the rule rather than the exception. Where homeowners pursue local and sustainable lawn alternatives, municipalities often intervene. One couple's efforts to allow tropical jungle plants to return to their Madeira Beach, Florida, yard–along with tree fruits, shade, and habitat for birds, butterflies and insects—won them a xeriscape award from their water district governing board (known as "Swiftmud"). City officials, on the other hand, described the concomitant "nuisance plants" and "dead undergrowth" as a potential habitat for rats and mice, resulting in threats to sue homeowners. In one Florida county alone, over 1,000 lots were cited in 1995 for being overgrown.[6]

A Houston lawyer, seeking to preserve a meadow of St. Augustine grass growing in the front and back yards by letting the lawn grow to full seeding height, had his 15-inch-tall grass mowed by the city and was subject to a $1,000 criminal fine by a municipal jury. Here, the city law makes illegal the "existence of weeds, brush, rubbish and all other objectionable, unsightly and unsanitary matter of whatever nature covering or partly covering the surface of any lots or parcels of real estate." More contentiously, Houston code defines "weeds" as any "uncultivated vegetable growth" taller than nine inches. As in most such cases, the city did not intervene until the case was brought to its attention by irate neighbors. Although one neighbor explicitly insisted that "it's not about conformity,"[7] the relationship between moral imperatives (like those of Kingberry Court [see Chapter 6]) and the imposition of legal action is evident.

These are but a few of the countless examples of such neighborhood/municipal interventions, which collectively demonstrate the power of law to control and homogenize domestic landscapes. But more than this, insofar as most of enforcement is not instigated by the city initially but rather at the behest of the violator's neighbors, these cases demonstrate the way lawn communities remain central enforcers of turfgrass landscapes. Some municipalities have dropped such cases, especially where weed statutes are based in public health policies and no credible risk can be demonstrated.[8] Even so, opposition, even if often articulated and defended by stressing individual private property rights, typically results in failure. The same can be said of struggles against restrictive deeds/covenants.

Deeds and Covenants

Deed restrictions are legally binding attachments to property that constrain an owner or renter. Covenants generally refer to deed restrictions that are not unique to a single property, but extend to a group of homes or lots, especially to property that is part of a specific development or subdivision. Although they vary, restrictions like these are often written by housing developers or local homeowner associations, presumably to protect property investments and maintain "community standards." Filed with the county clerk, they are usually activated through complaints.

Even as the primary purpose of deed restrictions is to enforce residential, rather than commercial or industrial use of a subdivision (including the restriction of businesses in residential homes), they have had a complex and politically fraught history. Racially restrictive covenants in particular were a fundamental part of U.S. residential segregation in the first half of the twentieth century (although some persisted for many years thereafter). Here, Anglo/white property owners specified covenants restricting the sale of property to people of color. This meant that no matter what your own political or social conscience, transferring property to nonwhites could be contested and restricted. Defended for decades, such restrictions were also used to exclude Jews, Catholics, and others from buying homes in some areas. Later courts, in the wake of the Civil Rights Movement and desegregation, overturned these rulings and such restrictions became unconstitutional, although deed restrictions controlling homeowner practices (especially around home exteriors) continue to exist throughout the country.

Of concern to lawn people, home deeds commonly contain provisions disallowing landscape changes without the consent of homeowner associations. These restrictions commonly tie the hands of owners and set neighbors against one another. The number of lawsuits against homeowners whose lawns (owing to length or presence of weeds) are in violation of such restrictions is hard to estimate. Anecdotal cases continue to mount in the press, however. Several homeowners in Boca Raton, Florida, and San Jose, California, were sued in 2003 for lawn problems: weeds and lack of mowing.[9] In the more arid West, another woman replacing her front yard bluegrass with xeriscaping was sued by her homeowners' association.[10] Other cases similarly pit the homeowner against the community in legal, and sometimes physical, confrontation.[11]

Countersuits sometimes occur, as where a Florida couple sued their homeowners' association for harassment over deed restriction violations including "spotty" grass. The householders sodded their yard at the association's urging, nonetheless, prior to settlement of the suit. Courts too, have vindicated homeowners occasionally, as where a Massachusetts man who had not mowed his lawn in fourteen years, when faced with state sanitary code violations, was found not guilty.[12]

Generally, however, such opposition ends in surrender. One Florida man, having replaced his brown and declining lawn with xeriscaping in 1998 (and cutting his water usage down from 9,000 to 4,000 gallons per month), was successfully sued by his homeowners' association, who described the lawn as "weed infested" and an "eyesore in the community." To avoid a possibly futile effort, he complied with their demands and planted grass again two years later. The homeowners' association dropped the suit, but only after he had paid the association's attorney's fees.[13]

Even where the city may rule in favor of a nonmonocultural lawn, neighbors may seek civil proceedings to force mowing and weeding. In the most dramatic cases, irate neighbors have themselves entered the property of lawn "dissidents" and mowed the grass and pulled up saplings and shrubs.[14] A remarkable and deeply held normative sense of the landscape is required for people to be motivated to act so radically and in concert. This depth and sense of "normalness" is as great a barrier to change as any legal restriction.

Signs of Change? Legal Reform

There are signs of reform in municipal, regional, and federal laws and institutions. These changes are ad hoc, but show some room for maneuvering in lawn reform. At the municipal scale, more formal legal efforts are apparent, especially in Canada, where over fifty cities and towns have banned pesticides. Most such bans began with efforts to ban chemicals on public lands, including schools and other public buildings, later expanding to include private lawns.[15] The Canadian municipal bans kicked off an acceleration of antipesticide municipal activity throughout that country and resulted in a critical change in industry response. Immediately following the decision by the Canadian Supreme Court, as a prominent example, the Toronto Board of Health finally endorsed a long-discussed ban on cosmetic use of pesticides on lawns in 2001. Industry representatives articulated their opposition as a problem of potential job losses in the spray application industry, rather than on the rights of the city to enforce a ban, or on the safety of the products themselves.[16] This may demonstrate a larger shift in the balance of power between the industry and communities/consumers.

Some evidence of similar municipal-level action has also begun to appear in the United States. In a prominent example, in Suffolk County, New York, the lawn-dominated suburbs of Long Island are beginning to shift towards experimental alternatives. Working through alliances between county water quality agencies and local grassroots organizations, organic lawn practices are finding their way into some of the most affluent communities in the country. The Water Authority has joined forces with the Long Island Organic Horticultural Association, the Long Island Neighborhood Network (a community organization), and the Long Island Groundwater Research Institute at the State University at Stony Brook. Together they have instituted a half–million-dollar, three-year program to compare chemical lawn care with organic alternatives. Unlike the route of municipal legislation favored in Canada, these U.S. community efforts operate on a more volunteer basis, in coordination with state agents.[17]

Real regulatory successes do emerge from these activities, moreover. Agitation by the Long Island Neighborhood Network resulted in New York State's Neighbor Notification Law in 2001, the first of its kind. The law mandates that written notice be given to all proximate neighbors (within 150 feet), at least forty-eight hours prior to the spraying, by any professional applicator who is spraying any pesticide. The law also requires any Do-It-Yourself applicators to place markers on treated areas, as professionals are already required to do. Finally, retailers that sell pesticides are required to post signs that inform applicators and consumers of the signage requirements, urge consumers to follow label instructions, and recommend notifying neighbors before application. The law has the double effect of providing vital information and also changing the moral community tone surrounding the use of pesticides; thus provoking embarrassment or even shame from the use of inputs, placing the burden of explanation on the user rather than the nonuser and so inverting the dominant relationship between of chemical use and community participation.

The so-called Madison "Permission" Law in Wisconsin represents another first of its kind, taking the form of an ordinance validating alternative landscaping. Because such landscaping commonly violates municipal weed laws, at least when they are broadly interpreted, this ordinance departs from most all city codes by allowing the creation of any form of natural landscaping, with the approval of a majority of neighbors.[18]

At the Federal/national scale, both lawn chemical controls and precedents to encourage alternatives, have been slower to emerge. In the United States, the Environmental Protection Agency (EPA) has testified on numerous occasions concerning the under-regulation of household and lawn pesticides and herbicides, especially relative to controls enforced in the agricultural sector.[19] In the last few years, however, the EPA has been more active, issuing cancellation orders for a range of pesticide registrations (including those products with the active ingredient chlorpyrifos [see Chapter 3]).[20] This effort has been resisted most visibly by manufacturers.[21]

Canadian Federal law has also advanced in the reform of pesticide laws, including those chemicals for home lawn application, with more stringent registration mandates and some chemical bans and phase-outs in currently pending legislation.[22] Past efforts to ban specific agricultural pesticides in Canada, however, have resulted in lawsuits under the "national treatment standards" of the North American Free Trade Agreement (NAFTA)'s Chapter 11, raising questions about the prospects for sustained legal opposition.[23] Even so, these joint national, regional, and local efforts represent a sea change in the relationship of consumers and regulators to the agrochemical economy.

Outside of North America, other central government efforts have also emerged. In 2003, new European rules established an international ban of some eighty products, almost all of which are lawn care chemicals (alongside a ban on another 135 agricultural chemicals). The Department for Environment Food and Rural Affairs (DEFRA) in the U.K. explained that the ban emerged when pesticide manufacturers failed to comply with the European Union's stringent licensing review process. "As a result it is no longer possible to guarantee the safety of these products and action has been taken to withdraw them from the market this summer."[24]

The differences in the forms of resistance in the United States, Europe, and Canada is notable. Where institutionally and ideologically, the Canadian and European states are more corporatist than that of the United States, culture and law in the United States tends to favor private property rights more directly. It is unsurprising then to see greater regulatory activity in Canada and Europe.

This need not mean the absence of environmental action in the United States, where grassroots efforts can potentially appeal to private property rights as an ideological lever against weed laws and other ordinances. While the lawn is subverted across North America, therefore, the difference in how this occurs in the United States and Canada reveals a kind of regional geography of dissent. But to what degree is this dissent a departure from the logics of the lawn, instead of an extension of them?

Are Lawn Alternatives Really an "Alternative"?

Whereas slow reforms in lawn chemical hegemony and its legal apparatus are encouraging, we have to wonder the degree to which alternatives to intensive lawn inputs are actually "alternative" and external to the larger structure at work on lawn people. Suspicion in this regard comes from our understanding (as laid out in Chapter 1) that capitalism is crisis-laden and tends simultaneously to lead to over-production of cheaper and cheaper goods in need of markets, and also to the constant shedding and externalizing of costs, therefore under-producing the ecological conditions required for its survival. This impulse in the economy, as we have seen throughout the book, leads to a shifting of risk ecology and risk consciousness downward and outward to lawn people, among countless consumer communities. But it may do something more.

In their research into obesity, the food economy, and the market for organic produce, Julie Guthman and Melanie DuPuis suggest that the growth of specialty food markets—"healthy" alternatives and indeed the entire movement against obesity—reflects not an overthrowing of the capital-driven efforts to maintain consumption, but instead the logical extension of those efforts. Even as overeating, fast food, and eating cheaply are an extension of global market needs (rife as the global economy is with an oversupply of cheap food), so too are the logics of dieting and organics, which force onto consumers additional burdens: guilt over their body, their daily eating, and their relationship to food. These in turn give rise to *whole new markets* for alternatives, which must be motivated by normative notions that there is a responsible and proper way to consume.

So under normal conditions of consumption, relatively affluent North Americans (by global standards anyway) buy and eat increasingly cheap and available foods in an accelerating cycle to provide outlets for overproduction. But as we reach a glut—there is only so much food we can eat—we begin to buy and eat healthier alternatives, rigorously diet, engage in endless exercise, and reduce consumption. Such efforts are directed at being "better" people, of course—morally self-controlled, proper nonobese citizens—but have the added advantage of providing new markets for new goods and making room for ongoing consumption of even traditional foods. Guthman and DuPuis point out that contemporary subjects of such a neoliberal economy exhibit an unstable personality, therefore, having trouble constantly negotiating the obligations placed

on them to both consume *enough* and consume *right*. They explain that "neoliberal governmentality produces contradictory impulses such that the neoliberal
subject is emotionally compelled to participate in society as both [an] out-of-
control consumer and a self-controlled subject."[25] They further state:

> neoliberalism produces a hyper-vigilance about control and deserving-
> ness. For in order to exercise choice freely one must be shaped guided
> and molded into one capable of exercising freedom . . . [the worthy indi-
> vidual] is expected to exercise choice, and to become responsible for
> his/her risks. . . [26]

What better captures and describes the embodied anxieties of lawn people?
If we replace "food" with the chemicals and other consumer goods required to
maintain lawn landscapes, we find the lawn as a sink for surplus and risk, but
also an acute location of anxiety, directing people to nervously consider and pursue alternatives.

And consider more obviously the degree to which "alternatives" are increasingly captured in the pre-existing logic of the lawn market economy. An explosion of organic lawn care services is emblematic in this regard. Such services
offer a range of products, all of which dodge the possibility of actually consuming less. Many organic care providers offer "beneficial" nematodes to manage
pests, especially grubs, in the turf soil. But as noted previously, nematodes are
naturally occurring soil agents, at least where intensive chemical controls have
not prevailed for long periods. Beyond marketing to people things they could
produce or find on their own, specifically by doing nothing, the nematode market stresses the complicated and specialized nature of organism-based insect
controls, rendering expert what is otherwise intuitive.

Beyond where organic alternatives are marketed as products, the landscaping market and its maintenance arm increasingly market whole alternative landscaping for the home. Firms sell wholesale remodeling of yards, planting of
species, and systems for runoff and water capture, among a host of other expensive domestic transformations. These efforts open new consumer communities
of people who may not have previously considered high-levels of landscape
management or maintenance, creating new demands and landscape desires,
equally rooted in the anxieties of lawn people.

So, while there are progressive movements afoot that challenge the enforcement of the lawn in both the legal and social spheres, the anxieties and fears of
lawn people that provide a foothold for such movements are located (at least in
part) within and not outside of the logics of the capital that produce the behaviors that haunt them in the first place. Still, if the core component of the system we have tried to portray in this volume is indeed the lawn itself, then efforts
to erode its ubiquity are the foundations of re-imagining a remarkably persistent hegemonic facet of North American daily life.

CHAPTER 8

Becoming Turfgrass Subjects

T HIS BRINGS US FULL CIRCLE back to the two alternatives for inter-
preting the lawn presented at the outset of the book. Lawns are either
the passive products of aggregated consumer choices, born of a quirky
regional culture, to which an industry responds by providing inputs as safe as they
can reasonably produce . . . or they are something else. This analysis has worked
to construct a political ecology of lawn people and the forces that act upon them
that departs from a different set of assumptions and pursues a divergent line of
evidence. The conclusion is that such volunteeristic accounts must be rejected
both on the merits of the evidence and the instability of their assumptions.

American turfgrasses are introduced cultivars incidentally promulgated in a
larger settlement of the continent with the various species that settlers brought
with them. The lawn as a sculpted, immaculate, atemporal, and emerald green
monoculture that harnessed these grasses is a borrowed aesthetic that was
extremely slow to take hold in the Americas. Such a lawn only developed as a
product of the economic growth conditions in suburban real estate development,
tied to proselytizing that connected the lawn with a certain kind of desirable
urban citizen and economic subject (Chapter 2).

Producing and maintaining a landscape that matches this "desirable" aesthetic requires inputs of capital and labor, applied in ways and times that are
determined by the specific ecological demands of such a system. Whole collective neighborhood rhythms are disciplined around these behaviors annually, sea-
sonally, and weekly (Chapter 3).

The necessary inputs into the system are also by no means ecologically inert
nor indisputably safe for human beings, especially children, wildlife, and ambient ecosystems. Neither has the increasing environmental consciousness that
has accompanied late twentieth century American sensibility resulted in a

reduction of these inputs, either in volume or in diversity. Rather, increased consciousness of risks has coincided with increased input application (Chapter 4).

The industry that produces and provides these inputs for the lawn finds itself in a situation of increasing competition, rising costs, falling revenues, debt, and consolidation. Such conditions require increased access and sales to consumers: more people must use inputs and users must apply more. The result has been a new approach, representing the lawn not just as a desirable individual household item, but as a community and family-oriented collective good. In the process, industry continues to shed costs and risks downward and outward towards consumers and workers (Chapter 5).

The management of this collective good is experienced by lawn people not so much as a choice, but as an obligation, which brings with it anxieties and mixed feelings. Notions of community pride and collective good, along with qualified trust in experts, offset the qualms people have in maintaining these landscapes, but never fully assuage the nagging sense that something might be wrong (Chapter 6).

Whereas alternatives to hazardous inputs are on the rise–in the form of anti-chemical activism, legal reform, and organic lawn care provision–fundamental barriers remain in the path of change. Property configurations, deeds, municipal codes, and homeowners' associations–especially in areas of new growth–all make nonintensive lawn care difficult. To a great degree, moreover, the logic of consuming alternatives matches that of maintaining the lawn, leaving the subjective experience of being lawn people largely unchallenged (Chapter 7).

How did lawn people get this way–dutiful, diligent, and anxious? Not by any simple choice. Rather, they have become "responsible" lawn managers because a number of things are simultaneously at work on them–including their communities, their families, and their property values–all mediated by an aesthetic designed far away in space and time. They become anxious for precisely the same reasons, however.

The data reviewed here actually suggest that the proper question might instead be: why do almost half the people in the United States not yet participate in being lawn people? And yet this very question is one that is receiving constant attention throughout the input industry and is also one where the answer shows a clearly visible trend. Chemical use holds steady on a per capita basis, despite vaunted alternatives. Owing to urban growth, moreover, more people maintain lawns every year, which are inherited in the purchase of a house, either new or used. More people are *becoming lawn people* all the time.

This fact has a number of practical implications for reducing the unnecessary hazards of chemical externalities. First, although some academics insist that "most evil is due to a lack of awareness of the consequences of our actions,"[1] lawn chemicals are used disproportionately by well-informed consumers, despite many of the effects of chemical use in turf care being acknowledged and pernicious. Providing yet more education to individuals so they can do "fifty simple things" to save the planet[2] is probably inadequate. In this case, as with many environmentally problematic behaviors, people act against their better judgment largely as a result of strong contextual pressure.

Nor can we necessarily depend on a radical transformation of "social" consciousness, especially a sense of responsibility to larger communities outside ourselves. Although some observers decry a declining sense of collective values,[3] the social world described in this book suggests something quite different. In this case, and arguably in the case of many unwanted outcomes in consumer ecology, it is the *presence* of normative community ethics as much as their absence that is important. Awareness of consequences weighs lightly in individual decision-making relative to the normative power of the community. It is not so much that community norms are vanishing (with unwanted ecological effects), as they are instead being remade into new persistent relationships. We might do better to critically interrogate the emergence of these new kinds of environmental and collective ethics than to bemoan the decay of lost or imaginary communities.[4]

To create the possibility of change, more generally, we cannot depend solely on the unit of the individual. Meaningful management needs to examine the powerful normative institutions that are unique to socially aggregated behaviors and the protection of collective interests. Environmental externalities, whether they flow out of the tailpipes of a sports utility vehicle (SUV) or the lawn at the end of a cul-de-sac, form a specifically social puzzle necessitating social-level intervention.

In fact, the social and cultural structures and incentives in the case of the lawn are so deeply ingrained that in the driest metropolitan areas in the United States, widely available and well-advertised alternatives to the lawn exist (including turf replacement and xeric landscaping), but are often prevalent only where covenants and restrictions *mandate* them.[5] The implementation of regulatory structures for lawn care remains urgent, therefore, both at the municipal level–as in Canada where communities have regulated lawn chemical use or the national level, as where the U.S. Environmental Protection Agency has pursued a ban on more pernicious substances. Action will have to be aimed at direct control rather than awaiting hopeful shifts towards green consciousness.

Anxiety, Objects, Subjects, and Political Economy

More fundamentally, the situation of lawn people suggests that apolitical ideas about consumer choice, identity, and anxiety hold little explanatory purchase. Lawn people, turfgrasses, input purveyors, communities, developers, and municipalities are all interlinked with one another in a network of enforcement that constitutes each, and that enforces the repeated and aggregated power-laden behaviors that we see throughout the system. Lawn people are citizens of a risk society, caught up in the contradictions of a larger economy, enrolled in a collective ecology. This raises questions about two larger issues in political ecological explanation. First, what is the role of anxiety in maintaining or breaking hegemony? Second, what is the role of objects in producing "subjects"?

Is Anxiety Emancipatory?

Lawn people are anxious. Their worries about over-consuming chemicals and wreaking ecological damage as a result of their choices are directly correlated with their behaviors; indeed such worries are fundamental to them. Are these anxieties a vehicle for critical change? Or are these concerns instead a necessary and logical product of the system through which lawn people are subjected, rather than external to it?

The answer is not immediately clear. On the one hand, as explored in Chapter 7, there are strong reasons to believe that people's anxieties are potentially part and parcel of the systems of accumulation built into the contradictions of capitalism. Worry produces the restless shouldering of responsibility for the economy's hazards and the desire to consume alternatives. This forms the economic bulimic "purging" that Guthman and DuPuis convincingly assert is necessary for later consumer "binging."[6] In this view, anxiety is produced by experts and state authorities, and acts to discipline people and make them more and more responsible for their own health, risk, and safety, rather than calling for truly alternative economic and ecological relationships.

On the other hand, as Maria Kaika has pointed out, anxiety is often produced through "domestic network crises," such as power failures or a loss of tap water, which grab hold of our attention and actually direct it to more fundamental relationships:

> One of the reasons why anxiety and discomfort is produced by a domestic network crisis is precisely because it forces us to reflect on the existence of things and social and economic relations to which the home is connected and which, when disrupted, render the normal function of our lives anomalous and reveal that the familiarity based on the supposed autonomy of the private space is itself a form of alienation.[7]

Following Heidegger, Kaika urges us to interrogate the familiar, presumably those familiar moments of unease, in order to peel back the surface layers of the household and find the complex networks and associations that lie beneath. In this case, anxiety is our guide to the "soft" plates in the armor of political economy; those things in our daily lives that when interrogated in detail give us glimpses into the nature of our political economies and the conditions of our subjection. *Anxious subjects need not be docile ones.*

The case of the lawn seems to suggest that anxiety cannot be considered emancipatory in and of itself, however, but that does present a kind of signal.

Lawn people are made anxious by the hazards generated in their homes but rarely interrogate the connection of their home to the broader economy Kaika describes. Suzanne connects the lawn to the dog's paws, but not to anything else. Rather, capitalizing on anxiety to resist subjection to things such as the lawn requires some kind of critical apparatus to interpret how we feel. Nor can we accept those interpretations that are ready-made.

These ready-made interpretations of hazards (and by implication of our anxiety) are typically provided to us by well-established experts who quantify our risks and identify our hazardous behaviors. As Guthman and DuPuis point out, these do not curb our compulsion "to participate in society as [an] out-of-control consumer," but do shift the blame and worry onto our shoulders to help us become "a self-controlled subject,"[8] effectively individuating our risk decisions, and further alienating us as citizens and consumers. To turn our worries about chemicals (or anything else for that matter) into progressive action instead therefore requires that we recognize ourselves as subjected. It is not enough to worry about what we do, or even why we do it, but rather how we are alienated from the sources of our own intimate fears. Anxiety does provide a window for political action, therefore, and an opportunity that requires far more attention in political ecological research, but not a phenomenon unmediated by the process of our becoming subjects (a process to which our anxiety points, but cannot name on its own).

The Lawn Speaks

Neither is naming that subjection a straightforward process. This is because our habits of explanation–as citizens, as consumers, and as lawn people–tend to overlook some of the most fundamental players in the process. If I feel I want to apply chemicals and yet am concerned about that fact; if I know I am making a choice, but one perhaps not of my own choosing; to what actors can I credit this force of desire? The most obvious choice, outside of myself, is the industry that depends on my participation.

As we have suggested, however, it cannot be argued that the industry and the advertising system it promulgates (showing happy people mowing beautiful lawns) produce the desires of the subject in any simple way. Industry, which does indeed depend on my purchase of these chemicals, is not inventing this desire, at least not in some way separate from the immediate visceral experience of daily life. It is rather reflecting and enforcing the images formed in the experience of lawn ownership. Community pressures, which are so essential to the continued use of inputs, are also not a simple product of the demands of industry. Rather, it seems apparent that individual and community desires respond most directly *the demands of turfgrass*. Neighbors respond to the needs of Poacea, not to shareholders, as they stare over their back fences at our brown patches and dandelions. The lawn makes these demands.

None of this is to say that the lawn is not itself produced or that it somehow preexists the capitalist economy of its creation. Nevertheless, the lawn itself has autonomy in the process of producing and reproducing that economy, its constituent agents, and the experiences of those agents. It is not the prime mover of such a system, no more than any other component, but it is an essential part. The lawn has its own interests too, mediated by the structured flows of fertilizer, water, and pesticides in the infrastructure where it is resident. Previously only assigned to social actors and institutions such as policemen, courts, offices, or families, this role in the process of interpellation must be extended to the nonhuman if there is any hope of dismantling the political economies of nature with which we are so tightly bound. One cannot undo the agrochemical system, even through active community and regulatory confrontation, without first understanding our profound social investment in, and essential ecological labor for, the lawn.

This suggests something more general about the problem of modernity, city and suburban living, nature, and culture. That is (as we asserted in Chapter 1), the enforcement of this specific kind of political economic subject–a concerned, active, communitarian, as well as an anxious, landscape producer and consumer– would be impossible without the lawn itself to enforce the daily practice, feeling, and experience of obligation and participation. The lawn interpellates the "subject."

That the needs of the lawn are interpreted through human cognition, culture, and meaning-making does little to change the urgency of the lawn's impressions on the people who do lawn work. Indeed the taken-for-granted obviousness of the lawn's needs is one of the things that makes these turf demands sound so loud. Consider legal theorist Christopher Stone, who notes in his classic essay *Should Trees Have Standing?* "I am sure that I can judge with more certainty and meaningfulness whether my lawn needs water, than the Attorney General can judge whether and when the United States wants (needs) to take an appeal from an adverse judgment by the lower court."[9] Based on this logic, Stone further argues, the needs of traditionally unrepresented parties–trees, rivers, fish–can be understood unproblematically in court, at least as unproblematically as the needs of abstract parties such as "the United States." The object's voice is crystal clear, whether or not it has been properly translated. And the subjection of the lawn worker by and to the lawn is predicated on just that apparently unambiguous ability to hear this voice.

This approach to the lawn holds epistemological implications for a far wider problem in explanation. How do objects matter in a world where culture mediates our experience of objects? How can the lawn matter independently of its own construction? To date, soft answers have been given to this problem. Objects are part of actor-networks, it has previously been suggested.

This answer, however satisfying and self-evidently true, underspecifies the character of interactions between subjects and objects and is perhaps altogether too uncritical and exculpatory in its mode of explanation. Actor-networks seem just to "happen" in such accounts, and all actors seem to have equal power and agency. Timothy Mitchell asserts that such an approach does much to dismantle the simple and problematic subject/object and human/nature dualisms that proliferate in modern thinking. He further insists that:

> to put in question these distinctions, and the assumptions about agency and history they make possible, does not mean introducing a limitless number of actors and networks, all of which are somehow of equal significance and power. Rather it means making the issue of power and agency a question, instead of an answer known in advance. [10]

I have not argued here, therefore, that turfgrass has a monopoly on the power to call the "subject" into being. Nor have I argued the reverse, on the other hand, that turfgrass technologies, aesthetics, and ideas exist prior to, or outside of, the material conditions detailed here. Mitchell says: "Ideas and technology did not precede this mixture as pure forms of thought brought to bear on the messy world of reality. They emerged from the mixture and were manufactured in the processes themselves."[10,11]

Instead I suggest, also following Mitchell, that "nature speaks." It does so by hailing into existence specific kinds of human "subjects," whose system of material ideological practices have ecological consequences as well as causes.

To examine this flow of power and chemicals is to begin to shed light on the active role of nonhumans in capitalized ecosystems. And these many nonhumans–including plants, animals, technical equipment, and infrastructure–all act in different (and potentially contradictory) ways to produce the "subject," we recognize as ourselves. And to the degree that these "objects" obey their own rules, as is so evident from ever-hungry turfgrass, it is their rules that set the pace and character of subjected lives. They do so tied to the exigencies of capitalist power, to be sure, but with independent, prior, and often ultimate authority.

Even more radically, these "objects" are recreated and re-domesticated in the process, and the place where we leave off and turfgrass starts (as well as the reverse) becomes extremely murky; neither of us, so late in this game, excludes the other. Nor are either of us masters or slaves of the other, fluid subjects to the other's fixed object. But instead, as Donna Haraway insists, we are *companion species*,[12] constantly subjecting and resubjecting one another.

Unthinking the North American lawn requires respecting the power of not only distant multinational capital to act on "subjects," therefore, but also of the intimate influences of nonhuman "objects" in our daily life. It means engaging the lawn itself, not simply attempting to disentangle ourselves from it–by buying something more "natural" (native species) or installing something more "artificial" (Astroturf)–but instead negotiating a relationship with these companion grasses, dandelions, and soils (which we have created and which have created us) that is sustainable, sensible, and less toxic than that which we have described here.

Epilogue: Rescuing the Environment from Determinism

Shortly after completing the first draft of this volume, I sold my house–with its lawn–in Columbus, Ohio. I never did apply any chemicals to the turf and the establishment of its biodiversity was complete by the time of my departure, including a vast coverage of the purple, minty, "Creeping Charlie" that had worried me so much. I had indeed absolutely ruined my lawn, just as one neighbor had long before warned. Nor did I feel good about it, even with the satisfaction of knowing that I had not sprayed a drop of any of the products whose flyers had filled my mailbox for so many years. A part of me honestly felt that I had let down the lawn. We packed the car and moved to Tucson, Arizona. Among the many startling differences between the two places is the overwhelming lack of turfgrass lawn in front of my new home. Instead, my front porch now looks out onto a landscape of mostly gravel, several cacti, some enormous agaves, and a few mesquite. Nor is my yard unique. Perhaps one in forty houses in my neighborhood has a lawn, and this proportion is likely high for the city overall. Even the wealthy suburbs, with their mini-mansion developments, are studded with saguaros rather than grass. And this landscape, although it does require care, has a very different kind of influence, though I have yet to name it or discern exactly what it is. I certainly feel less anxious. Perhaps it is simply a question of personal taste, but I think something else is going on.

Which is why I was intrigued when I discovered that the landscapes of nearby Phoenix, Arizona, are literally covered in lawns. Lawns are the standard development practice throughout the region, as it turns out, especially on the suburban fringe in equally water-poor cities such as Denver, Colorado, Las Vegas, Nevada, and Palm Springs, California. There are some obvious questions that might come out of the natural experiment formed by these near adjacent municipalities. Why do the people of Phoenix plant lawns and not the people of Tucson? Why is one city dominated by turfgrass and the other by gravel? We have a wealth of variables to pick from in formulating our answer and explanation, including economics (water prices), culture (origins of settlers), and law (zoning and real estate subsidies), among many others. These are certainly the kinds of questions that preoccupy geographers, many of whom specialize in explaining land cover change, and the human (social, political, and economic) origins of nonhuman outcomes. And even as these are all very interesting questions, they dodge perhaps more fundamental ones, hinted at in the research described here. What does turfgrass do to the people of Phoenix? What does it require in their daily lives, their demands for municipal services, their relationship to industry and immigrant labor, indeed to a whole range of turf-grass identity politics? How does it affect their communities, their politics? Does it influence their recycling habits? Their school board participation? Their voting? Could tearing up the turfgrass influence, in some small way, the political character of a city? I have to think it might.

Such a question about the influence of nonhumans on humans is currently difficult to ask in the discipline of geography, however, for fear of unearthing the corpse of environmental determinism–that long-ago dismissed set of theories that ascribed to place-based conditions (temperature, moisture, hilliness) the power to control the fate and progress of civilizations. A dead mode of explanation, the theory served empires in the dawning twentieth century and justified colonial domination over subject(ed) people around the world; those unfortunate, largely nonwhite communities, seen as developmental infants constrained by their forests, deserts, and hills. The degree to which this abandoned theory still haunts the field of geography can be seen in the controversy within the discipline surrounding Jared Diamond's *Guns, Germs and Steel*, a book centered on continental scale influences on the history of civilization. Even that volume, with its arguably overbold pronouncements on ultimate factors in human history, was cautious to emphasize that landscapes only have capacities, proclivities, limits, and barriers for human population development, not an active role in the history of human affairs.[12]

But if the case of the lawn tells us anything, it is that the nonhuman world does have an active, ongoing, and crucial role in directing the conditions of the economy and the character of human culture. To examine the political ecology of this role seems prerequisite to progressive political and economic change. This is because the most persistent and powerful influences in making us who we are seem to populate the world around us as a concrete universe of things: cars, airport terminals, dogs, potted plants, insects, swimming pools, elk, icemakers, trees, and automatic teller machines. Beyond the lawn the landscape is filled to the horizon with co-inhabitants of our ecological metropolis, all "working on us" in different ways. And yet, like the lawn, they all can be moved, removed, broken-down, or rebuilt. The fact is, that as tenacious as the modern lawn seems to be (indeed as the entire stubborn postwar world), it is actually not much older than the Baby Boom and is pretty easy to kill in an hour with a systemic herbicide. It is certainly fixed but it is incredibly fragile. Indeed, the case of the lawn is one that reveals just how much terrific effort (in labor-hours, advertising dollars, daily conversation) is required to prop up an inevitable and directional vision of the world, the energy necessary to actually produce the normal, and the ease with which it might therefore give way towards something else.

Moreover, the lawn teaches the surprising way that new objects and subjects happen all the time, with the encounter between humans, plants, and insects constantly rolling out new landscapes and new sorts of people. We and the lawn

are really terrifically new, unplanned, and surprising. Although profoundly problematic, lawns and lawn people were not invented in any simple way, and so provide opportunities for all kinds of new trajectories.

Such new landscapes may never be the ones of some idealized green utopia,
but they need not be the worst of our historical precedent–sterile, monocultural,
soaked in poison. These people may never be the ones we most revolutionarily
(and quixotically) desire or imagine ourselves to be, but neither must they always
be the ones we loathe in historical retrospect–environmentally callous, exploita-
tive, and uncooperative. Happily, neither can these landscapes nor these selves
be totally controlled, directed, anticipated, or foreseen; not subject to some sovereign power, some master planbecause there are too many players, too many
surprises. Influencing the "objects" all around us may indeed be the easiest way
to change ourselves. It might seem like an odd conclusion, both freeing and
frightening, to suggest that the world is both profoundly structured but also
totally malleable, that no one is driving this train and that it has no track, but
this is exactly what the lawn suggests. Unthinking the lawn is only the beginning, it seems. So we really ought to start now.

Suggestion and Sources for Alternatives

Some General Rules

Most of us aren't immediately concerned about our subjection to community ideology. Rather, we want to know how to manage our yards so we do not hurt wildlife, children, and one another. The following "rules" summarize some important things to keep in mind in this regard.

Rule No.1: You do not have to have a turfgrass lawn   Unless there are specific deed restrictions stating otherwise, you do not have to grow grass in your yard. The range of alternative ground covers is staggering and regionally diverse, but include such things as xeriscaping (low-water demanding succulents, attractive nonorganic materials, etc.), nongrass plant beds (perennials, groundcover, or shrubs around existing trees or shrubs, or along a fence line), legumes (such as birdsfoot trefoil, crownvetch, clover), or vines, among others. Where opposition to such ground covers has been offered up by neighbors on the basis of municipal law, cities are increasingly siding with homeowners, provided the cover is not a threat to health (unlike pesticides!), which it rarely is. But mostly, such ground covers encourage almost nothing in the way of active antagonism, as they enhance rather than detract the attractiveness of the property (and property values) while lowering labor demands for you. Consult a nonprofit information organization such as the Wild Ones or a university extension agent (see below).

Rule No. 2: If you have a turf lawn, it does not have to be the grasses you inherited   Grass cultivars vary tremendously. Most often, however, we do not actually choose the kind of grasses we have in our lawn, either because we bought or rented the house with the current lawn, or because a new home was created with lawn grasses chosen by the developer (usually for reasons of cost and convenience, rather than ecological good sense). By selecting the right cultivar to go with local soil and water conditions, you can reduce the workload and input demands for your lawn substantially. In Ohio, for example, Kentucky Bluegrass tends to dominate as a lawn cultivar. In fact, it is a poor choice in many places, since it demands more water and care for many local soil conditions. Blending a number of grass species and cultivars detracts from the "putting green effect" but provides the most robust and manageable lawn. To determine what grass is right for your conditions consult a University Turfgrass Extension Service (see below).

Rule No. 3: Encourage diversity   Aesthetic variability in your lawn is something you should encourage. More importantly, so-called weeds help to combat pests and diseases by increasing the overall diversity of your yard, whereas monoculture is inherently vulnerable. By having a range of nongrass species, especially including legumes such as clover, soil quality is usually improved. Weeds (often flowers) also provide food and nesting sites for insects and birds. Properly mowed (neither too short nor too often), moreover, grasses always tend to dominate other species. By tolerating biodiversity and doing as little as possible in the way of labor, you will encourage a healthy and productive ecosystem without losing your grasses.

Rule No. 4: Tolerate dynamism   Things change. This is especially true of living things. It is perfectly normal to expect the landscape outside your home to look different not only over the course of the year, but even year to year. This is a result of entirely natural patterns of dormancy. Cool season grasses (bluegrass, ryegrass, fescue), for example, are specifically adapted to go into a low-growth and photosynthesis phase during the hottest months of the summer. This means they turn a little pale and somewhat grey/brown, before returning to their growing state in the fall. This is all perfectly normal, and efforts to make July grass look like May grass will only result in frustration and waste. The same can be said for inter-annual variability. Complex ecosystems tend to change from one year to the next: with new growth, the arrival of new species, and the expansion and contraction of different floral communities. Unless such change represents the dominance of a single undesirable plant species, it should also be looked on favorably. What you are seeing is succession, competition, and natural variability–part of the extremely complex pattern of life.

Rule No. 5: Consult extension before industry   Lawn care service providers appear to have an answer for all of your problems. Indeed, their job is to identify problems *you didn't even think you had!* Professional services, even the very best and most responsible of them, have a vested interest in selling you products and procedures. Especially deceptive are practices where companies provide free or reduced cost evaluations of the problems you have in your lawn, suggest some apparently inexpensive remedies, and then over time expand services to meet "new problems" as they arise (TruGreen ChemLawn recently faced a class action lawsuit from clients who were charged for or received unauthorized services). Always take the effort to determine for yourself whether or not you have a problem, and consult a University Extension Service (see below) before going to a professional. Extension agents are paid by the state to meet the needs of the public. Their paycheck is based on realizing their mission to help people, not how much product they sell. Extension agents usually have years of specialized training (or even a Ph.D.), where their professional counterparts have only been trained in sales, if anything at all. And their services are free!

Rule No. 6: Nonturf landscapes are legal Most municipal restrictions regarding front yards are based on health code restrictions, many of which were laid down decades ago. A range of precedents (Chapter 5) have been established to protect natural landscaping and xeriscaping. Not only that, but municipal weed laws are themselves changing, largely in response to opposition to and actions taken by natural landscapers. New setback laws and landscaping exceptions are being written into many town codes, allowing for natural landscaping if the area is set back somewhat from the sidewalk or if it follows specific standards. There is typically nothing a municipality will do if you keep your yard mowed, even if it is a riotously diverse and healthy six-inch ecosystem filled with soil-enriching clover and lemon-yellow dandelions.

Rule No. 7: Beware of deed restrictions Most deed restrictions, including those that enforce the maintenance of turf landscaping in specific ways, have an average life span of twenty-five to thirty years. Some are in effect "in perpetuity." In many cases, such restrictions have a sunset clause, and after the initial term of twenty-five to thirty years expires, are renewed only by written approval of a specified percent of property owners in a subdivision. Many more restrictions, however, will be automatically renewed unless the owners take action to *prevent* reactivation. This suggests that vigilance is essential for homeowners interested in alternative landscaping, both at the time of purchase and beyond.

Rule No. 8: Beware of "Organic" Alternatives Happily, many lawn care companies and formulator firms have noticed the "green" trend in consumer spending, and are busily devising "organic" alternatives for lawn care. This is commendable in every sense, except perhaps in the service of clarity. There are currently no accepted or official standards for what constitutes "organic" lawn care, and the actual treatments offered by different vendors will probably vary hugely. Some will be organic in only the crudest sense (overusing "organic" fertilizers is no better than overusing "inorganic" ones). On the other hand, other vendors may provide excellent Integrated Pest Management, and the use of many creative alternatives. The label "organic" is no guarantee of improved environmental or human safety. As such, you will want to know exactly what the service provides, in precisely what quantities, and at what times. If you are confused on any details, consult a university extension agent. The most truly "organic" form of management is simply not to use any inputs at all, or replace your lawn altogether.

Resources and Allies

The range of resources and allies available to those wishing to learn about and oppose the use of cosmetic pesticides or to engender alternatives is vast. Here are a few.

The Long Island Neighborhood Network

The Long Island Neighborhood Network is a longstanding grassroots organization with a history of successes, including obtaining federal Superfund clean up of local sites, closing hazardous facilities, opposing overdevelopment, and revealing state cleanup policy failures. More than this, the Network functions as a clearinghouse for information to help individual homeowners avoid lawn chemical usage and seek organic alternatives, including the creation and release of surveys showing stores that sell alternatives, staging organic trade shows to promote horticultural services and pesticide-free products, and establishing organic lawn educational forums for communities and homeowners. In terms of regulation, the Network pushed and won passage of the New York State Neighbor Notification Law (Chapter 5).

According to the Network's Mission Statement, they are:

> dedicated to reclaiming the suburban and rural character of community life on Long Island by preserving our environmental resources; initiating policies to prevent exposures to environmental hazards; proposing government consolidations designed to reduce the local tax burden; and holding our governmental officials accountable by advancing reforms which set higher ethical standards and keep the operation of government open to the public.

Their website, (http://longislandnn.org/) is a model for coordinating community level information and activity.

The Rachel Carson Council

The Rachel Carson Council follows in the footsteps of its namesake to inform the general public about the effects of pesticides not only on human beings–especially children–but also on other living organisms and biological systems.

The council promotes awareness about risks, but also serves as a clearinghouse for alternative benign pest management strategies. Their efforts include regular workshops around the United States; links to small businesses (e.g., bed and breakfasts) that observe and direct ecologically sustainable alternatives; sponsorships of events (such as "Pesticide-Free Day"); and the production of videos, conference proceedings, and books with pesticide-related information.

The Council's mission is to foster:

> a sense of wonder and respect toward nature and to helping society realize Rachel Carson's vision of a healthy and diverse environment . . . [and to provide] information at both scientific and layperson levels on pesticide-related issues, which provides answers to the public, produces various publications clarifying pesticide dangers, brings alternative pest controls to the public's attention, and presents conferences and workshops for the public and the scientific community.

The information provided at their website (http://members.aol.com/rccouncil/ourpage/) is meant to scientifically inform the average homeowner, and uses academic references, newsletters, and moving anecdotes to provide real and intuitive alternatives. The site provides information and linkages in both English and Spanish.

The Wild Ones

The Wild Ones is a national not-for-profit organization providing an umbrella for local chapters (some fifty chapters in twelve states) that seek landscaping alternatives. Their work includes efforts to advocate native plants in natural landscapes, including the establishment of native plant communities around both residences and commercial properties. Their other efforts include the preservation and restoration of native communities in situ, working in natural areas to promote biodiversity, as well as promoting environmental education for both children and adults. They produce both a handbook and a journal that give straightforward "how to" advice on creating and maintaining landscapes. And they also push for change, especially in "weed law" ordinances that stand in the way of more ecologically benign and diverse environments. The mission of the Wild Ones also includes putting activists in touch with one another to compare notes on things as simple as killing weeds in walkways and as complex as reforming city laws.

Their stated mission is :

> to educate and share information with members and community at the "plants-roots" level and to promote biodiversity and environmentally sound practices. We serve as a resource for private individuals, schools,

commercial property owners, and community decision makers as they move toward ethical choices in land use and in the redefinition of current guidelines and ordinances affecting our landscape. Because we are a "plants-roots" organization, our organizational goals are accomplished through local chapters and their individual members.

The Wild Ones website (http://www.for-wild.org/) is a link-filled clearinghouse with questions and answers on practical problems facing ecological restoration advocates, as well as connections to conferences, local chapters and events.

Xeriscape Colorado! Inc.

Xeriscape Colorado! is a non-profit organization working to extend low water-demanding landscape options. Founded in the 1980s as an outgrowth of encounters between the Denver Water Board and landscaping organizations, the organization lays claim to the invention of the term "xeriscape." Their activities include operating demonstraion gardens; providing "how to" information on low water landscapes; publishing the Xeriscape Management Journal; and hosting a series of workshops, tours, classes, and programs.

According to their mission, they are:

> a network of interested volunteers representing all aspects of the landscape industry, municipal and public agencies and the general public. All are brought together by a common interest in more efficient and regionally representative landscapes for the Colorado Rocky Mountain region. The organization is committed to helping people improve their landscapes and to reduce demands upon water, maintenance and other resources.

Though focused predominantly on xeriscaping in Colorado, their website (http://www.xeriscape.org/) is most notable for its extensive bibliography, providing information for potential xeriscapers throughout the country.

Useful Extension Services

All land grant universities—one in every state in the United States—have an agricultural campus. Of these, several have a turfgrass extension service. While historically these services have been tied to maintaining and promoting traditional lawns, the tide of ecological commitment in these schools has long since turned. This makes extension services one of the best sources for advice on managing yard problems (turfgrass, shrubs, and trees) using the lowest levels of chemicals inputs, time, and labor.

In particular, extension services provide excellent information on Integrated Pest Management: systems of insect and weed control that emphasize cultural (growing and managing), rather than chemical, solutions to pest problems. They also provide regionalized suggestions on which turf cultivars homeowners can grow with a minimum of trouble and time. Many universities catalogue common problems on line, so that homeowners can look up pests, identify their specific problems and needs, and implement controls that are most locally appropriate. Of the many available extension services, some of the finest include:

- The University of Illinois (http://www.turf.uiuc.edu/extension/ extension.html)
- Colorado State University (http://www.ext.colostate.edu/)
- Iowa State University (http://www.extension.iastate.edu/ag/ lawngard.html)
- University of Tennessee (http://www.utextension.utk)
- Cornell University (http://www.explore.cornell.edu/scene.cfm?scene= home%20gardening)
- University of California IPM Online (http://www.ipm.ucdavis.edu/)
- Pennsylvania State University Turfgrass Management (http:// turfgrassmanagement.psu.edu/)

Unusual in its emphasis on the city, the Urban Landscape Ecology program at Ohio State University is notable for its commitment to integrating urban systems through sustainable practices and landscapes (http://ohioline.osu.edu/ lines/hygs.html). The program seeks "to develop new technologies and environmentally friendly approaches to landscape planning, establishment and maintenance. At the same time, it aims to educate citizens about the risks associated with excessive chemical applications and get them involved in fostering healthier, sustainable landscapes."

Data Development and Analysis

The National Homeowner Survey

This national survey was conducted by the Center for Survey Research at Ohio State University during the summer of 2001. It comprises 594 interviews with respondents across the United States, stratified by the four U.S. census-defined regions (West, South, Midwest, and Northeast), and selected through random digit dialing. Screening sought to identify households with lawns and interview the adults who were "responsible" for the lawn: "a grassy area at the front, the side or behind your residence."

Our initial exploratory analysis used log-linear modeling of the categorical data to identify relationships between the response variables and a number of perception, community attachment, and demographic variables from the national survey data.[1] Using the relationships suggested by the log-linear models, we developed the final logistic regression models for each of the response variables. We assessed the fit of all logistic regression models using the Hosmer and Lemeshow goodness-of-fit statistic[2] and found that all models provided good fits to the data. In addition, all explanatory variables in the final models were judged statistically significant from zero at $p < 0.10$ using the Wald Statistic.

Notably, in logistic regression–like other multivariate analyses–the effects of causal variables can be shown to influence probabilities of outcomes in response variables independently of one another. The likelihood of using a lawn care company is significantly higher for women than men, for example, no matter the income or education of individuals.

The Applicator Survey

Surveys of professional lawn chemical applicators were conducted during the summer and fall of 2004. Subjects recruited included participants in Ohio State University's OARDC (Ohio Agricultural Research and Development Center)–sponsored turf care professional educational seminars (Northeast Ohio Lawn Care Seminars). Approximately 300 professionals attended these events (held at the Wooster campus of Ohio State) to inform practitioners of best management practices, new technology, and health and safety issues. Participants included those who own and work in the lawn care industry in Ohio, spanning companies from small, one-person owner operated firms to large franchised national outfits. Professionals attend these seminars for purposes of certification; participation in the survey was optional.

The Kingberry Court Interviews

Kingberry Court is a pseudonym for a cul de sac in which interviews were conducted between April and October 2003. These were tape-recorded and transcribed, and lasted between one and two hours. When initiating the interview, we asked to speak with the member of the household who did most of the yard work. In all but one case we were directed toward the adult male in the family. In four of the eight interviews, only the adult male was present. In three of the interviews, however, the wife also sat down with us or hovered nearby and often added her own observations, which usually confirmed the husband's opinions.

The interviews were semi-structured, but commonly took the form of a free-form discussion, allowing residents to set the agenda for discussion and stress their own priorities. While emphasizing their opinions about chemicals–including why they used them and their feelings about any possible environmental concerns–respondents often diverged into other aspects of yard work such as mowing, pruning, planting, and planning landscaping.

Table B.1 shows how Kingberry Court and its residents compare with the local census region, the metropolitan area, the Midwest, and the United States as a whole. These figures indicate that the residents of Kingberry Court–and the wider census tract of which it is a part–are substantially better educated and wealthier, and own larger and more expensive homes than the metropolitan area, the region, or the country as a whole. As a result, Kingberry Court provides an insight into upper-middle-class life in a somewhat better-to-do, but largely typical American suburb. Demographically, Kingberry Court is the kind of place where residents can be expected to care about the environment, and to have knowledge of and concern over the human health and environmental risks of lawn chemical use.

APPENDIX TABLE B.1   Comparison of Kingberry Court to General Population

	Median family income[1]	Percent population white[2]	Percent population with a postgraduate degree[3]	Median market value of one-family houses[4]	Median square footage of new one-family houses[5]
United States	$50,000	75	9	$120,000	1,755
Midwest	$51,000	84	8	$106,000	1,740
Metro area	$55,000	81	10	$121,000	na
Local census tract	$117,000	90	38	$232,000	na
Kingberry Court	$150,000	100	87	$337,000	3,337

[a]All figures are rounded to nearest $1,000 and nearest whole percent.

[1] Source: Table P77: Median Family Income in 1999 (Dollars) [1] – Universe: Families. Census 2000 Summary File 3 (SF3), U.S. Census Bureau; U.S. Census Bureau. (2000) Median family income in 1999 (dollars) [1]–Universe: Families. Census 2000 Summary File 3 (SF3), Washington, D.C.: U.S. Census Bureau.

[2] Source: Table QT-P3: Race and Hispanic or Latino 2000: Census 2000 Summary File 1 (SF1) 100-Percent Data, U.S. Census Bureau.

[3] Source: Table QT-P20: Educational Attainment by Sex, 2000. Census 2000 Summary File 3 (SF3), U.S. Census Bureau.

[4] Source: Table H76, Median Value (Dollars) for Specified Owner-Occupied Housing Units [1], Census 2000 Summary File 3 (SF3), U.S. Census Bureau.

[5] Data are from 1987, the year Kingberry Court was built. Source: Median and Average Square Feet of Floor Area in New One-Family Houses Completed by Location. 2003. Manufacturing, Mining, and Construction Statistics, U.S. Census Bureau.

The Land Cover Survey

Compiling tax assessor data, we developed two measures of lawn size that can be calculated at either the household or census tract levels: the Potential Lawn Area (PLA) and the Potential Lawn Ratio (PLR). The PLA of a residence is determined by subtracting the footprint of the house, calculated as the house square footage (h) divided by number of floors (s), from the overall lot size (l).

$$PLA = l - (h/s)$$

This provides a measure of the *maximum possible* extent of residential space given over to lawns.

The PLR of a residence is the ratio of the PLA to residential lot size (l):

$$PLR = PLA / l$$

High PLR values indicate large lawns relative to the footprint area of the house. This provides a test for not only whether actual lawn size varies, as would be expected under variations in lot size, but also whether the proportion of the lawn committed to nonhouse coverage varies.

The selected study area inFranklin County, Ohio, encompasses the city of Columbus as well as the city's suburban growth zone. We utilized Franklin County Tax Assessor data, updated in October 2000, as our database for analysis. The Franklin County Tax Assessor database contains 378,092 records, each representing a tax-lot within Franklin County. Of these 378,092 records, 79,894 were suitable for analysis. Many records had to be eliminated because of missing values in essential data fields: number of stories, lot square feet, house square feet, year built, or street address.

The remaining 79,894 records were geocoded with ESRI's ArcView, version 3.2 and 1999 U.S. Census Bureau's Tiger street centerline data. The geocoded points were then intersected with Census Tract polygon data-layer. This adds a field to each point that contains the census tract number. Any census tract containing fewer than 30 points was then eliminated from further study. This left 205 census tracts containing more than 30 points out of the 252 total tracts in the county. The remaining data points were then grouped by census tract and summary statistics created for particular fields: PLR and PLA.

For use in analysis, this raw figure must be further altered through calibration to a more conservative figure that excludes impervious surfaces around the household (including driveways and sidewalks) as well as nonlawn pervious surfaces such as trees and gardens. For this purpose, we used aerial photos to calibrate a correction for PLA and determine the proportion of actual lawn to PLA, using 1:600 orthorectified black-and-white aerial photography from the Franklin County Assessor's office. After subtracting out the house footprint from the l (overall lot size), it was determined that 0.816 of the remaining lot could be classified as lawn. The 0.816 multiplier, with a standard deviation of 0.052, resulted from aerial photo interpretation of 63 lots spatially stratified across Franklin County. For each sample point, the house footprint and all nonlawn areas were digitized to determine PLA and the lawn multiplier. Removed in the process were areas of shrub and tree cover, garden cover, sidewalks, driveways, and porches (Fig. B.1), producing a corrected measure of PLA × 0.816 of total lot area excluding the house footprint (h). This figure can be generated for the household, census tract, or municipal level–for any city–with digital assessor's data. Note that this figure exceeds the one reported by homeowners in a statewide survey conducted in Ohio during 2000, where the mean percentage of open lot reported by lawn-owning residents to be under turfgrass was 66.18%. Ours is not the first attempt to establish pervious/impervious area multipliers for single-family residential units. Cappiella and Brown used direct measurement methods of variously zoned residential areas in four U.S. cities to create impervious cover coefficients. They used direct measurement to assess residential lots ranging from 2 acres to 1/8 of an acre, finding that 90% to 68%, respectively, of the residential lots were forest or open space.[3] This speaks to

0   25   50   Feet

FIGURE B.1 Measuring how much of a lot is actually a lawn using air photography. TL = total lot (100%); AL = area under lawn (70.75%); NLA = non-lawn area, including mulch, concrete and other areas (15.25%); H = house footprint (14%). Reprinted with permission from Robbins, P., and T. Birkenholtz. (2003). Turfgrass revolution: measuring the expansion of the American lawn. *Land Use Policy* 20:181–194, with permission from Elsevier.

two issues in our calculation. Our 0.816 multiplier is consistent with the above, though stratifying the figure between zones may improve precision. We derived our multiplier across different zones and the largest parcel of land we sampled was less than one acre; we had no outliers in the sample. Additionally, we multiplied the PLA (PLA $= l - h/s$) *not* the total lot by 0.816. Therefore, our calculation is highly conservative.

To model the relationship between PLA and PLR, we used each of these in ordinary least squares (OLS) multiple regression to explore the relationship between the dependent variables Mean PLR or Mean PLA and the independent variables (Berry and Feldman, 1985).[4] OLS regression was used because data satisfied OLS assumptions for the model as the best linear unbiased estimator (BLUE). Distribution of errors (residuals) is normal, they are uncorrelated with each other, and homoscedastic (constant variance among residuals), with the mean of 0. We also analyzed predicted values plotted against residuals, as they are a better indicator of non-normality in aggregated data, and found them also to be homoscedastic and independent of one other.

Modeling Lawn Cover Growth
The model with Mean PLR as the dependent variable required no data transformations. In the Mean PLA model, we transformed the positively skewed dependent variable with a natural logarithm to achieve a normal distribution, creating the ln Mean PLA. The data contain no influential outliers.

Recall that we eliminated census tracts with over-small population; we are working with population data, so we therefore eliminate bias associated with sample data. The independent variable Median Income was transformed with a natural logarithm to eliminate positive skewness and to ensure a standard normal distribution for proper analysis. The independent variable Mean House Value was eliminated in preliminary analysis due to low t values and multicollinearity with Median Income; income and housing value co-vary. The results of the regression showed new housing starts in affluent neighborhoods tend to have larger lawns (PLA) and that the size of the lawn in any given unit of construction is increasing annually. This relationship forms a specific geography of relative lawn coverage, as well, since Mean Year Built not only indicates the year the home was built, but also explains its location. Newer homes—at increasing distance from the city center in the growth zone—tend to have higher ratios of lawn to lot (PLR). In Franklin County, with new housing starts on the rise and increasing lateral growth, lawn size as a proportion of total lot size is getting larger.

Another finding worth noting from the survey is the relatively large total area and proportion of lawn cover across both urban and suburban across the County. On average, 82% of the home property area not under the house was a turfgrass lawn. This means that roughly 23% of the land cover for the entire county is lawn. This is a staggering figure, and removes any doubt that what happens on

the lawn, for better or for worse, is a major determinant of what happens ecologically in the city. The relationship between home age and lawn size further
suggests that the total lawn area and proportion of lot under lawn definitely
increase, not only in areas of higher income and housing value (which seems
intuitive), but also in areas of more recent construction and growth, no matter
the housing value or income. This means that every new housing start, on average, has more lawn, and that each year that proportion grows.

So even while lot size is decreasing, and despite increases in house sizes, there
is more lawn for each new house constructed. This apparent contradiction is reconciled when the nature of new house construction is considered. Only 17% of
homes built in 1970 had two or more floors. This continuation of ranch style construction, leftover from the housing boom of the 1950s and 1960s, meant that
single-story homes continued to dominate. By 1996 on the other hand, newly
constructed two-story homes comprised half the market.[5] This shift in construction style to "pop-top" suburban structures means more lawns, of greater
size, even in a period of more densely concentrated suburban development.

NOTES

Introduction

1. Press coverage of the struggle was ongoing Crumbley, Ray. (2000). Neighborhood dispute over unmanicured yard headed to court. *Columbus Dispatch*. Columbus: January 3, D7. Crumbleyay, R. (2000). Reynoldsburg says resident can let back yard grow wild. *Columbus Dispatch*. Columbus: September 15, B4. Crumbley, Ray. (2000). Neighbors sue over high grass. *Columbus Dispatch*. Columbus: October 19, 4C. Crumbley, R., and R. Albrecht.(2000). It's mowing versus growing in area's turf war grass-height laws. *Columbus Dispatch*. Columbus: August 14, 1B.

2. Detailed in Chapter 1 and Appendix B.

3. Approximately 14 million hectares (mha) of turfgrass in the United States; the state of Iowa is 14.5 mha in size.

4. All figures are from the National Gardening Association, whose annual survey tracks consumer spending in each sector of the industry National Gardening Association. (2000). *National gardening survey*. Burlington, VT: National Gardening Association.

5. Ibid.

6. Adler, R. W., J. C. Landman, et al. (1993). *The Clean Water Act: 20 years later*. Washington D. C.: Island Press.

7. United States Environmental Protection Agency. (1996). Pesticides industry aales and usage eport (http://www.epa.gov/oppbead1/pestsales/95pestsales/market_estimates1995.pdf), (accessed February 13, 2007)

8. Research on the selective effects of antibiotic soaps on bacteria are not yet far advanced, but initial evidence suggests that they are used far too frequently, with the possible risk of producing infections resistant to the best available antibiotics. See Larson, E., A. Aiello, et al. (2003). Short- and long-term effects of handwashing with antimicrobial or plain soap in the community. *Journal of Community Health* 28(2): 139–150.

9. Bormann, F. H., D. Balmori, et al. (1993). *Redesigning the American lawn: A search for environmental harmony*. New Haven and London: Yale University Press.

10. Pollan, Michael. (1991). Why mow? In *Second Nature: A Gardener's Education*, 65–78. New York: Dell Publishing.

11. Jenkins, V. S. (1994). *The lawn: A history of an American obsession*. Washington and London: Smithsonian Institute Press.

12. Teyssot, George., Ed. (1999). *The American lawn*. New York: Princeton Architectural Press.

13. Schroeder, F. E. H. (1993). *Front yard America: The evolution and meanings of a vernacular domestic landscape*. Bowling Green, OH: Bowling Green State University Popular Press.

14. Steinberg, Ted. (2006). *American green: The obsessive quest for the perfect lawn*. New York: W. W. Norton and Co.

15. Wasowski, A., and S. Wasowski. (2002). *The landscaping revolution: Garden with Mother Nature, not against her*. New York: McGraw-Hill. Wasowski, Sally. (2004). *Requiem for a lawnmower, revised edition: Gardening in a warmer, drier, world*. Lanham, MD: Taylor Trade Publishing.

16. For a comprehensive summary of turfgrass benefits see Beard, J. B., and R. L. Green. (1994). The role of turfgrasses in environmental-protection and their benefits to humans. *Journal of Environmental Quality* 23(3): 452–460.

17. Schroeder, F. E. H. (1993). *Front yard America: The evolution and meanings of a vernacular domestic landscape*. Bowling Green, OH: Bowling Green State University Popular Press. 5.

Chapter 1

1. Buttel, F. H., and W. L. Flinn (1978). The politics of environmental concern: The impacts of party identification and political ideology on environmental attitudes. *Environment and Behavior* 10: 17–32, Widegren, Örjan. (1998). Environmentally friendly behaviour as collective action: Some aspects of "non-rational" motivation. *Tidsskrift for Samfunnsforskning* 39(2): 231–258. Diamantopoulos, A., B. B. Schlegelmilch, and R. R. Sinkovics, et al. (2003). Can socio-demographics still play a role in profiling green consumers? A review of the evidence and an empirical investigation. *Journal of Business Research* 56(6): 465–480.

2. Schahn, J., and E. Holzer. (1990). Studies of environmental concern: The role of knowledge, gender, and background variables. *Environment and Behavior* 22(6): 767–786. Scott, D., and F. K. Willits. (1994). Environmental attitudes and behavior: A Pennsylvania survey. *Environment and Behavior* 26(2): 239–260. Berger, I. E. (1997). "The demographics of recycling and the structure of environmental behavior. *Environment and Behavior* 29(4): 515–531. Widegren, Örjan. (1998). Environmentally friendly behaviour as collective action: Some aspects of "non-rational" motivation. *Tidsskrift for Samfunnsforskning* 39(2): 231–258.

3. Jacobs, H. E., J. S. Bailey, et al. (1984). "Development and analysis of a community-based resource recovery program. *Journal of Applied Behavior Analysis* 17: 127–145. Granzin, K. L., and E. J. Olsen (1991). Characterizing participants in sctivities protecting the environment. *Journal of Public Policy & Marketing* 10: 1–27.

4. See Samdahl, D. M., and R. Robertson. (1989). Social determinants of environmental concern: A specification and test of the model. *Environment and Behavior* 21: 57–81.

5. For a summary comparison of apolitical ecology with political ecology, see Robbins, Paul. (2004). *Political ecology: A critical introduction*. New York, Blackwell . . . And see: Neumann, R. P. (2005). *Making political ecology*. London, Hodder Arnold.

6. Fishbein, M., and I. Ajzen. (1975). *Belief, attitude, intention, and behavior: An introduction to theory and research*. Reading, MA: Addison-Wesley. Tarrant, M. A., and H. K. Cordell. (1997). The effect of respondent characteristics on general attitude-behavior correspondence. *Environment and Behavior* 29(5): 618–637.

7. Wasik, J. F. (1993). *The green supermarket shopping guide*. New York, Warner Books. Widegren, Örjan. (1998). Environmentally friendly behaviour as collective action: Some aspects of "non-rational" motivation. *Tidsskrift for Samfunnsforskning* 39(2): 231–258.

8. Weiner, J. L., and T. A. Doescher. (1991). A Framework for Promoting Cooperation. *Journal of Marketing* 55: 38–47.

9. Roberts, J. A., and D. R. Bacon. (1997). Exploring the subtle relationships between environmental concern and ecologically conscious consumer behavior'. *Journal of Business Research* 40(1): 79–89.

10. Diamantopoulos, A., B. B. Schlegelmilch, et al. (2003). Can socio-demographics still play a role in profiling green consumers? A review of the evidence and an empirical investigation." 56(6): 465–480.

11. Berger, I. E., and R. M. Corbin (1992). Perceived consumer effectiveness and faith in others as moderators of environmentally responsible behaviors. *Journal of Public Policy and Marketing* 11(2): 79–89. Pickett, G. M., N. Kangun, et al. (1993). Is there a general conserving consumer? A public policy concern. *Journal of Public Policy and Marketing* 12(2): 234–243. Scott, D. and F. K. Willits (1994). "Environmental attitudes and behavior: A Pennsylvania survey." *Environment and Behavior* 26(2): 239–260. Gooch, G. D. (1995). "Environmental beliefs and attitudes in Sweden and the Baltic states." *Environment and Behavior* 27: 513–539. Diamantopoulos, A., B. B. Schlegelmilch, et al. (2003). Can socio-demographics still play a role in profiling green consumers? A review of the evidence and an empirical investigation. *Journal of Business Research* 56(6): 465–480.

12. Gooch, G. D. (1995). Environmental beliefs and attitudes in Sweden and the Baltic states. *Environment and Behavior* 27: 513–539.

13. Pickett, G. M., N. Kangun, et al. (1993). Is there a general conserving consumer? A public policy concern. *Journal of Public Policy and Marketing* 12(2): 234–243.

14. Blaikie, P., and H. Brookfield (1987). *Land degradation and society*. New York: Routledge, 68. PAUL NOTES: original publication by Methuen, reprinted by Routledge same year. The page numbers are from the Routledge edition.

15. Ibid., 27.

16. Marx, Karl. (1898). *The Eighteenth Brumaire of Louis Bonaparte (1852) by Karl Marx. Translated from the German for the people, organ of the socialist labor party, by Daniel De Leon*. New York: International Publishing Co.

17. Blaikie, P., and H. Brookfield (1987). *Land degradation and society*. New York: Routledge, 35.

18. Althusser, Louis. (1971). Ideology and ideological state apparatuses: Notes towards an investigation. *Lenin and philosophy and other essays*, 127–186. New York: Monthly Review Press.

19. Scotts Company (2000). Business Segments Overview: North American Consumer (www.smgnyse.com/html/consumerlawn.cfm). (Last accessed July, 2001)

20. Mitchell, Don. (2000). *Cultural geography: A critical introduction*. Oxford: Blackwell, 82.

21. Zukin, Sharon. (1991). *Landscapes of power: From Detroit to Disney World*. Berkeley: University of California Press.

22. Gramsci, Antonio. (1973). *Prison notebooks*. London, Lawrence and Wishart. For discussions of hegemony see especially page 12, and for discussions of hegemony and the ideology of the liberal state, see 245–246.

23. Burton, I., R. W. Kates, et al. (1993). *The environment as hazard*. New York: The Guilford Press.

24. Beck, Ulrich. (1992). *Risk society: Towards a new modernity*. London: Sage Publications.

25. Allen, James. 1992. Lawn chemicals are safe," *USA TODAY*, April 22, 14A.

26. O'Connor, James. (1996). The second contradiction of capitalism. in *The Greening of Marxism*, 197–221.ed. Ted Benton. New York: Guilford Press, 207.

27. Ibid.

28. The classic reference here is Bullard, R. D. (1990). *Dumping in Dixie*. Boulder, CO: Westview. And more recently, Pulido, Laura. (2000). Rethinking environmental racism: White privilege and urban development in Southern California. *Annals of the Association of American Geographers* 90(1): 12–40.

29. Swyngedouw, Erik. (2004). *Social power and the urbanization of water: Flows of power*. Oxford: Oxford University Press, 11.

30. Beck, Ulrich. (1992). *Risk society: Towards a new modernity*. London: Sage Publications.

31. Beck, Ulrich. (1999). *World risk society*. Oxford: Blackwell Publishers.

32. Williams, Raymond. (1973). *The country and the city*. New York: Oxford University Press.

33. Gandy, Matthew. (2002). *Concrete and clay: reworking nature in New York City*. Cambridge, MA: MIT Press 2.

34. For a paramount statement of such an approach, see David Harvey's classic: Harvey, David. (1982). *The limits to capital*. Oxford: Basil Blackwell.

35. Cronon, William. (1995). "The trouble with wilderness or, getting back to the wrong nature." in Willliam. Cronon *Uncommon Ground: Rethinking the Human Place in Nature*, 69–90. New York: W. W. Norton and Co., 86.

36. For much more on the human/animal interface in the city, see Wolch, Jennifer. (2002). "Anima urbis." *Progress in Human Geography* 26(6): 721–742.

37. Latour, Bruno. (1988). *The pasteurization of France*. Cambridge, MA: Harvard University Press.

38. Wood, Denis. (2003). *Five billion years of global change: A history of the land*. New York: Guilford Press, 121.

39. Murdoch, Jonathan. (1997). Inhuman/nonhuman/human: actor-network theory and the prospects for a non-dualistic and symmetrical perspective on nature and society. *Environment and Planning D: Society and Space* 15: 137.

Latour, Bruno. (1987). *Science in action: how to follow scientists and engineers through society*. Cambridge, MA: Harvard University Press.

Haraway, Donna. (2003). *The companion species manifesto: dogs, people, and significant otherness*. Chicago: Prickly Paradigm Press.

40. For details on Foucaultian methodological approaches to power, see especially Foucault, Michel. (1990). *The history of sexuality volume I: An introduction*. New York: Vintage Books.

41. Althusser, Loius. (1971). Ideology and ideological state apparatuses: Notes towards an investigation. *Lenin and philosophy and other essays*, 127–186. New York, Monthly Review Press.

42. Ibid.

43. Ibid., 182.

44. Compare this to Agrawal's similar understanding of the environmental subject, which is equally tied to modern ecological governance and community, but perhaps less hinged to the economy. Agrawal, Arun. (2005). *Environmentality: Technologies of government and the making of subjects*. Durham, NC: Duke University Press.

45. Kaika, Maria. (2005). *City of flows: Modernity, nature, and the city*. New York: Routledge.

Chapter 2

1. Richards, John F. (1990). Land transformation. In *The earth as transformed by human action*. B. L. T. Turner, W. C. Clark, R. W. Kates, et al. Cambridge: Cambridge University Press: 163–178.

2. Schroeder, Fred E. H. (1993). *Front yard America: The evolution and meanings of a vernacular domestic landscape.* Bowling Green, OH: Bowling Green State University Popular Press.

3. Hoad, T. F. (1986). *The concise Oxford dictionary of English etymology.* Oxford: Oxford University Press.

4. Mosser, Monique. (1999). The saga of grass: From the heavenly carpet to fallow fields. In *The American lawn.* Georges Teyssot. New York: Princeton Architectural Press: 40–63.

5. Ibid.

6. O'Malley, Therese. (1999). The lawn in early American landscape and garden design. In *The American lawn.* Georges Teysot. New York: Princeton Architectural Press: 65–87, 82.

7. Hickman, K. R., D. C. Hartnett, R. C. Cochran, and C. E. Owensby. (2004). Grazing management effects on plant species diversity in tallgrass prairie. *Journal of Range Management* 57(1): 58–65.

8. Malin, James C. (1984). *History and ecology: Studies of the grassland.* Lincoln: University of Nebraska Press.

9. Brown, Lauren. (1979). *Grasses: An identification guide.* New York: Houghton Mifflin, 12.

10. Cronon, William. (1983). *Changes in the land: Indians, colonists, and the ecology of New England,* New York: Hill and Wang.

11. Carrier, Lyman, and Katherine S. Bort. (1916). History of the Kentucky bluegrass and white clover in the United States. *Journal of the American Society of Agronomy* 8: 256–66.

12. Fuhlendorf, S. D., and D. M. Engle. (2001). Restoring heterogeneity on rangelands: Ecosystem management based on evolutionary grazing patterns. BioScience 51(8): 625–632.

13. Brown, Lauren. (1979). *Grasses: An identification guide.* New York: Houghton Mifflin, 13.

14. Crosby, Alfred W. (1986). *Ecological imperialism: The biological expansion of Europe, 900–1900.* Cambridge: Cambridge University Press.

15. O'Malley, Therese. (1999). The lawn in early American landscape and garden design. In *The American lawn.* Georges Teysot. New York: Princeton Architectural Press: 65–87.

16. Ibid.

17. Jenkins, Virginia Scott. (1994). *The lawn: A history of an American obsession.* Washington and London: Smithsonian Institute Press.

18. Downing, Andrew Jackson. (1844). *A treatise on the theory and practice of landscape gardening, adapted to North America; with a view to the improvement of country residence., 2nd edition.* New York: Wiley and Putnam, 55–56.

19. Ibid. 80.

20. O'Malley, Therese. (1999). The lawn in early American landscape and garden design. In *The American lawn.* Georges Teysot. New York: Princeton Architectural Press: 65–87. 81.

21. Jenkins, Virginia Scott. (1994). *The lawn: A history of an American obsession.* Washington and London: Smithsonian Institute Press, 24.

22. Downing, Andrew Jackson. (1844). *A treatise on the theory and practice of landscape gardening, adapted to North America; with a view to the improvement of country residences, 2nd edition.* New York: Wiley and Putnam, *viii–ix.*

23. Ibid. *x.*

24. O'Malley, Therese. (1999). The lawn in early American landscape and garden design. In *The American lawn.* Georges Teysot. New York: Princeton Architectural Press: 65–87, 84.

25. Ibid. 85.

26. Gandy, Matthew. (2002). *Concrete and clay: Reworking nature in New York City.* Cambridge, MA: MIT Press, 98.

27. Olmsted, Frederick Law. (1870). *Public parks and the enlargement of towns.* Cambridge, MA: American Social Science Association, 23.

28. Ibid. 23.

29. Fein, Albert. (1972). *Frederick Law Olmsted and the American environmental tradition*. New York: George Brazilier, 35.

30. Spirn, Anne Whiston. (1996). Constructing nature: The legacy of Frederick Law Olmstead. In *Uncommon ground: Rethinking the human place in nature*. William. Cronon. New York: Norton, 91.

31. These key public features were likely influential as well on public aesthetics, though it is questionable, in the case of golf, the degree to which such landscapes were popularly accessible. See Jenkins for the case for the role of recreational sports in accelerating the acceptance of the lawn aesthetic. Jenkins, Virginia Scott. (1994). *The lawn: A history of an American obsession*. Washington and London: Smithsonian Institute Press.

32. Parsons, Samuel. (1891). *Landscape gardening*. New York: G.T. Putnam and Sons, 6.

33. Ibid., 8.

34. Ibid., 3.

35. Jackson, Kenneth T. (1985). *Crabgrass frontier: The suburbanization of the United States*. New York: Oxford University Press.

36. Ibid., 93.

37. Ibid., 135.

38. Ibid., 205; 239.

Chapter 3

1. Brown, Lauren. (1979). *Grasses: An identification guide*. New York: Houghton Mifflin.

2. Kaufmann, John E. (1994). Principles of turfgrass growth and development. In *Integrated pest management for turf and ornamentals*. A. E. Leslie. Boca Raton, FL: Lewis Publishers: 91–97, 91.

3. Hitchcock, A. S. (1971). *Manual of grasses of the United States*. New York: Dover. Emmons, Robert D. (2000). *Turfgrass science and management*. Albany: Delmar.

4. Emmons, Robert D. (2000). *Turfgrass science and management*. Albany: Delmar.

5. Kaufmann, John E. (1994). Principles of turfgrass growth and development. In *Integrated pest management for turf and ornamentals*. A. E. Leslie. Boca Raton, FL: Lewis Publishers: 91–97, 93.

6. Emmons, Robert D. (2000). *Turfgrass science and management*. Albany: Delmar, 34.

7. Dukes, J. S. (2002). Species composition and diversity affect grassland susceptibility and response to invasion. *Ecological Applications* 12(2): 601–617.

8. Brady, N. C. (1984). *The nature and properties of soil*. New York: Macmillan Book Co.

9. Craul, P. J., and C. J. Klein. (1980). Characterization of streetside soils of Syracuse, N.Y. *Metria* 3: 33–41.

10. Patterson, J. C., and D. L. Mader. (1982). Soil compaction. In *Urban forest soils: A reference workbook*. P. J. Craul, USDA Forest Service Consortium for Environmental Forestry Studies, Syracuse: SUNY College of Environmental Science and Forestry. Washington, D.C.

11. Pyšek, Petr. (1995). On the terminology used in plant invasion studies. In *Plant invasions: General aspects and special problems*. P. Pyšek, K. Prach, M. Rejmánek, and M. Wade. Amsterdam: SPB Academic Publishing: 71–81.

12. Baker, H. G. (1974). The evolution of weeds. *Annual Review of Ecological Systems* 5: 1–24.

13. Baker, H. G. (1965). Characteristics and modes of evolution of weeds. In *The genetics of colonizing species*. H. G. Baker, and G. L. Stebbins. New York: Academic Press: 147–169.

14. Emmons, Robert D. (2000). *Turfgrass science and management*. Albany: Delmar.

15. Roy, J. (1990). In search of the characteristics of plant invaders. In *Biological invasions in Europe and the Mediterranean basin*. A. J. di Castri, A. J. Hansen, and Debushe. Dordecht (Netherlands): Kluwer.

16. Lowney, K. S., and J. Best. (1998). Floral entrepreneurs: Kudzu as agricultural solution and ecological problem. *Sociological Spectrum* 18(1): 93–114.

17. Richmond, Douglas S., Parwinder S. Grewal, and John Cardina. (2004). Billbug infestations increase weed invasions in lawns. Wooster, OH: Ohio State University - Urban Landscape Ecology Program (ULEP): 8–9. This is an extension paper published by ULEP in WOOSTER.

Chapter 4

1. Jenkins, Virginia Scott. (1994). *The lawn: A history of an American obsession*. Washington and London: Smithsonian Institute Press, 183.

2. Barron, Leonard. (1923). *Lawn making: Together with the proper keeping of putting greens*. New York: Doubleday, Page and Co., 77.

3. Ibid., 78.

4. Sprague, Howard B. (1940). *Better lawns for homes and parks*. New York: McGraw Hill Book Company, 167.

5. Marco, Gino J., Robert M. Hollingsworth, and William Durham, eds. (1987). *Silent Spring revisited*. Washington D. C.: American Chemical Society, 162.

6. Shepard, H. H. (1939). *The chemistry and toxicology of insecticides*. Minneapolis: Burgess Shepard, H. H. (1951). *The chemistry and action of insecticides*. New York: McGraw-Hill.

7. Russell, Edmund. (2001). *War and nature: Fighting humans and insects with chemicals from World War I to Silent Spring*. Cambridge: Cambridge University Press.

8. Mitchell, Timothy. (2002). *Rule of experts: Egypt, techno-Politics, modernity*. Berkeley: University of California Press, 22.

9. Leary, James C., William I. Fishbein, and Lawrence C. Salter. (1946). *DDT and the insect problem*. New York: McGraw-Hill Book Company, 39.

10. Date from Dunlap, Thomas R. (1981). *DDT: Scientists, citizens, and public policy*. Princeton: Princeton University Press, 253–254.

11. Kohn, Gustave K. (1987). Agriculture, pesticides, and the American chemical industry. In *Silent Spring revisited*. G. J. Marco, R. M. Hollingworth and W. Durham. Washington D. C.: American Chemical Society, 164.

12. Leary, James C., William I. Fishbein, and Lawrence C. Salter. (1946). *DDT and the insect problem*. New York: McGraw-Hill Book Company, 1.

13. Dawson, R. B. (1954). *Practical lawn craft*. London: Crosby Lockwood and Son.

14. Turusov, V., V. Rakitsky, and L. Tomatis. (2002). Dichlorodiphenyltrichloroethane (DDT): Ubiquity, persistence, and risks. *Environmental Health Perspectives* 110(2): 125–128, 125.

15. Schery, Robert. (1961). *The lawn book*. New York: Macmillan Company, 169.

16. Barron, Leonard. (1923). *Lawn making: Together with the proper keeping of putting greens*. New York: Doubleday, Page and Co.
Dickinson L. S. Lawrence S. (1931). *The lawn: The culture of turf in park, golfing, and home areas*. New York: Orange Judd Publishing.

17. Sprague, Howard B. (1940). *Better lawns for homes and parks*. New York: McGraw Hill Book Company.

18. Turusov, V., V. Rakitsky, and L. Tomatis (2002). Dichlorodiphenyltrichloroethane (DDT): Ubiquity, persistence, and risks. *Environmental Health Perspectives* 110(2): 125–128, 125.

19. Carson, Rachel. (1962). *Silent spring*. New York: Houghton Mifflin, 80.

20. United States Environmental Protection Agency. (1975). *DDT: A review of scientific and economic aspects of the decision to ban its use as a pesticide.* Washington D.C.: United States Environmental Protection Agency.

21. His 1961 edition was called *The Lawn Book.* Schery, Robert. (1961). *The lawn book.* New York: Macmillan Company.

22. Schery, Robert W. (1973). *A perfect lawn: The easy way.* New York: MacMillan, 14.

23. Land was converted from nondeveloped to developed coverage at an average rate of 22,000 ha/year in the state of Ohio between 1982 and 1997, and 675,000 ha/year in the United States over the same period. With the proportion of lawn within total municipal area estimated at approximately 23%, over the same period, there were slightly larger proportions of urban growth given over to turfgrass every year. This change is especially acute in the states with the most rapid urban land cover growth, including Florida, Georgia, Texas, and California. Natural Resources Conservation Service (2000). *Summary report: 1997 national resources inventory (revised December 2000).* Washington D.C.: United States Department of Agriculture.

24. Per-hectare calculations are based on total usage figures supplied by the EPA for 1995 and land coverage from the NRCS Resource Inventory for 1997 United States Environmental Protection Agency. (1996). *Pesticides industry sales and usage report* (http://www.epa.gov/oppbead1/pestsales/95pestsales/market_estimates1995.pdf) (Last accessed February, 2007) Natural Resources Conservation Service. (2000). *Summary report: 1997 national resources inventory (revised December 2000).* Washington D.C.: United States Department of Agriculture. Lawns were calculated at 23% of developed land total based on air photography and modeling results (see Appendix B). Environmental Protection Agency residential figures include those for lawn and garden, but survey figures from the National Gardening Foundation suggest that a vast majority of active ingredients are used on lawns. National Gardening Association (2000). *National gardening survey.* Burlington, VT: National Gardening Association.

25. National trends tend toward the decline of land in cultivation. Roughly 17 million hectares were removed from cultivation between 1982 and 1997. This has clearly led to net decreases in chemical inputs; herbicide usage has decreased by almost 20 million kilograms (kg) of active ingredients, and total chemical use has likely decreased by more than 34 million kg.

26. Emmons, Robert D. (2000). *Turfgrass science and management.* Albany: Delmar.

27. Briggs, Shirley A., and Rachel Carson Council Staff. (1992). *Basic guide to pesticides: Their characteristics and hazards.* Boca Raton, FL: CRC Press.

28. Extension Toxicology Network. (2004). Ecotoxnet (http://extoxnet.orst.edu/pips/ghindex.html) (Last accessed February, 2007)

29. Kidd, H., and D. R. James, eds. (1991). *The agrochemicals handbook.* Cambridge, UK: Royal Society of Chemistry Information Services - Weed Science Society of America. (1994). *Herbicide handbook.* Champaign, IL: Weed Science Society of America.

30. Cox, Caroline. (1999). 2,4-D: Ecological effects. *Journal of Pesticide Reform* 19(3): 14–19.

31. de Duffard, A. M., C. Orta, and R. Duffard. (1990). Behavioral changes in rats fed a diet containing 2,4-dichlorophenoacetic butyl ester. *Neurotoxicology* 11(4): 563–572.

32. Ibrahim, M. A., G. G. Bond, T. A. Burke, et al. (1991). Weight of Evidence on the Human Carcinogenicity of 2,4-D. *Environmental Health Perspectives* 96: 213–222.

33. The original study is Hayes, H. M. (1991). Case-control study of canine malignant lymphoma: positive association with dog-owner's use of 2,4-dichlorophenoxyacetic acid herbicides. *Journal of the National Cancer Institute* 83(17): 1226–1231. Responses from the industry are summarized in Welterlen, Mark S. (2000). 2,4-D and canine-cancer link debunked. *Grounds Maintenance* 35(4): 8. More recent findings can be found in Glickman, L. T., M. Raghavan, D. W. Knapp, P. L. Bonney, and M. H. Dawson. (2004). Herbicide exposure

and the risk of transitional cell carcinoma of the urinary bladder in Scottish Terriers. *Journal of the American Veterinary Medical Association* 224(8): 1290–1297.

34. Hamilton, Martha A. (1997). Monsanto's green thumb; From agricultural roots, firm has blossomed–and ao has a spinoff. *Washington Post*: H2.

35. Weed Science Society of America. (1994). *Herbicide handbook*. Champaign, IL: Weed Science Society of America. United States Environmental Protection Agency. (1997). Glyphosate: Pesticide tolerances: *Federal Register*: April 11, 1997 (Volume 62, Number 70).

36. Briggs, Shirley A., and Rachel Carson Council Staff (1992). *Basic guide to pesticides: their characteristics and hazards*. Boca Raton, FL: CRC Press.

37. Callimachi, Rukmini. (2004). Scotts turf viewed with caution. *Columbus Dispatch*. Columbus: C1–C2. Kintisch, Eli. (2004). Biotechnology offers new grass for golf courses: Monsanto is partner in product that worries federal scientists. *St. Louis Post-Dispatch*: A1.

38. Rissler, Jane, and Margaret Mellon (1996). *The ecological risks of engineered Crops*. Cambridge, MA: The MIT Press.

39. Emmons, Robert D. (2000). *Turfgrass science and management*. Albany: Delmar.

40. Extension Toxicology Network (2004). Ecotoxnet (http://extoxnet.orst.edu/pips/ghindex.html) (Last accessed February, 2007)

41. Briggs, Shirley A., and Rachel Carson Council Staff (1992). *Basic guide to pesticides: Their characteristics and hazards*. Boca Raton, FL: CRC Press.

42. Russell, Edmund. (2001). *War and nature: Fighting humans and insects with chemicals from World War I to Silent Spring*. Cambridge: Cambridge University Press. 86–87.

43. Ibid.

44. Extension Toxicology Network (2004). Ecotoxnet (http://extoxnet.orst.edu/pips/ghindex.html) Last accessed February, 2007.

45. Lewis, R. G., R. C. Fortmann, and D. E. Camann (1994). Evaluation of Methods for Monitoring the Potential Exposure of Small Children to Pesticides in the Residential Environment. *Archives of Environmental Contamination and Toxicology* 26(1): 37–46. Quackenboss, J. J. et al. (2000). Design strategy for assessing multi-pathway exposure for children: the Minnesota Children's Pesticide Exposure Study (MNCPES). *Journal of Exposure Analysis and Environmental Epidemiology* 10(2): 145–158. Clayton, C. A., E. D. Pellizzari, et al. (2003). Distributions, associations, and partial aggregate exposure of pesticides and polynuclear aromatic hydrocarbons in the Minnesota Children's Pesticide Exposure Study (MNCPES). *Journal of Exposure Analysis and Environmental Epidemiology* 13(2): 100–111.

46. Barr, Dana B., et al. (2004). Concentrations of dialkyl phosphate metabolites of organophosphorus pesticides in the U.S. population. *Environmental Health Perspectives* 112(2): 186–200. Greenlee, A. R., T. M. Ellis, and R. L. Berg. (2004). Low-dose agrochemicals and lawn-care pesticides induce developmental toxicity in murine preimplantation embryos. *Environmental Health Perspectives* 112(6): 703–709.

47. Blondell, Jerome. (1999). Review of Poison Control Center data for residential exposures to organophosphatepesticides, 1993–1996. U.S. EPA Memorandum.

48. Russell, Edmund. (2001). *War and nature: Fighting humans and insects with chemicals from World War I to Silent Spring*. Cambridge: Cambridge University Press. Pages 198–199.

49. Extension Toxicology Network. (2004). Ecotoxnet (http://extoxnet.orst.edu/pips/ghindex.html). (Last accessed February, 2007)

50. Smalley, H. E., J. M. Curtis, and F. L. Earl. (1968). Teratogenic action of carbaryl in Beagle dogs. *Toxicological Applications in Pharmacology* 13: 392–403. Smalley, H. E., P. J. O'Hara, C. H. Bridges, and R. D. Radeleff. (1969). The effects of chronic carbaryl administration on the neuromuscular system of swine. *Toxicological Applications in Pharmacology* 14: 490–494. United States Department of Health Education and Welfare. (1969). Report of the

secretary's commission on pesticides and their relationship to environmental health. Washington D.C.: United States Department of Health Education and Welfare.

51. Anger, W. K. (1981). Effects of carbaryl on variable interval response rates in rats. *Neurobehavioral Toxicology* 2: 21–24. Bear, D. M. (1986). Aggression in cat and human precipitated by a cholinesterase inhibitor. *Psychosomatics* 27: 535–536. Branch, R. A. (1986). Is carbaryl as safe as its reputation? Does it have a potential for causing chronic neurotoxicity in humans? *American Journal of Medicine* 80: 659–664.

52. Extension Toxicology Network (2004). Ecotoxnet (http://extoxnet.orst.edu/pips/ghindex.html). (Last accessed February, 2007)

53. Hummel, Norman W. (1996). *Lawn fertilization.*, Cornell Cooperative Extension.

54. Emmons, Robert D. (2000). *Turfgrass science and management*. Albany, Delmar.

55. Proportion from United States International Trade Commission (1998). Industry and trade summary–fertilizers. Raw totals of national consumption from The Fertilizer Institute, http://www.tfi.org/factsandstats/statistics.cfm. (Last accessed February, 2007)

56. Osmond, D. L., and D. H. Hardy. (2004). Characterization of turf practices in five North Carolina communities. *Journal of Environmental Quality* 33(2): 565–575.

57. Muller, Franz. (2000). *Agrochemicals: Composition, production, toxicology, applications*. Weinheim: Wiley-VCH.

58. Turner, R. E., and N. N. Rabalais. (2003). Linking landscape and water quality in the Mississippi river basin for 200 years. *Bioscience* 53(6): 563–572. page 563.

59. Watson, J., and P. Baker. (1990). *Pesticide transport through soils*. Tucson, Arizona Cooperative Extension, College of Agriculture, University of Arizona.

60. Figures from Smith, R. A., R. B. Alexander, and K. J. Lanfear. (1996). *United States Geological Survey water supply paper no. 2400–Stream water quality in the coterminous United States: Status and trends of selected indicators during the 1980s*, Reston, VA: United States Geological Survey.

61. Goodman, Peter S. (1998). Greener grass vs. cleaner water; Effort to cure bay does little about doctoring lawns. *The Washington Post*: B01.

62. Emmons, Robert D. (2000). *Turfgrass science and management*. Albany: Delmar.

63. King, K. W., and J. C. Balogh. (2001). Water quality impacts associated with converting farmland and forests to turfgrass. *Transactions of the American Society of Agricultural Engineers* 44(3): 569–576.

64. Emmons, Robert D. (2000). *Turfgrass science and management*. Albany: Delmar. 259.

65. Busey, P., T. K. Broschat, and D. L. Johnston. (2003). Injury to landscape and vegetable plants by volatile turf herbicides. *Horttechnology* 13(4): 650–652.

66. Bernard, C. E., et al. (2001). Environmental residues and biomonitoring estimates of human insecticide exposure from treated residential turf. *Archives of Environmental Contamination and Toxicology* 41(2): 237–240.

67. Leonas, K. K., and X. K. Yu. (1992). Deposition patterns on garments during application of lawn and garden chemicals–A comparison of six equipment types. *Archives of Environmental Contamination and Toxicology* 23(2): 230–234.

68. Lewis, R. G., et al.(1991). Preliminary results of the EPA House Dust Infant Pesticides Exposure Study (HIPES). *Abstracts of the Papers of the American Chemical Society* 201(89-Agro Part 1, April 14). Lewis, R. G., R. C. Fortmann, and D. E. Camann. (1994). Evaluation of methods for monitoring the potential exposure of small children to pesticides in the residential environment." *Archives of Environmental Contamination and Toxicology* 26(1): 37–46. Nishioka, Marcia, G., Marielle C. Brinkman, and Hazel M. Burkholder. (1996). *Evaluation and selection of analytical methods for lawn-applied pesticides*. Research Triangle Park, NC: US Environmental Protection Agency, Research and Development. Nishioka, M. G., et al. (1996). Measuring transport of lawn-applied herbicide acids from turf to home: Correlation of

dislodgeable 2,4-D tuff residues with carpet dust and carpet surface residues. *Environmental Science and Technology* 30(11): 3313–3320. Nishioka, Marcia, et al. (1999). *Transport of lawn-applied 2,4-D from turf to home: Assessing the relative importance of transport mechanisms and exposure pathways.* Research Triangle Park (NC), National Exposure Research Laboratory. Nishioka, Marcia G., et al. (1999). Distribution of 2,4-dichlorophenoxyacetic acid in floor dust throughout homes following homeowner and commercial applications: Quantitative effects on children, pets, and shoes. *Environmental Science and Technology* 33(9): 1359–1365.

69. Zartarian, V. G., et al. (2000). A modeling framework for estimating children's residential exposure and dose to chlorpyrifos via dermal residue contact and nondietary ingestion. *Environmental Health Perspectives* 108(6): 505–514.

70. Leiss, J. K., and D. A. Savitz. (1995). Home pesticide use and childhood-cancer: A case control study. *American Journal of Public Health* 85(2): 249–252. Zahm, Sheila H., and Mary H. Ward. (1998). Pesticides and childhood cancer. *Environmental Health Perspectives* 106(Suppl. 3): 893–908.

71. Tinker, J. R. (1991). An analysis of nitrate-nitrogen in ground-water beneath unsewered subdivisions. *Groundwater Monitoring and Remediation* 11(1): 141–150.

72. King, K. W., et al. (2001). Impact of a turfgrass system on nutrient loadings to surface water. *Journal of the American Water Resources Association* 37(3): 629–640.

73. Iskander, F. Y. (1994). Measurements of 27 elements in garden and lawn fertilizers using instrumental neutron-activation. *Journal of Radioanalytical and Nuclear Chemistry-Articles* 180(1): 25–28.

74. Potter, D. A. (1993). Pesticide and fertilizer effects on beneficial invertebrates and consequences for thatch degradation and pest outbreaks in turfgrass. *ACS Symposium Series* 522: 331–343.

75. Adapted from Muller, Franz. (2000). *Agrochemicals: Composition, production, toxicology, applications.* Weinheim, Wiley-VCH. 498.

76. Potter, D. A. (1993). Pesticide and fertilizer effects on beneficial invertebrates and consequences for thatch degradation and pest outbreaks in turfgrass. *ACS Symposium Series* 522: 331–343.

77. Grewal, P. S., R. U. Euhlers, and D. Shapiro-Ilan, eds. (2005).*Nematodes as biocontrol agents.* Wallingford, UK: CABI Publishing.

78. Schery, Robert. (1961). *The lawn book.* New York: Macmillan Company. 173.

79. Nelson, B. K., David L. Conover, and W. Gregory Lotz. (1994). Combined chemical, physical hazards make exposure harder to calculate." *Occupational Safety and Health* 63(6): 52–54.

80. Briggs, Shirley A., and Rachel Carson Council Staff. (1992). *Basic guide to pesticides: Their characteristics and hazards.* Boca Raton, FL: CRC Press. 4.

81. Ibid. 16.

82. Priest, M. W., D. J. Williams, and H. A. Bridgman. (2000). Emissions from in-use lawn-mowers in Australia. *Atmospheric Environment* 34(4): 657–664. Sawyer, R. F., R. A. Harley, S. H. Cadle, J. M. Norbeck, R. Slott, and H. A. Bravo. (2000). Mobile sources critical review: 1998 NARSTO assessment. *Atmospheric Environment* 34(12–14): 2161–2181. Christensen, A., R. Westerholm, and J. Almen. (2001). Measurement of regulated and unregulated exhaust emissions from a lawn mower with and without an oxidizing catalyst: A comparison of two fuels. *Environmental Science and Technology* 35(11): 2166–2170.

83. Marzluff, J. M., and K. Ewing. (2001). Restoration of fragmented landscapes for the conservation of birds: A general framework and specific recommendations for urbanizing landscapes. *Restoration Ecology* 9(3): 280–292.

84. Maddock, T. A. (2004). Fragmenting regimes: how water quality regulation is changing political-economic landscapes. *Geoforum* 35(2): 217–230.

85. Goodman, Peter S. (1998). Greener grass vs. cleaner water; Effort to cure bay does little about doctoring lawns. *The Washington Post*: B01.

86. Colt, J. S., J. Lubin, et al. (2004). Comparison of pesticide levels in carpet dust and self-reported pest treatment practices in four US sites. *Journal of Exposure Analysis and Environmental Epidemiology* 14(1): 74–83.

Chapter 5

1. Lewis, R. G., et al. (1991). Preliminary results of the EPA House Dust Infant Pesticides Exposure Study (HIPES). *Abstracts of the Papers of the American Chemical Society* 201(89-Agro Part 1, April 14).

2. Anon. (1999). EPA chlorpyrifos assessment draws criticism. *Pest Control Technology* 27(12).

3. Gots, Ronald E. (1997). EPA must avoid "junk science" justification. *The Tampa Tribune*: 8.

4. And indeed much was learned about methodologies for assessing exposure risks. The scrutiny of several important studies and techniques over this period led to an improved understanding of how to measure and predict pesticide exposure and how not to. See Lewis, R. G., R. C. Fortmann, and D. E. Camann. (1994). Evaluation of methods for monitoring the potential exposure of small children to pesticides in the residential environment. *Archives of Environmental Contamination and Toxicology* 26(1): 37–46 Quackenboss, J. J.,et al. (2000). Design strategy for assessing multi-pathway exposure for children: the Minnesota Children's Pesticide Exposure Study (MNCPES). *Journal of Exposure Analysis and Environmental Epidemiology* 10(2): 145–158. Sexton, K., et al. (2003). Predicting children's short-term exposure to pesticides: Results of a questionnaire screening approach. *Environmental Health Perspectives* 111(1): 123–128.

5. *Lawn & Landscape Magazine (2001). Canadian municipalities allowed to restrict use of pesticides.* (http://www.lawnandlandscape.com/news/news.asp?ID=595&SubCatID= 108&CatID=20). (Last accessed February, 2007)

6. Carmichael, Amy. (2002). Chemical industry fighting lawn pesticide bans with increasing success. *Canadian Press Newswire*, May 26.

7. Stephens, R. J. (1982). *Theory and practice of weed control*. London: The Macmillan Press Ltd.

8. Green, M. B., G. S. Hartley, and T. F. West. (1987). *Chemicals for crop improvement and pest management,* Third edition. Oxford: Pergamon Press.

9. Young, Ronald D., D. G. Westfall, and Gary W. Colliver. (1985). production, marketing, and use of phosphorous fertilizers. In *Fertilizer technology and use*, Third Edition. O. P. Englestad. Madison, WI: Soil Science Society of America.

10. Green, M. B., G. S. Hartley, and T. F. West. (1987). *Chemicals for crop improvement and pest management,* Third edition. Oxford: Pergamon Press.

11. United States Department of Commerce. (1985). *A competitive assessment of the U.S. herbicide industry.* Washington, D.C.: International Trade Administration, U.S. Department of Commerce.

12. British Medical Association. (1992). *The British Medical Association guide to pesticides, chemicals, and health.* London: Edward Arnold, a division of Hodder and Stoughton.

13. Eveleth, William T., ed. (1990). *Kline guide to the U.S. vhemical industry*, Fifth edition. Fairfield, NJ: Kline and Company, Inc. Zimdahl, Robert L. (1999). *Fundamentals of weed science,* Second edition. San Diego: Academic Press.

14. Reich, Marc S. (2000). Seeing green. *Chemical and Engineering News*. April 10: 23–27.

15. British Medical Association. (1992). *The British Medical Association guide to pesticides, chemicals, and health.* London: Edward Arnold, a division of Hodder and Stoughton.

16. United States Department of Commerce. (1985). *A competitive assessment of the U.S. herbicide industry.* Washington, D.C.: International Trade Administration, U.S. Department of Commerce.

17. British Medical Association. (1992). *The British Medical Association guide to pesticides, chemicals, and health.* London: Edward Arnold, a division of Hodder and Stoughton.

18. Zimdahl, Robert L. (1999). *Fundamentals of weed science,* Second edition. San Diego: Academic Press. Rao, V.S. (2000). *Principles of weed science,* Second edition. Enfield, NH: Science Publishers, Inc.

19. Reich, Marc S. (2000). Seeing green. *Chemical and Engineering News.* April 10: 23–27.

20. Staggers, D. T. (1976). The search for new herbicides. *Herbicides: Physiology, biochemistry, ecology,* Second edition, Volume II. L. J. Audus. London: Academic Press.

21. Anderson, Wood Powell. (1996). *Weed science: principles and applications.* St. Paul MN: West Publishing Company.

22. Hess, Glenn. (2000). Pesticide manufacturers are unhappy with EPA's crackdown on chlorpyrifos. *Chemical Market Reporter.* 257: 1,13.

23. Hanson, David J. (1998). Pesticide law off to a rough start. *Chemical and Engineering News:* September 28: 20–22. Thayer, Ann M. (1999). Transforming agriculture. *Chemical and Engineering News* April 19: 21–35.

24. Hess, Glenn. (2000). Pesticide manufacturers are unhappy with EPA's crackdown on chlorpyrifos. *Chemical Market Reporter.* 257: 1,13.

25. Whitten, Jamie L. (1966). *That we may live.* Princeton, NJ,:Van Nostrand Company, Inc.

26. British Medical Association. (1992). *The British Medical Association guide to pesticides, chemicals, and health.* London: Edward Arnold, a division of Hodder and Stoughton.

27. United States Department of Commerce. (1985). *A competitive assessment of the U.S. herbicide industry.* Washington, D.C.: International Trade Administration, U.S. Department of Commerce.

28. The fertilizer industry differs somewhat from the pesticide industry, but the value of agricultural shipments in the industry worldwide is also decreasing, presenting similar challenges for sales. Fertilizer makers are also affected by agricultural market saturation and rising raw material costs. Gale Group. (2001). *Nitrogenous fertilizers,* Gale Business Resources.

29. Biotechnological applications are one area of opportunity for agricultural chemical makers, although with its own drawbacks. Because biotechnology research is expensive, smaller firms are usually taken over by larger, better-capitalized firms, hastening the concentration of the industry. In addition, the expansion of genetic modification strategies has increased competition among nonenhanced products, as all other manufacturers clamor for the remaining portion of the market, increasing the ferocity with which nonbiotechnological manufacturers must compete. Thayer, Ann M. (1999). Transforming agriculture. *Chemical and Engineering News* April 19: 21–35.

30. Zimdahl, Robert L. (1999). *Fundamentals of weed science,* Second edition. San Diego: Academic Press.

31. The Scotts Company. (2001). The Scotts Company annual report pursuant to Section 13 or Section 15(D) of the Securities Exchange Act of 1934 for the Fiscal Year Ended September 30, 2000, Marysville (OH). The Scotts Company (2001).The Scotts Company Quarterly Report Pursuant to Section 13 or Section 15(D) of the Securities Exchange Act of 1934 for the Quarterly Period Ending March 31, 2001, Marysville (OH).

32. Agrow Reports. (2000). *World non-agricultural pesticide markets,* London: PJB publications.

33. New Jersey Department of Environmental Protection. (2003). Final Report of the New Jersey comparative risk project, Draft report. Trenton, NJ.

34. Richmond, Douglas S., et al. (2004). A survey of home lawns: The story so far. In *Urban Landscape Ecology Program (ULEP): Research Update 2004.* P. S. Grewal. Wooster, OH: The Ohio State University Ohio Agricultural Research and Development Center: 4–7.

35. Churchville, Victoria. (1985). Greening of America's lawns elicits warnings on chemicals; Groups worry about health risks. *The Washington Post*: April 21, A1.

36. Dougherty, P. H. (1983). Chemlawn Campaign Spreading. *New York Times*. New York: Advertising (D): 21.

37. American Bar Association. (1988). Lawn care firms: Let us spray. *American Bar Association Journal* 74: 20–21.

38. Meier, Barry. (1990). Lawn care concern says it will limit safety claims. *New York Times*. New York: June 30, 30.

39. National Association of Attorneys General. (1993). Orkin; Unsubstantiated safety claims for pesticides. *National Association of Attorneys General, Consumer Protection Report*: 32. Washington, D.C.: NAAG.

40. Williams, Fred O. (1999). TrueGreen to pay $600,000 fine for violating pesticide laws. *Buffalo News*. Buffalo, NY, July 27: 6D.

41. Pennsylvania Law Journal. (1992). Cancer suit leveled against lawn service; Plaintiff claims chemicals caused deadly foot cancer. *Pennsylvania Law Journal*: 11.

42. National Association of Attorneys General. (2003). Pennsylvania settles with lawn care company. *National Association of Attorneys General, Consumer Protection Report*: 9. Washington, D.C.: NAAG.

43. Dunn, Kathleen A., et al. (1998). Teens at work: A statewide study of jobs, hazards, and injuries. *Journal of Adolescent Health* 22: 9–25.

44. Bambarger, Brad. (1987). O. M. Scott and Sons. *Lawn and Garden Marketing* October: 24. Cook, Adrienne. (1990). Digging for dollars. *American Demographics*July: 40–41.

45. Williams, Brian. (1997). Storms past, Scotts finds seeds of change yield a blooming success. *The Columbus Dispatch*. Columbus, OH: July 27: 1H, 2H.

46. Williams, Brian. (1997). Storms past, Scotts finds seeds of change yield a blooming success. *The Columbus Dispatch*. Columbus, OH: 1H, 2H.

47. Bambarger, Brad. (1987). "O. M. Scott and Sons." *Lawn and Garden Marketing* October: 24.

48. Scotts Company. (2002). *The Scotts company: 2001 summary annual report and 2001 financial statements and other information.* Marysville, OH: The Scotts Company.

49. The Scotts Company. (2001). The Scotts Company annual report pursuant to Section 13 or Section 15(D) of the Securities Exchange Act of 1934 for the Fiscal Year Ended September 30, 2000, Marysville (OH).The Scotts Company (2001).The Scotts Company quarterly report pursuant to Section 13 or Section 15(D) of the Securities Exchange Act of 1934 for the Quarterly Period Ending March 31, 2001, Marysville (OH).

50. Scotts Company. (2004). Press Release: Scotts named 'partner of the year' by home depot: Award presented for commitment to growing the lawn and garden category, September 23. Marysville (OH): Scotts Co.

51. Baker, George P., and Karen Wruck (1991). Lessons from a middle market LBO: The case of O.M. Scott. *The Continental Bank Journal of Applied Corporate Finance*. 4(1): 46–58. Chemical Week. (1998). Monsanto completes pesticide sales; more divestments to come. *Chemical Week*. 160: 13.

52. Cleveland Plain Dealer. (2000). At Scotts they call it pull. *Cleveland Plain Dealer*. Cleveland, OH, June 23: 44.

53. The Scotts Company. (2001). The Scotts Company annual report pursuant to Section 13 or Section 15(D) of the Securities Exchange Act of 1934 for the Fiscal Year Ended

September 30, 2000, Marysville (OH).The Scotts Company (2001).The Scotts Company quarterly report pursuant to Section 13 or Section 15(D) of the Securities Exchange Act of 1934 for the Quarterly Period Ending March 31, 2001, Marysville (OH).

54. United States Department of Commerce. (1985). A competitive assessment of the U.S. herbicide industry. Washington, D.C.: International Trade Administration, U.S. Department of Commerce.

55. Scotts Company. (2002). *The Scotts Company: 2001 summary annual report and 2001 financial statements and other information.* Marysville, OH: The Scotts Company.

56. Ibid.

57. The Scotts Company. (2001). The Scotts Company annual report pursuant to Section 13 or Section 15(D) of the Securities Exchange Act of 1934 for the Fiscal Year Ended September 30, 2000, Marysville (OH).The Scotts Company (2001).The Scotts Company quarterly report pursuant to Section 13 or Section 15(D) of the Securities Exchange Act of 1934 for the Quarterly Period Ending March 31, 2001, Marysville (OH).

58. In addition, the harvesting of peat for potting soils is subject to environmental regulation in both the United States and Britain. The U.S. Army Corps of Engineers is currently suing Scotts Company over surface water contamination from their peat-harvesting activities at a New Jersey plant, and the company only recently reached an agreement with British environmental officials to close down peat harvesting at several sensitive sites in the United Kingdom. Schoon, N. (1992). Peat deal angers campaigners. The Independent. London, January 31: HOME NEWS PAGE; Page 6. The Scotts Company. (2001). The Scotts Company annual report pursuant to Section 13 or Section 15(D) of the Securities Exchange Act of 1934 for the Fiscal Year Ended September 30, 2000, Marysville (OH).The Scotts Company (2001).The Scotts Company quarterly report pursuant to Section 13 or Section 15(D) of the Securities Exchange Act of 1934 for the Quarterly Period Ending March 31, 2001, Marysville (OH).

59. Scotts Company. (2002). *The Scotts Company: 2001 summary annual report and 2001 financial statements and other information.* Marysville, OH: The Scotts Company. (2001). The Scotts Company annual report pursuant to Section 13 or Section 15(D) of the Securities Exchange Act of 1934 for the Fiscal Year Ended September 30, 2000, Marysville (OH).

60. Cleveland Plain Dealer. (2000). At Scotts they call it pull. *Cleveland Plain Dealer.* Cleveland, OH, June 23: 44.

61. Chemical Week. (1998). Monsanto completes pesticide sales; more divestments to come. *Chemical Week.* 160: 13.

62. The Scotts Company. (2001). The Scotts Company annual report pursuant to Section 13 or Section 15(D) of the Securities Exchange Act of 1934 for the Fiscal Year Ended September 30, 2000, Marysville (OH).The Scotts Company (2001). The Scotts Company quarterly report pursuant to Section 13 or Section 15(D) of the Securities Exchange Act of 1934 for the Quarterly Period Ending March 31, 2001, Marysville (OH).

63. United States Securities and Exchange Commission. (2001). The Scotts Company Annual Report, United States Securities and Exchange Commission (2001). The Scotts Company Quarterly Report, U.S. Securities and Exchange Commission, Scotts Company (2002). *The Scotts Company: 2001 summary annual report and 2001 financial statements and other information.* Marysville, OH: The Scotts Company.

64. The Scotts Company. (2001). The Scotts Company annual report pursuant to Section 13 or Section 15(D) of the Securities Exchange Act of 1934 for the Fiscal Year Ended September 30, 2000, Marysville (OH). The Scotts Company (2001).The Scotts Company quarterly report pursuant to Section 13 or Section 15(D) of the Securities Exchange Act of 1934 for the Quarterly Period Ending March 31, 2001, Marysville (OH).

65. Engel, J. F., W. N. Harnish, and C. A. Staetz. (1990). Challenges: The industrial viewpoint. In *Safer insecticides: Development and use.* E. Hodgson and R. J. Kuhr. New York: Marcel Dekker.

66. Baker, George P., and Karen Wruck. (1991). Lessons from a middle market LBO: The case of O. M. Scott. *The Continental Bank Journal of Applied Corporate Finance*. 4(1): 46–58. Williams, Brian. (1997). Storms past, Scotts finds seeds of change yield a blooming success. *The Columbus Dispatch*. Columbus, OH: 1H, 2H.

67. Ibid.

68. Journal of Business Strategy. (1989). Why I bought the company. *Journal of Business Strategy*. 10: 4–8.

69. Williams, Brian. (1997). Storms past, Scotts finds seeds of change yield a blooming success. *The Columbus Dispatch*. Columbus, OH July 27: 1H, 2H Cleveland Plain Dealer. (2000). At Scotts they call it pull. *Cleveland Plain Dealer*. Cleveland, OH, June 23: 44.

70. Journal of Business Strategy. (1989). Why I bought the company. *Journal of Business Strategy*. 10: 4–8. Cleveland Plain Dealer. (2000). At Scotts they call it pull. *Cleveland Plain Dealer*. Cleveland, OH:, June 23: 44 Robbins, P., and J. Sharp. (2003). Producing and consuming chemicals: The moral economy of the American lawn. *Economic Geography* 79(4): 425–451.

71. Journal of Business Strategy. (1989). Why I bought the company. *Journal of Business Strategy*. 10: 8.

72. Hagedorn, James. (2001). Priorities for the future: from James Hagedorn, President and Chief Executive Officer of The Scotts Company, Marysville (OH): The Scotts Company. The Scotts Company. (2001). The Scotts Company annual report pursuant to Section 13 or Section 15(D) of the Securities Exchange Act of 1934 for the Fiscal Year Ended September 30, 2000, Marysville (OH).

73. Hagedorn, James. (2001). Priorities for the future: from James Hagedorn, President and Chief Executive Officer of The Scotts Company, Marysville, OH: The Scotts Company.

74. Jaffe, Thomas. (1998). Lean green machine. *Forbes*. 162: 90. Scotts Company. (2000). Business segments overview: North American consumer (www.smgnyse.com/html/consumerlawn.cfm). (Last accessed July, 2001)

75. Reich, Marc S. (2000). Seeing green. *Chemical and Engineering News*. April 10: 23–27.

76. Jaffe, Thomas. (1998). Lean green machine. *Forbes*. 162: 90. Scotts Company. (2002). *The Scotts company: 2001 summary annual report and 2001 financial statements and other information*. Marysville, OH: The Scotts Company.

77. National Gardening Association. (2000). *National gardening survey*. Burlington, VT: National Gardening Association.

78. Mann, Susan, and James Dickenson. (1978). Obstacles to the development of a capitalist agriculture. *Journal of Peasant Studies* 5(4): 466–81.

79. Henderson, George. (1999). *California and the fictions of capital*. New York: Oxford University Press. 29.

Chapter 6

1. National Gardening Association. (2000). *National gardening survey*. Burlington, VT: National Gardening Association.

2. All individual and place names have been changed.

3. See especially Beck, Ulrich. (1992). *Risk society: towards a new modernity*. London: Sage Publications.

4. Linder, Staffan B. (1970). *The harried leisure class*. New York: Columbia University Press. Templeton, Scott R., David Zilbermand, and Seung Jick Yoo (1998). An economic perspective on outdoor residential pesticide use. *Policy Analysis* 32(17): 416A–423A.

5. Olson, M. (1971). *The logic of collective action: Public goods and the theory of groups*. Cambridge, MA: Harvard University Press. Weiner, J. L., and T. A. Doescher. (1991). A framework for promoting cooperation. *Journal of Marketing* 55: 38–47.

6. Beck, Ulrich. (1999). *World risk society*. Oxford: Blackwell Publishers. 9.

7. O'Connor, James. (1996). The Second Contradiction of Capitalism. In T. Benton *The Greening of Marxism*, 197–221. New York: Guilford Press.

Chapter 7

1. Crumbley, Ray, and Robert Albrecht. (2000). It's mowing versus growing in area's turf war grass-height laws. *Columbus Dispatch*. Columbus, OH: 1B.

2. Rappaport, Brett. (1993). As natural landscaping takes root we must weed out the bad laws: How natural landscaping and Leopold's land ethic collide with unenlightened weed laws and what must be done about it. *The John Marshall Law Review*. 26(4). (http://www.epa.gov/greenacres/weedlaws/index.html) (Last accessed February , 2007)

3. Ibid.

4. Ibid.

5. Ibid.

6. Martin, John. (1997). No, the grass isn't always greener. *The St. Petersburg Times*. St. Petersburg: FLJuly 18: 4.

7. Nissimov, Ron. (1999). MetFront mowed down: Homeowner refuses to give up his dream of St. Augustine 'meadow' despite court ruling. *The Houston Chronicle*. Houston, December 13: A19.

8. Long, Cheryl. (1996). Joe Friday, lawn cop! *Organic Gardening* 43(1): 15. Crumbley, Ray. (2000). Reynoldsburg says resident can let back yard grow wild. *Columbus Dispatch*. Columbus, OH: September 15: B4.

9. Coats, Bill. (2003). For sake of order, a lockstep culture. *The St. Petersburg Times*. St. Petersburg, FL: December 28: 1.

10. Martin, John. (1997). No, the grass isn't always greener. *The St. Petersburg Times*: St. Petersburg, FL: July 18: 4.

11. Van Sickler, Michael. (2003). Lawsuit springs from lawn dispute. *St. Petersburg Times*. St. Petersburg, FL: June 9: 4.

12. Martin, John. (1997). No, the grass isn't always greener. *The St. Petersburg Times*. St. Petersburg, FL: July 18: 4.

13. Alberto, Deborah. (2000). Couple using xeriscape method agrees to put sod back in yard. *The Tampa Tribune*. Tampa, FL: March 16: 4.

14. Crumbley, Ray. (2000). Neighborhood dispute over unmanicured yard headed to court. *Columbus Dispatch*. Columbus, OH: January 3: D7. Crumbley, Ray. (2000). Neighbors sue over high grass. *Columbus Dispatch*. Columbus, OH, October 19: 4C. Crumbley, Ray, and Robert Albrecht. (2000). It's mowing versus growing in area's turf war grass-height laws. *Columbus Dispatch*. Columbus, OH: 1B.

15. Carmichael, Amy. (2002). Chemical industry fighting lawn pesticide bans with increasing success. *Canadian Press Newswire*, May 26.

16. Mittelstaedt, Martin. (2001). Toronto closer to pesticide ban: Board of health, wary of childhood cancer, wants an end to spraying around homes. *The Globe and Mail*. Toronto, July 17: A4.

17. Paquette, Carole. (2003). Organic methods are urged for lawns and farms. *New York Times*, February 16: 7.

18. Rappaport, Brett. (1993). As natural landscaping takes root we must weed out the bad laws: How natural landscaping and Leopold's land ethic collide with unenlightened weed laws and what must be done about it. *The John Marshall Law Review*. 26(4). (http://www.epa.gov/greenacres/weedlaws/index.html). (Last accessed February, 2007)

19. Guerrero, Peter F. (1990). Lawn Care Pesticides Remain Uncertain While Prohibited Safety Claims Continue. In *Statement of Peter F. Guerrero before the Subcommittee on*

Toxic Substances, Environmental Oversight, Research and Development of the Senate Committee on Environment and Public Works. Washington D. C.: US General Accounting Office.

20. Pesticide & Toxic Chemical News. (2000). EPA announces cancellation of end-use pesticide products containing chlorpyrifos. *Pesticide & Toxic Chemical News.* 29(5).

21. Hess, Glenn. (2000). Pesticide manufacturers are unhappy with EPA's crackdown on chlorpyrifos. *Chemical Market Reporter.* 257: 1,13.

22. Bailey, Sue. (2002). Grass may not be greener under new legislation to update pesticide laws. *Canadian Press Newswire,* March 21.

23. Crompton Corp. v. Government of Canada. (2001). Notice of Intent to Submit a Claim of Arbitration under Section B of chapter Eleven of the North American Free Trade Agreement. (http://www.international.gc.ca/tna-nac/disp/crompton_archive-en.asp) (Last accessed February, 2007)

24. Clover, Charles, and David Millward. (2003). Gardeners were banned from buying dozens of pesticides from yesterday under new European rules. *The Daily Telegraph.* London: 7.

25. Guthman, J., and M. DuPuis. (2006). Embodying neoliberalism: Economy, culture, and the politics of fat. *Environment and Planning D: Society and Space.* 24(3): 444.

26. Ibid., 443.

Chapter 8

1. Sack, R. D. (1999). A sketch of a geographic theory of morality. *Annals of the Association of American Geographers* 89(1): 26–44. 35.

2. See for example Lamb, Marjorie. (1991). *Two minutes a day for a greener planet: Quick and simple things you can do to save our Earth.* New York: Harper.

3. Putnam, Robert D. (1993). The prosperous community: Social capital and economic growth. *Current* 356: 4–9. Birdsall, S.S. (1996). Regard, respect, and responsibility: Sketches for a moral geography of the everyday. *Annals of the Association of American Geographers* 86(4): 619–629.

4. For a more extensive critique of "community" and its dysfunctions, see Joseph, M. (2002). *Against the romance of community.* Minneapolis: University of Minnesota Press.

5. Martin, C. A., K. A. Peterson, and L. B. Stabler. (2003). Residential landscaping in Phoenix, Arizona, U.S.: Practices and preferences relative to covenants, codes, and restrictions. *Journal of Arboriculture* 29(1): 9–17.

6 . Guthman, J., and M. DuPuis (2006). Embodying neoliberalism: Economy, culture, and the politics of fat. *Environment and Planning D: Society and Space.* 24(3): 427–448.

7. Kaika, Maria. (2005). *City of flows: Modernity, nature, and the city.* New York: Routledge. 70.

8. Guthman, J. and M. DuPuis (2006). Embodying neoliberalism: Economy, culture, and the politics of fat. *Environment and Planning D: Society and Space.* 24(3): 444.

9. Stone, Christopher D. (1974). *Should trees have standing? Towards legal rights for natural objects.* Los Altos, CA: William Kaufmann. 24.

10. Mitchell, Timothy. (2002). *Rule of experts: Egypt, techno-politics, modernity.* Berkeley: University of California Press. 52–53.

11. Ibid. 52.

12. Haraway, Donna. (2003). *The companion species manifesto: Dogs, people, and significant otherness.* Chicago: Prickly Paradigm Press. 6.

13. The merits and drawbacks to Diamond's argument are well beyond the scope of this volume. Readers should be directed to critiques by James Blaut, in particular, however, for discussion. Blaut, J. M. (1999). Environmentalism and eurocentrism. *Geographical Review* 89(3): 391–408. Blaut, J. M. (2000). *Eight Eurocentric historians.* New York: Guilford

Press. Diamond, J. (1997). *Guns, germs, and steel: The fates of human societies*. New York: W. W. Norton.

Appendix B

1. Agresti, Alan. (1996). *An introduction to categorical data analysis*. New York: Wiley.

2. Hosmer, D. W., and S. Lemeshow, (1989). *Applied logistic regression*. New York: Wiley.

3. Capiella, Karen, and Kenneth Brown. (2001). *Impervious cover and land use in the Chesapeake Bay watershed*. Annapolis, MD: United States Environmental Protection Agency Chesapeake Bay Program.

4 . Berry, W. D., and S. Feldman (1985). *Multiple regression in practice*. Newbury Park, Sage Publications.

5. United States Bureau of the Census. (1997). *Statistical abstract of the United States*, 117th edition. Washington D. C.: Bureau of Census.

RECOMMENDED READINGS

Introduction

Adler, R. W., J. C. Landman, et al. (1993). *The Clean Water Act: 20 years later*. Washington D. C.: Island Press.

Beard, J. B., and R. L. Green. (1994). The role of turfgrasses in environmental-protection and their benefits to humans. *Journal of Environmental Quality* 23(3): 452–460.

Bormann, F. H., et al. (1993). *Redesigning the American lawn: A search for environmental harmony*. New Haven and London: Yale University Press.

Jenkins, V. S. (1994). *The Lawn: A history of an American obsession*. Washington and London: Smithsonian Institute Press.

Pollan, Michael. (1991). Why mow? *Second Nature: A Gardener's Education*, 65–78. New York: Dell Publishing.

Schroeder, F. E. H. (1993). *Front yard America: The evolution and meanings of a vernacular domestic landscape*. Bowling Green, OH: Bowling Green State University Popular Press.

Steinberg, Ted. (2006). *American green: The obsessive quest for the perfect lawn*. New York: W. W. Norton and Co.

Teyssot, Georges., ed. (1999). *The American lawn*. New York: Princeton Architectural Press.

Chapter 1

Agrawal, Arun. (2005). *Environmentality: Technologies of government and the making of subjects*. Durham, NC: Duke University Press. Althusser, Louis. (1971). Ideology and ideological state apparatuses: Notes towards an investigation. In *Lenin and Philosophy and Other Essays*, 127–186. New York: Monthly Review Press.

Beck, Ulrich. (1992). *Risk society: towards a new modernity*. London: Sage Publications.

Berger, I. E. (1997). The demographics of recycling and the structure of environmental behavior. *Environment and Behavior* 29(4): 515–531.

Blaikie, P., and H. Brookfield. (1987). *Land degradation and society*. London and New York: Routledge. Buttel, F. H., and W. L. Flinn. (1978). The politics of environmental concern: The impacts of party identification and political ideology on environmental attitudes. *Environment and Behavior* 10: 17–32.

Cronon, William. (1995). The trouble with wilderness or, getting back to the wrong nature. In
    W. Cronon *Uncommon Ground: Rethinking the Human Place in Nature*, 69–90. New York:
    W. W. Norton and Co.
Diamantopoulos, A., B. B. Schlegelmilch, et al. (2003). Can socio-demographics still play a role
    in profiling green consumers? A review of the evidence and an empirical investigation.
    Journal of Business Research 56(6): 465–480.
Gandy, Matthew. (2002). *Concrete and clay: Reworking nature in New York City*. Cambridge,
    MA: MIT Press.
Harvey, David. (1996). *Justice, Nature, and the Geography of Difference*. Cambridge, MA: Black-
    well Publishers.Mitchell, Don. (2000). *Cultural geography: A critical introduction*. Oxford:
    Blackwell.
Neumann, R. P. (2005). *Making political ecology*. London: Hodder Arnold.
O'Connor, James. (1996). "The Second Contradiction of Capitalism." Ted. Benton (ed). *The
    greening of Marxism*, 197–221. New York: Guilford Press.
Pickett, G. M., N. Kangun, et al. (1993). Is there a general conserving consumer? A public pol-
    icy concern. *Journal of Public Policy and Marketing* 12(2): 234–243.
Robbins, Paul. (2004). *Political ecology: A critical introduction*. New York Blackwell.
Schahn, J., and E. Holzer. (1990). Studies of environmental concern: the role of knowledge, gen-
    der, and background variables. *Environment and Behavior* 22(6): 767–786.
Widegren, Örjan. (1998). Environmentally friendly behaviour as collective action: Some aspects
    of non-rational motivation. *Tidsskrift for Samfunnsforskning* 39(2): 231–258.
Zukin, Susan. (1991). *Landscapes of power: From Detroit to Disney World*. Berkeley: Univer-
    sity of California Press.

Chapter 2

Brown, Lauren. (1979). *Grasses: An identification guide*. New York: Houghton Mifflin.
Crosby, A. W. (1986). *Ecological imperialism: The biological expansion of Europe, 900–1900*.
    Cambridge: Cambridge University Press.
Downing, A. J. (1844). *A treatise on the theory and practice of landscape gardening applied to
    North America with a view to the improvement of country residences*. New York: Wiley and
    Putnam.
Fein, Albert. (1972). *Frederick Law Olmsted and the American environmental tradition*. New
    York: George Brazilier.
Jackson, K. T. (1985). *Crabgrass frontier: The suburbanization of the United States*. New York:
    Oxford University Press.
Jenkins, V. S. (1994). *The lawn: A history of an American obsession*. Washington and London:
    Smithsonian Institute Press.
Malin, J. C. (1984). *History and ecology: Studies of the grassland*. Lincoln: University of Nebraska
    Press.
Olmsted, F. L. (1870). *Public parks and the enlargement of towns*. Cambridge, MA: American
    Social Science Association.
Schroeder, F. E. H. (1993). *Front yard America: The evolution and meanings of a vernacu-
    lar domestic landscape*. Bowling Green, OH: Bowling Green State University Popular
    Press.
Spirn, A. W. (1996). Constructing nature: The Legacy of Frederick Law Olmsted. In William.
    Cronon. *Uncommon ground: Rethinking the human place in nature*. New York: Norton.

Chapter 3

Baker, H. G. (1974). The evolution of weeds. *Annual Review of Ecological Systems* 5: 1–24.
Brady, N. C. (1984). *The nature and properties of soil*. New York: Macmillan Book Co.
Emmons, R. D. (2000). *Turfgrass science and management*. Albany: Delmar.
Hitchcock, A. S. (1971). *Manual of grasses of the United States*. New York: Dover.

Chapter 4

Barron, Leonard. (1923). *Lawn making: Together with the proper keeping of putting greens.* New York: Doubleday, Page and Co.

Bernard, C. E., H. Nuygen, et al. (2001). Environmental residues and biomonitoring estimates of human insecticide exposure from treated residential turf. *Archives of Environmental Contamination and Toxicology* 41(2): 237–240.

Branch, R. A. (1986). Is carbaryl as safe as its reputation? Does it have a potential for causing chronic neurotoxicity in humans? *American Journal of Medicine* 80: 659–664.

Briggs, S. A., and Rachel Carson Council Staff. (1992). *Basic guide to pesticides: Their characteristics and hazards.* Boca Raton, FL, CRC Press.

Carson, Rachel. (1962). *Silent spring.* New York: Houghton Mifflin.

Colt, J. S., J. Lubin, et al. (2004). Comparison of pesticide levels in carpet dust and self-reported pest treatment practices in four US sites. *Journal of Exposure Analysis and Environmental Epidemiology* 14(1): 74–83.

Cox, Caroline. (1999). 2,4-D: Ecological effects. *Journal of Pesticide Reform* 19(3): 14–19.

Dunlap, T. R. (1981). *DDT: Scientists, citizens, and public policy.* Princeton: Princeton University Press.

Extension Toxicology Network. (2004). Ecotoxnet (http://ace.ace.orst.edu/info/extoxnet/).

Ibrahim, M. A., G. G. Bond, et al. (1991). Weight of Evidence on the Human Carcinogenicity of 2,4-D. *Environmental Health Perspectives* 96: 213–222.

Iskander, F. Y. (1994). Measurements of 27 elements in Garden and lawn Fertilizers Using Instrumental Neutron-Activation. *Journal of Radioanalytical and Nuclear Chemistry-Articles* 180(1): 25–28.

Kidd, H., and D. R. James, eds. (1991). *The agrochemicals handbook.* Cambridge, UK: Royal Society of Chemistry Information Services.

Leary, J. C., W. I. Fishbein, et al. (1946). *DDT and the insect problem.* New York: McGraw-Hill Book Company.

Lewis, R. G., A. E. Bond, et al. (1991). Preliminary results of the EPA House Dust Infant Pesticides Exposure Study (HIPES). *Abstracts of the Papers of the American Chemical Society* 201(89-Agro Part 1, April 14).

Maddock, T. A. (2004). Fragmenting regimes: how water quality regulation is changing political-economic landscapes. *Geoforum* 35(2): 217–230.

Nishioka, M. G., H. M. Burkholder, et al. (1996). Measuring transport of lawn-applied herbicide acids from turf to home: Correlation of dislodgeable 2,4-D tuff residues with carpet dust and carpet surface residues. *Environmental Science and Technology* 30(11): 3313–3320.

Nishioka, M. G., H. M. Burkholder, et al. (1999). Distribution of 2,4-dichlorophenoxyacetic acid in floor dust throughout homes following homeowner and commercial applications: Quantitative effects on phildren, pets, and shoes. *Environmental Science and Technology* 33(9): 1359–1365.

Osmond, D. L., and D. H. Hardy. (2004). Characterization of turf practices in five North Carolina communities. *Journal of Environmental Quality* 33(2): 565–575.

Rissler, J., and M. Mellon. (1996). *The ecological risks of engineered crops.* Cambridge, MA: The MIT Press.

Russell, Edmund. (2001). *War and nature: Fighting humans and insects with chemicals from World War I to Silent Spring.* Cambridge: Cambridge University Press.

United States Environmental Protection Agency. (1975). *DDT: A review of scientific and economic aspects of the decision to ban its use as a pesticide.* Washington D.C.: United States Environmental Protection Agency.

Chapter 5

Dunn, K. A., C. W. Runyan, et al. (1998). Teens at work: A statewide study of jobs, hazards, and injuries. *Journal of Adolescent Health* 22: 9–25.

Engel, J. F., W. N. Harnish, and C.A. Staetz. (1990). Challenges: The industrial viewpoint. In E. Hodgson and R. J. Kuhr *Safer insecticides: Development and Use*. New York: Marcel Dekker.

Eveleth, W. T., ed. (1990). *Kline guide to the U.S. chemical industry*, Fifth Edition. Fairfield, N.J.: Kline and Company, Inc.

Henderson, George. (1999). *California and the fictions of capital*. New York: Oxford University Press.

Mann, S., and J. Dickenson (1978). Obstacles to the development of a capitalist agriculture. *Journal of Peasant Studies* 5(4): 466–81.

Meier, Barry. (1990). Lawn care concern says it will limit safety claims. *New York Times*. New York: June 30, 30.

Staggers, D. T. (1976). The search for new herbicides. In L. J. Aldus. *Herbicides: Physiology, biochemistry, ecology*. Second edition, Volume II. London: Academic Press.

Chapter 6

Beck, Ulrich. (1992). *Risk society: towards a new modernity*. London: Sage Publications.

Joseph, M. (2002). *Against the Romance of Community*. Minneapolis (MN), University of Minnesota Press.

Olson, Mancur. (1971). *The logic of collective action: Public goods and the theory of groups*. Cambridge, MA: Harvard University Press.

Templeton, S. R., David Zilbermand, and Seung Jick Yoo. (1998). An aconomic perspective on outdoor residential pesticide use. *Policy Analysis* 32(17): 416A–423A.

Chapter 7

Guthman, J. and M. DuPuis (2006). "Embodying Neoliberalism: Economy, Culture, and the Politics of Fat." *Environment and Planning D: Society and Space* 24(3): 427–448.

Rappaport, Brett. (1993). "As natural landscaping takes root we must weed out the bad laws: how natural landscaping and Leopold's Land Ethic collide with unenlightened weed laws and what must be done about it." *The John Marshall Law Review* 26(4), (http://www.epa.gov/greenacres/weedlaws/index.html). (Last accessed February 2007)

Chapter 8

Haraway, Donna. (2003). *The companion species manifesto: Dogs, people, and significant otherness*. Chicago: Prickly Paradigm Press.

Latour, Bruno. (2005). *Reassembling the Social: An Introduction to Actor-Network-theory*. Oxford: Oxford University Press.

Mitchell, Timothy. (2002). *Rule of experts: Egypt, techno-politics, modernity*. Berkeley: University of California Press.

Stone, C. D. (1974). *Should Trees have standing? Towards legal rights for natural objects*. Los Altos, CA: William Kaufmann.

Appendixes

Capiella, K., and K. Brown. (2001). *Impervious cover and land use in the Chesapeake Bay watershed*. Annapolis, MD: United States Environmental Protection Agency Chesapeake Bay Program.

Hosmer, D. W., and S. Lemeshow. (1989). *Applied logistic regression*. New York: Wiley.

Robbins, P., and T. Birkenholtz. (2003). "Turfgrass revolution: measuring the expansion of the American lawn." *Land Use Policy* 20:181–194.

Robbins, P., A.-M. Polderman, et al. (2001). "Lawns and toxins: An ecology of the city." *Cities: The International Journal of Urban Policy and Planning* 18(6): 369–380.

Robbins, P., and J. Sharp. (2003). "Producing and consuming chemicals: The moral economy of the American lawn." *Economic Geography* 79(4): 425–451.

Robbins, P., and J. Sharp. (2006). Turfgrass subjects: the political economy of urban monoculture. In N. Heynan, M. Kaika, and E. Swyngedouw. *In the nature of cities: Urban political ecology and the politics of urban metabolism.* New York: Routledge.

Robbins, P., and J. T. Sharp. (2003). "The lawn chemical economy and its discontents." *Antipode* 35(5): 955–979.

INDEX